How It Works®

Science and Technology

Third Edition

Marshall Cavendish
99 White Plains Road
Tarrytown, NY 10591

Website: www.marshallcavendish.com

Third edition updated by Brown Reference Group plc.

Library of Congress Cataloging-in-Publication Data
How it works: science and technology.—3rd ed.
p. cm.
Includes index.
ISBN 0-7614-7314-9 (set)   ISBN 0-7614-7325-4 (Vol. 11)
1. Technology—Encyclopedias. 2. Science—Encyclopedias.
[1. Technology—Encyclopedias. 2. Science—Encyclopedias.]
T9 .H738 2003
603—dc21   2001028771

Consultant: Donald R. Franceschetti, Ph.D., University of Memphis

Brown Reference Group
Editor: Wendy Horobin
Associate Editors: Paul Thompson, Martin Clowes, Lis Stedman
Managing Editor: Tim Cooke
Design: Alison Gardner
Picture Research: Becky Cox
Illustrations: Mark Walker, Darren Awuah

Marshall Cavendish
Project Editor: Peter Mavrikis
Production Manager: Alan Tsai
Editorial Director: Paul Bernabeo

Printed in Malaysia
Bound in the United States of America
08 07 06 05 04   6 5 4 3 2

Title picture: Laboratory testing of sticky foam, see *Nonlethal Weapon*

How It Works®

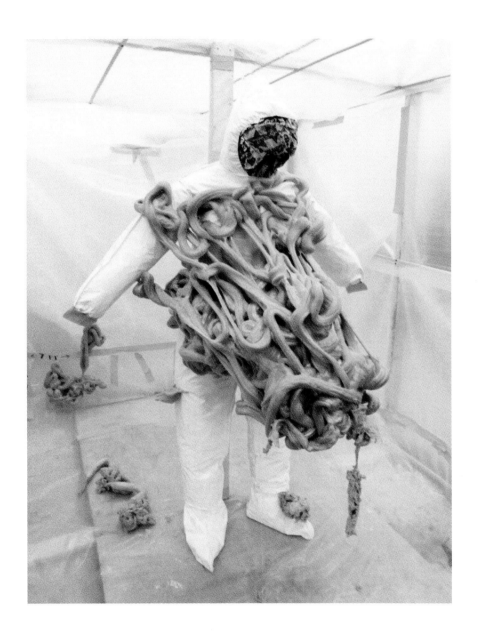

Science and Technology

Volume 11

Microtome

Operating Room

Marshall Cavendish

New York • London • Toronto • Sydney

Contents

Volume 11

Microtome

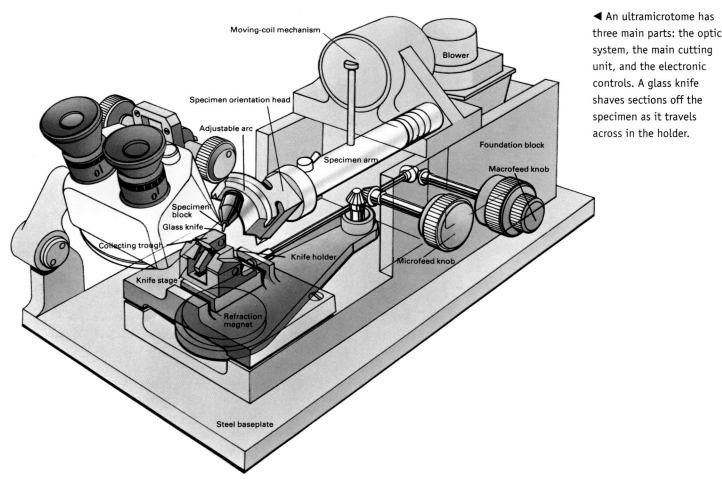

Moving-coil mechanism

Blower

Specimen orientation head

Adjustable arc

Foundation block

Specimen arm

Macrofeed knob

Specimen block

Glass knife

Collecting trough

Knife holder

Microfeed knob

Knife stage

Refraction magnet

Steel baseplate

◀ An ultramicrotome has three main parts: the optic system, the main cutting unit, and the electronic controls. A glass knife shaves sections off the specimen as it travels across in the holder.

The microtome, invented in 1865 by the German anatomist Wilhelm His, is an instrument used to cut very thin sections of specimens for examination under a light microscope. Even thinner sections are needed when using an electron microscope, and this problem was resolved with the development of the ultramicrotome.

The optical resolution of the light microscope is such that specimens are often best examined as thin sections, rather than whole. Today, medical and biological techniques requires specimens of the order of 1 to 50 µm (micrometer), the usual thickness being 4 to 5 µm. (A micrometer, or micron, is one-millionth of a meter.) Specimens are usually chemically preserved in a solution such as formalin (formaldehyde in water), dehydrated, and embedded in wax. The wax block is firmly clamped onto a microtome—originally known as a cutting engine—and sections are cut with a specially prepared sharp steel knife.

Types of microtomes

There are three main types of microtomes: the rocking, the rotary, and the sliding microtome. On the rocking design, the knife is clamped in a fixed horizontal position with the edge uppermost. The wax block is attached to the end of an arm pivoted near the knife and is moved or rocked in an arc past the knife edge. On the downward stroke, the knife removes a thin section of the specimen. The block is advanced toward the knife by a ratchet mechanism with a micrometer thread for adjusting section thickness.

On a rotary microtome, the specimen block moves up and down in a vertical plane, and the feed mechanism is actuated by a large hand wheel, one rotation of which produces a complete cutting cycle. Larger and harder specimens can be sectioned on these machines, and their rotary action is adapted easily to automatic power drive.

Sliding microtomes are the heaviest of all, enabling small and large sections to be cut of whole human lung and brain. One type of sliding microtome has a moving knife, drawn horizontally across the block, and is particularly useful for specimens that have been embedded in cellulose nitrate. The other most common and versatile type is the base sledge, where the specimen is mounted on a moving carriage, or sledge, and the knife is fixed.

Ultramicrotomes

The greater resolution of the electron microscope over the light microscope requires even thinner sections. To obtain these sections, small (0.5 to 1.0 cubic millimeter) biological specimens are embedded in very hard synthetic resins, such as methacrylate (thermoplastic), epoxy, and polyester. Microtomes capable of cutting ultrathin sections of these hard embedments—ultramicrotomes—have developed since 1950 and allow reliable and reproducible sections of even thickness to be obtained. A range of thickness for most machines is 5 to 150 nm (1 nm is equal to one-billionth of a meter); biological specimens are sectioned between 20 and 100 nm.

The embedded specimen is attached to a metal arm or tube that moves in a vertical plane past the knife edge. The knives are usually small pieces of plate glass broken in a controlled way to produce a fine edge 0.24 in. (6 mm) long and much sharper than any steel knife. Alternatively, expensive diamond knives are used with a long-lasting edge only 0.06 in. (1.5 mm) in length. As sections are cut, they float out onto water contained in a trough, attached to the knife, and are often so small (0.1 mm^2 or less) that a stereoscopic binocular microscope is needed to see them. They are then collected onto small metal grids for insertion into the electron microscope.

The fine precision of the feed mechanism on these machines can be obtained either mechani-

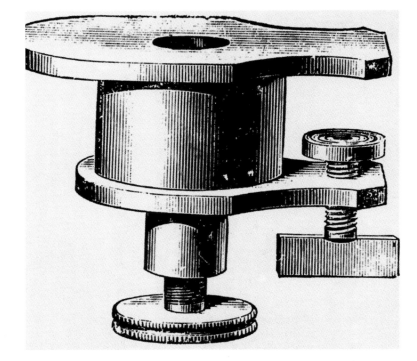

▲ The earliest microtomes were far less complex in design and usage than current models. Biological specimens, for example, were simply placed in the hole and sliced with a knife.

◄ The greater resolution of the electron microscope requires very thin sections, which are seen here being cut on an ultramicrotome. The specimen is attached to the metal arm.

cally by a micrometer thread, reduced 250 times by a lever and leaf-spring system, or more often by electrically controlled thermal expansion of the rod or tube carrying the specimen. The rate of expansion and therefore section thickness will depend not only on the current applied but also on cutting speed.

During the cutting cycle, the specimen block must not damage the knife edge on the return stroke, and this problem can be avoided by the specimen arm being displaced sideways on a D-ring movement after the section is cut. A less common but more advanced method is to retract the knife about 25 μm from its cutting position by means of a large electromagnet in the base of the machine, which is energized momentarily after a section is cut, while the specimen arm returns ready for another cutting stroke. Most ultramicrotomes can be operated automatically, the automatic models having complicated electric circuitry.

Freezing microtomes

Both the microtomes and the ultramicrotomes have attachments capable of allowing sections to be cut from frozen unembedded specimens, thus avoiding damage to cells and tissue structures from chemical reagents and resins. Some microtomes are made to freeze a specimen as well as slice it. They are used with a cryostat—a refrigerated cabinet at –4°F (–20°C) in which the microtome is placed.

SEE ALSO: Microscope, electron • Microscope, optical • Pathology

Microwave Oven

Microwave ovens are among the most visible products of microwave technology. Originally used in commercial environments, these ovens now supplement conventional stoves in many homes. They cook faster—cooking times are expressed in seconds or minutes rather than minutes and hours—than any conventional method of cooking and offer considerable energy savings.

Microwave ovens are a variation on devices that have found uses in drying wood, heating ceramics and ceramic products, and melting glass and other materials. Commercially, microwave ovens are used in bakeries and in cooking meat.

There are many accounts of how microwaves were discovered as a cooking method. No one is certain of the truth, but one of the best stories relates how, in 1945, an American engineer, Percy Spencer, passed too close to a microwave source, causing the chocolate bar in his pocket to melt.

Microwave ovens first saw use in hospital kitchens and military canteens in 1947. The first model was the size of a refrigerator. Since then, microwave ovens have reduced in size, and their use has spread so that millions of domestic models are now in homes worldwide.

In the home, microwave ovens have three basic uses—defrosting, reheating, and primary cooking. By using a fraction of full power, frozen food can be quickly and easily defrosted. This method can save a great deal of time, especially in the case of chicken, for example, which needs to be properly defrosted for health reasons. In reheating, microwave ovens are often far more effective than conventional ovens, particularly for some foods, such as rice and pasta, because they retain their original texture. Primary cooking with microwaves saves time. For example, a baked potato takes about five minutes in a microwave, compared with approaching one hour in a conventional oven.

Dielectric heating

The principle behind microwave cooking is called dielectric heating. Strictly speaking, dielectrics are materials that are not conductors of electricity, but nonetheless become electrically polarized, that is, experience a rearrangement of charge on the molecular level when placed in an electromagnetic field. If the field is varying at a frequency that matches one of the natural rotational

▲ Microwave ovens provide rapid and easy cooking of food, and today 90 percent of American homes possess one. Some of the problems with microwave-cooked food, such as the inability of microwaves to produce browning on meat, have been overcome with the introduction of combination microwaves, which include a conventional heating element.

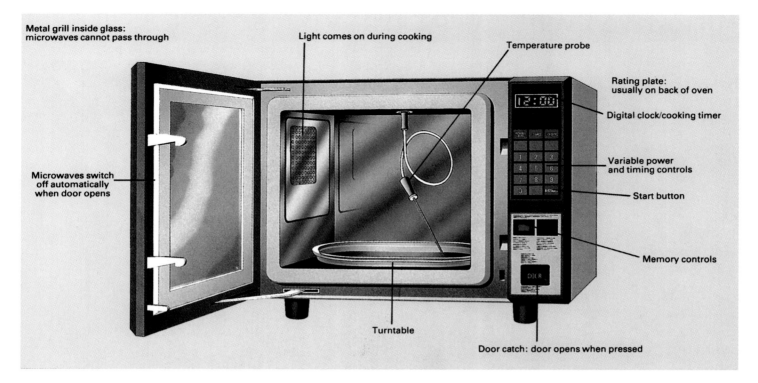

Metal grill inside glass:
microwaves cannot pass through

Light comes on during cooking

Temperature probe

Rating plate:
usually on back of oven

Digital clock/cooking timer

Microwaves switch
off automatically
when door opens

Variable power
and timing controls

Start button

Memory controls

Turntable

Door catch: door opens when pressed

or vibrational frequencies characteristic of the molecules in the dielectric, the material will absorb energy from the field and it will be converted into heat.

Microwave ovens typically operate at frequencies of about 2,450 megahertz, a frequency that is absorbed well by water, sugars, fats, and other food molecules, causing them to vibrate rapidly. Foodstuffs are generally somewhat conductive in that they contain ions that can move about in response to an electric field. They are not nearly as conductive as metals, however, in which there are so many mobile electrons that any applied field results in very large currents and very rapid heating. Thus, metal containers cannot be used with a microwave, since very dangerous levels of heating could occur.

Microwave cooking

The vibration induced by microwaves causes a rapid build-up of heat in the food and results in a faster rate of cooking. Microwave cooking is, therefore, very different from conventional cooking. Instead of heat penetrating the food from the outside, the heat is generated from within the food itself.

Microwaves penetrate food to a depth of only about 1.5 in. (4 cm). Thus, only thin items will cook rapidly by microwave. Thicker items will cook but not through the direct action of microwaves. Instead, cooking thicker food relies on a mechanism that has something in common with conventional cooking. Heat from the microwaved layer is conducted into areas that the

microwaves are unable to penetrate. Thus, in the instructions for microwave cooking, the cook is told to remove some foods after a certain period of time and then leave them to stand for a few minutes before serving. The food continues to cook through conduction.

Although microwave cooking has many advantages over conventional cooking, it is not without its drawbacks. As the heat originates from inside the food, the food will not brown. Therefore, it is often the case that people who are unfamiliar with microwave cooking expect the food to look cooked, with the result that the food becomes overcooked. Certain foods that rely on long cooking times to develop flavors are less satisfactory when cooked by microwaves. In addition, whole eggs should not be cooked in a microwave oven—the moisture in the egg generates heat, causing the shell to burst.

Oven construction

At the heart of a microwave oven is a magnetron, a device that generates microwaves. A magnetron is a particular kind of cathode-ray tube that has something in common with television and the cathode-ray oscilloscope.

A magnetron is a small vacuum tube with a large potential difference (voltage) held between the anode and the cathode; the microwaves are emitted from the cathode. Magnetrons are characterized by a small interelectrode spacing. The interelectrode capacitance and the capacitance of any electrical leads in the magnetron must also be kept to a minimum. The beam of microwaves is

▲ First used in 1947 in hospital kitchens, microwave ovens have since been used in millions of homes worldwide. Their great advantage is that they cook very fast— baking a potato in five minutes rather than a whole hour, as in a traditional oven.

controlled by crossed electric and magnetic fields forming an electromagnetic wave.

Magnetrons are available in many different power ratings, according to the application. Some magnetrons are capable of generating pulses of up to 10^7 watts. In home microwave ovens, typical magnetron ratings of about 750 watts are used.

In a microwave oven, the magnetron is connected to a waveguide, which channels the waves toward the metal-lined cooking chamber. These simple components, plus an on-off switch and a timer, are all that is needed to make a microwave oven. However, the extremely directional waves resulting from the narrow dispersion from the end of the waveguide causes particular hot spots in the oven and can result in uneven cooking, especially with large pieces of food.

Microwave oven makers have solved this problem in two ways. First, a rotating paddle device can be placed near the end of the waveguide, thus deflecting the microwaves and allowing a more even distribution of energy within the oven.

▶ Electromagnetism aligns food molecules (A) from their usual random patterns (B). If an electrostatic field is added (C), their positive and negative charges point in the same direction. Reversing the electrostatic field (D) flips the molecules, causing frictional heating that then cooks the food from within.

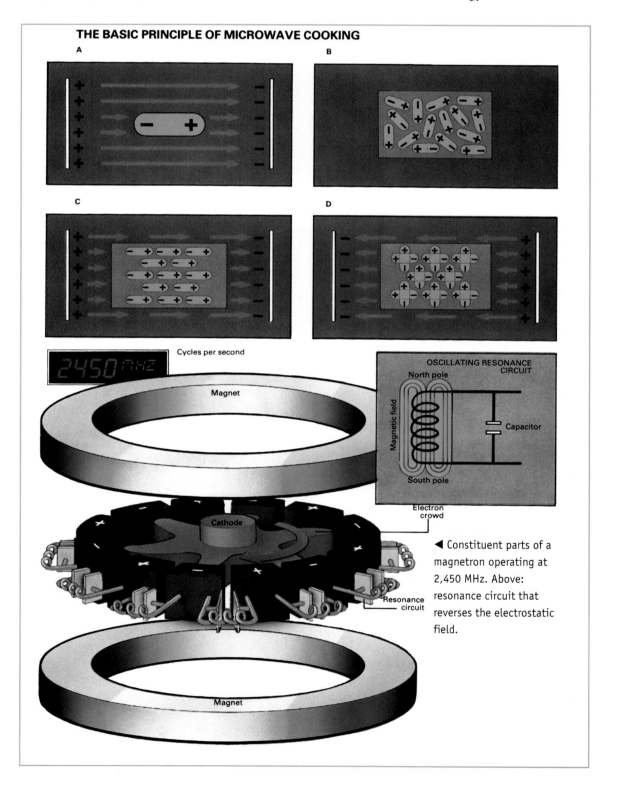

THE BASIC PRINCIPLE OF MICROWAVE COOKING

◀ Constituent parts of a magnetron operating at 2,450 MHz. Above: resonance circuit that reverses the electrostatic field.

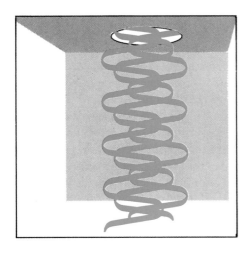 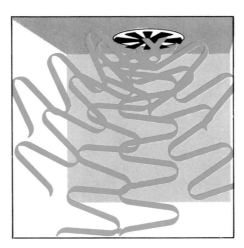 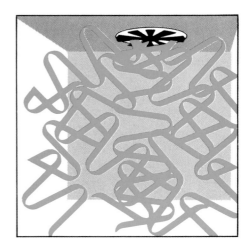

Second, the food can be placed on a rotating turntable, which also helps to negate the hot spots.

There have been safety issues in connection with microwaves. Escaping microwaves can agitate water molecules in living humans or animals just as well as they can in meat or vegetables. The dangers inherent in microwaves are made obvious by the horrifying fact that a major cause of death in NATO exercises has been from soldiers straying into the paths of microwaves used for communications purposes.

To ensure the safety of ovens in the home, safety regulations are stringent. The sides of the cooking compartment are lined with metal to confine the microwaves within the compartment. Even the glass door is lined with a metal grid so that microwaves do not escape. The gap around the door is also a point of potential microwave loss. The usual solution is to fit a quarter-wave choke to cancel out any escaping microwaves. Another safety device causes the magnetron to automatically switch off as soon as the door is opened.

Cooking vessels

Cooking vessels suitable for traditional methods of cooking are not always suitable for use in microwave ovens. Vessels must be made of a material that does not interfere with the passage of microwaves so that maximum power reaches the food. Manufacturers talk in terms of transparent vessels—because, like light, microwaves are electromagnetic waves, suitable containers are those that behave as glass does toward light.

Metal vessels are not suitable for use with microwaves. The biggest danger is that they will reflect the microwaves back toward the walls of the oven and cause damage to the magnetron. Saucepans, metal molds, and aluminum foil are all unsuitable for use in microwave ovens. Users must be very careful to avoid vessels that have even the smallest amount of metal—such as in

some kinds of decoration on nonmetallic dishes—because damage may still result.

Glass that can withstand the high temperatures that food will reach during cooking is often recommended. Glazed china and porcelain are also suitable, provided the glaze is nonmetallic. Unglazed earthenware may absorb moisture; it must be avoided because the water content will become agitated and cause the vessel to shatter.

The problems with using traditional cooking vessels have caused manufacturers to make special plastic microwave-proof vessels, which will not cause damage. In addition, special browning dishes, which absorb energy from the microwaves without causing harm to either the magnetron or the dishes themselves, are available. Browning dishes sear meat to make it look more like meat cooked by traditional methods.

New technology

Manufacturers are now designing microwaves that make cooking even more effortless. One recent development is a microwave oven that uses a barcode reader to scan food packaging for information on cooking time and ingredients. This device saves the user from having to read the packaging to find out the cooking time and may also give warning if the food contains any ingredients the user does not like or has an allergy toward.

Another recent development is the Internet microwave. It can download recipes and be used to shop for groceries and is also linked to the user's bank account for the payment of bills. These facilities are especially useful for people who do not possess a computer. Some manufacturers believe this progress is only the start for appliances that are linked to the Internet and to each other to make peoples' lives easier.

▲ Left: energy enters the oven cavity through an opening in the metal case, usually at the top. Hot spots occur if heat is not distributed evenly throughout. Center: a concealed mechanism distributes microwaves to different parts of the oven. Many ovens have a turntable that rotates the cooking food. Right: microwaves cannot penetrate metal, so they are reflected off the oven walls at right angles, making a random pattern that cooks the food evenly.

 SEE ALSO: CATHODE-RAY TUBE • ELECTROMAGNETIC RADIATION • ELECTROMAGNETISM • RADAR

Milking Machine

The first vacuum-operated milking machine was developed over 100 years ago, and since then, levels of automation have gradually increased. The first reference to the use of wheat straws as milk tubes, inserted into the cow's teat, appeared in Egypt in about 380 B.C.E., and the idea reappeared in Britain in 1831 in a more advanced form. The susceptibility, however, of teats and udders to disease stopped the development of such devices. From 1870 onward, attempts were made to milk cows with pressure devices, which on the whole, failed because of their complexity and the fact that they did not milk any faster than a good hand milker.

In 1879, the Royal Agricultural Society of England offered a £50 prize for a milking machine; the first to show promise was that of William Murchland in Kilmarnock, Scotland, patented in 1889. This machine used continuous suction (vacuum) and required a great deal of labor and, for that reason, was not a success. The second major development was that of Dr. Shiels of Glasgow who, between 1895 and 1903, attempted to overcome the problem of swollen teats caused by continuous suction by using a pulsator, which alternated the suction level between 0.14 and 0.6 bar (100–380 mm of mercury, Hg).

In 1913, the Royal Agricultural Society again offered prizes, and this time there were 11 entries from countries including Australia, New Zealand, the United States, Sweden, and Britain. During World War I, machine milking became established with moderate success, but several companies failed to survive the economic depression of the 1920s. Today, the vast majority of dairy farmers in industrialized nations use milking machines, saving time and reducing the incidence of disease.

Machine milking

All milking machines follow similar principles in the extraction of milk from the cow: a stainless steel cup, lined with natural or synthetic rubber, fits around the cow's teat, and a continuous vacuum of about 0.6 bar (380 mm Hg) is applied to the teat from the bottom of the cup. An alternating vacuum is applied between the cup and the lining, causing it to collapse around the teat intermittently, thus providing a massaging action and making and breaking the constant vacuum applied to the teat.

The vacuum to operate both the milk removal and the pulsator action is provided by a vacuum pump situated remotely from the cow and providing vacuum sufficient for one or more units.

▲ An illustration from a 19th-century book, showing the Colvin vacuum-operated milking machine. Milking machines did not become established until World War I.

The vacuum level is regulated by a vacuum controller—a simple valve of varying design, but normally weight-loaded, which is preset to maintain a constant vacuum within the system. A vacuum gauge provides the operator with a visual check that the system is operating within the limits prescribed by the manufacturer.

The alternating vacuum applied to the teat cup liner is provided by a pulsator; several systems are used throughout the world. In general, the pulsator operates between 45 and 70 pulsations per minute but should be preset for each installation

◀ Cows being milked in a herringbone-type milking parlor. Each cow's output is measured in the recording jars seen on the left.

so that cows are milked at a constant rate each day. The ratio of the vacuum phase to the atmospheric phase is termed the pulsation ratio. The vacuum phase of the system should not be less than 50 percent (1:1) and not more than 75 percent (3:1) of the pulsation cycle, otherwise the interruption to the blood supply, caused by excessive squeezing within the teat, could prove harmful.

The procedures adopted during machine milking should be designed to take advantage of the physiological mechanism that is responsible for milk ejection from the cow and be completed as quickly as possible without causing damage or injury to the animal.

Further developments in dairy farming, including programmed feeding (during milking time) linked with cow identification, automatic teat cup removal, and automatic cow-washing devices, have increased levels of automation.

Ultimately, total mechanization of feeding, watering, manure removal, and milking can be achieved, and research carried out in Germany has indicated savings in labor and feeding costs by moving the cow in a portable compartment from function to function. The system, which links the compartments, moves a herd of cows in ventilated conditions, rather like a train, from the feeding station to the watering station and on to the milking station.

Robotic milking

Robotic systems of milking cows have been in use for several years in Europe, and in 2000, the first experimental systems were installed in the United States. Computer-operated robots use lasers to accurately position milking cups on the cow's udders. In some systems, the cows may have some choice over when they want to be milked; the cows wear identification collars so that when they enter the stall, a computer automatically registers which cow is present. The computer stores information on how much milk the cow usually produces and its stage of lactation. On the basis of this information, the computer decides whether to allow the cow to be milked or not. The computer also determines when to stop milking individual teats to avoid overmilking, and when milking is finished, the robot automatically washes the cups and sprays the cow's udders to clean them. If the system runs out of materials, such as feed, the computer may automatically page the farmer to inform him or her of the situation.

Although the cost of installing robotic systems is comparatively high, long-term savings are possible through reduced labor costs.

▲ This dried milk factory can process 44,000 gallons (1.5 million l) of milk per day. There are more than 210 million dairy cows in the world, whose output becomes about 475 million tons (427 million tonnes) of milk and 5.5 million tons (5 million tonnes) of milk powder per day. In the West, the dairy industry relies on high technology to produce and process this milk for human consumption.

 SEE ALSO: Agricultural machinery • Agriculture, intensive • Dairy industry • Food processing

Mine, Explosive

Mines can be used at sea or on land and differ from most other weapons of war in that they are not directed against specific targets. Once laid they can remain active for many years, and modern types are very difficult to detect and destroy.

The term *mine* is derived from the medieval practice of digging, or mining, tunnels under enemy fortifications and filling them with explosive, which was then detonated to destroy or breach the fortifications. This type of mining still finds occasional application in modern warfare.

The modern land mine, however, is generally an explosive device used on, or just below, the ground surface and of two main types—antipersonnel and antiarmor. Antipersonnel mines are related to the older trip-wire guns while the first antitank mines, used by the Germans in World War I following the introduction of tanks by the British, consisted of artillery shells buried fuse uppermost. Subsequent development has resulted in a variety of modern mines of both types.

Antipersonnel mines

Antipersonnel mines, which may be of either fragmentation or blast type, are small devices mainly intended to injure or disable rather than kill outright. Subsequent care of wounded soldier uses up enemy resources (such as other troops and transportation) that would otherwise be used in attack. Generally, nonmagnetic and nonconducting materials are used for these mines to make them difficult to detect. They can be fired by pressure fuses, trip-wires, and tilting rods or under direct control by a hidden operator.

Blast designs have a limited range, and their effect is limited to the enemy who sets them off; typically, such a mine would be no more than 3 to 4 in. (7.5–10 cm) in diameter and simply scattered on the surface. When stepped on, they explode with sufficient force to blow a foot off.

Fragmentation mines produce a large number of high-velocity fragments, which are spread over a comparatively large target area. Mines of this type can be placed on the ground or buried just below the surface, and when fired, they project the fragments upward and outward in all directions. In bounding mines, the fragmentation projectile is thrown up from the ground and exploded in the air at a height of around 6 ft. (2 m) to spread the fragments horizontally in all directions. Another type is the fixed directional mine, such as the Claymore, which is mounted on legs just above the ground and aligned to cover the desired target area. The Claymore has a

▶ An automatic mine-laying machine of the British Army being towed behind an armored truck. The mines are made of plastic to avoid detection.

curved-plate explosive charge covered with some 700 steel ball projectiles, and when fired, the casualty area covers a 60 degree arc for a range of 150 ft. (50 m) at a height of 3 ft. (1 m).

Antiarmor mines

Conventional antiarmor mines contain a large explosive charge, up to 20 lbs. (9 kg) or more in some cases, and are laid below ground level. They are triggered by the force, typically 300 to 400 lbs. (136–180 kg), of the tank passing over them and destroy the vehicle by the blast effect. Other designs use charges shaped to give an incandescent jet of gases that have an armor-piercing effect. A small uncovering charge may be used to clear the earth covering before the main charge is exploded to penetrate the armor, while another variant is designed to be installed above ground at the side of a road to fire horizontally at the target.

An increasing trend with antiarmor mines is the use of microelectronics to create an intelligent mine, which can, for example, use acoustic sensors to sense the approach of a tank and then fire an armor-piercing warhead when the target is in

range. A related trend is toward the use of smaller antiarmor mines or minelets, with the increasing sophistication of the firing system making the best use of the smaller charge. To increase the difficulty of detection, antiarmor mines make extensive use of plastics and even wood, while metal parts are restricted to a minimum or even totally eliminated.

Another type of mine is the chemical mine, which is designed to disperse both gaseous and liquid agents. Such mines are considered to be most effective when laid in antiarmor minefields, which slow down the progress of the enemy and so result in greater exposure to the chemical.

Mine laying

For maximum effect, mines are normally laid in groups or minefields, with antipersonnel mines and antilift devices being used in conjunction with antiarmor mines to restrict clearing operations. Often, safe paths have to be left through minefields to allow passage to the layer's forces, while the positions of mines are mapped to simplify clearing when the minefield is no longer required. Hand laying is still used for some types of antiarmor mine, but many modern mines can be laid by machines at high rates. For example, the British bar mine is an antiarmor type that is laid underground using a plow system at a rate of 600 to 700 an hour, the laying furrows rapidly blending back into the surface to make detection difficult.

▲ Antipersonnel mines. Above left: (1) an Argentine FMKI plastic mine, (2) an Israeli trip-wire mine, (3) a Spanish P4B plastic mine. Above right: (1) an Italian SB33 antipersonnel mine, (2) an Argentine antitank mine, (3) an Israeli No. 6 antitank mine, made of metal.

Another way of laying minefields rapidly to meet the conditions of modern warfare is the U.S. FASCAM (FAmily of SCAtterable Mines) system, which includes a variety of antipersonnel and antitank mines. A typical member of the FAS-CAM family is the Area Denial Artillery Munition (ADAM), which consists of a 155 mm howitzer projectile with a range of over 55,000 ft. (17,000 m) and carries 36 antipersonnel mines. These mines are dispersed from the shell over the target area and armed after contact with the ground, and they are fired by a trip wire arrangement. Similarly, the Remote Antiarmor Mine System (RAAMS) uses a 155 mm shell to deliver a group of nine antiarmor mines. Other members of the FASCAM family include the Ground Emplacement Mine Scattering System (GEMSS), portable mine projectors, and the Volcano, which can deliver mines either by helicopter or ground vehicle.

Naval mines

The use of mines as a sea weapon was pioneered by the Dutch who, in 1585, succeeded in using clockwork mechanisms to explode casks of gunpowder in small boats that were drifted against Spanish ships in Antwerp harbor. In 1776, the U.S. inventor of the submarine, David Bushnell, devised the first underwater mine, known as Bushnell's keg, in the form of a watertight keg and fuse mechanism that had to be attached to the target ship by hand. This system was used, without any real success, during the War of Independence. During the American Civil War, however, Bushnell's kegs were deployed by the Confederates and were successful in damaging 43 Federal ships, 27 of which sank. Another U.S. inventor, Robert Fulton, produced the first true contact mine, while Samuel Colt, inventor of the revolving firearm, introduced the electrically controlled mine. Large-scale mining operations occurred in 1904 during the Russo-Japanese war, and by World War I, mines had become a major weapon, with some 240,000 being laid between 1914 and 1918, leading to the sinking of nearly 600 Allied ships and over 180 German warships (including 36 U-boats). Usage during World War II was also on a large scale, with around one mine in 40 proving effective, though in some areas this estimate increased to one-in-five.

Modern naval mines are a comparatively cheap and effective way of preventing the movement of shipping and enemy sea forces and demand from the enemy a considerable effort in clearing safe lanes and then keeping them clear (during World War II, some 60 percent of German seagoing naval personnel were involved a detonator, which in turn sets off the high-explosive filling of the mine. This type of mine is laid in a safe condition with a hydrostatic device arming the firing circuit when the mine has sunk to a preset depth. Generally, they are moored or tethered to the seabed with cables although they may also be free floating.

Influence mines

With influence mines, the target ship does not have to make contact with the mine; a sensor system is used to fire the explosive charge when the ship is close enough for the explosive shock wave to be effective. Magnetic mines make use of the permanent and induced magnetic fields of a ship to trigger the firing mechanism. Pressure mines rely on the variation in pressure, caused when a ship passes over the mine, to trigger them, while acoustic mines are fired by the sound produced by a ship. Mines of this type are normally laid on the seabed and rely on the water to transmit the blast to the ship, thus restricting their use to comparatively shallow waters except in cases where they are used against submarines. However, moored mines have been developed for use in deeper water (such as at the edge of the continen-

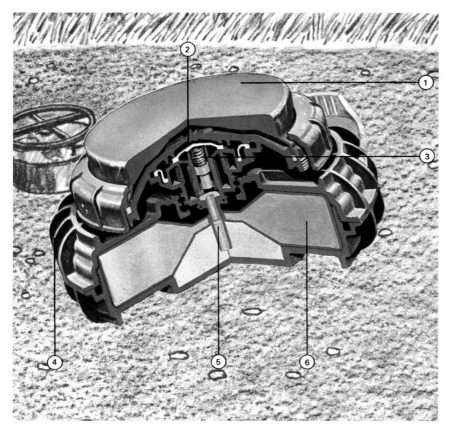

▲ Cutaway of modern antitank mine: (1) pressure plate, (2) pressure membrane, (3) striker, (4) plastic case, (5) detonator, (6) explosive charge.

▼ An antipersonnel mine: (1) fuse cap, (2) strikers, (3) mine fuse, (4) splinters, (5) ejection charge, (6) mine body, (7) arming wire, (8) explosive charge, (9) detonator.

in minesweeping). They have the advantage of attacking a ship in its weakest area—under the waterline—and are particularly effective because of the noncompressibility of water, which is very effective in transmitting the explosive blast to the target. There are two main types of mines: controlled and independent. Controlled mines are connected by a cable to an observation and control station and are fired when a target ship is in range. They are normally used for applications such as harbor defense, where they allow safe passage for wanted shipping. Independent mines may be moored to float at a set distance below the surface, grounded on the seabed and triggered automatically by passing vessels, or they may even float freely at or near the surface without any anchoring device. (Free-floating, or drifting, mines are no longer used by the U.S. Navy.) Independent mines use two main types of firing mechanisms: contact and influence.

Contact mines

As the name suggests, the contact mine is fired by contact with the target, the mine generally being spherical in shape with a number of contact horns positioned around its surface. When struck, the horns bend and pass an electric current to fire

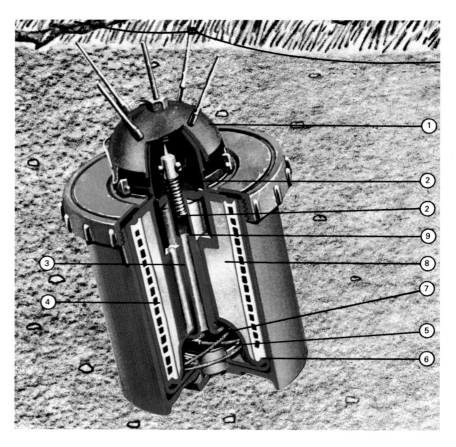

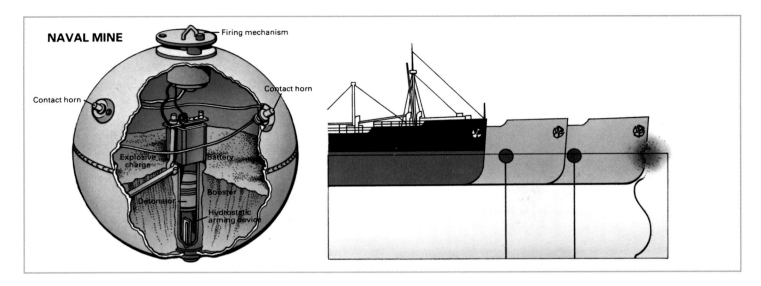

NAVAL MINE

Firing mechanism

Contact horn

Contact horn

Explosive charge

Battery

Detonator

Booster

Hydrostatic arming device

tal shelf), while an alternative approach uses a rocket unit to propel the explosive charge up toward the target ship before firing. Another design houses a homing torpedo that, when fired, either actively or passively seeks the target.

In many cases, mines use a combination of activation devices so that, for example, both acoustic and magnetic sensors have to be activated to fire the mine, making the process of sweeping much more difficult. Further sophistication is given by timing devices that allow a mine to remain dormant for some time before it is activated or counter units that allow a set number of ships to pass before the mine is exploded.

Recent developments include the use of intelligent sensors that are able to differentiate between one type of ship and another, so as to select the most valuable target, and units that can be laid in a safe condition for remote activation when required.

Laying naval mines

There are three methods available for laying naval mines, and they are classified according to the vehicle used for deployment: submarine, air, or ship (surface).

Aircraft deployment has many advantages over other methods. Existing minefields that have lost some of their mines to explosions may be easily replenished by air, a task impossible by other means. In addition, delivering mines by air permits the mining of waterways under control of enemy forces. Mines deployed in this way, however, must have certain adaptations to reduce the problems of impact with the water when dropped from a great height. Parachutes are used to slow the fall of the mine—on contact with water, or when the mine has reached a predetermined depth, the mine automatically releases the parachute and both sink, helping to avoid detection.

▲ Above left: a naval mine of the contact type; when it sinks to a preset depth, a hydrostatic device automatically arms the firing circuit. Above right: a naval mine is designed to detonate when one of the contact horns is hit by a ship or submarine.

Tail fins and nose fairings may be included to improve flight stability and reduce drag. Airplanes that deliver bombs are also suitable for delivering mines. One aircraft that provides accurate delivery is the P-3 Orion, but others, such as the A-6 Intruder, the F/A 18 Hornet, and the S-3 Viking, are also suitable.

Mines delivered by submarines are launched from the torpedo tubes. This method of deployment is particularly useful when the covert laying of mines is necessary. In addition, submarines are able to operate in poor weather conditions and in enemy territory far from friendly bases. However, submarines are slow in comparison to airplanes, and this drawback combined with their relatively low payload capacity reduces the number of mines that can be deployed.

Using ships to deploy mines (surface-laid mines) lacks many of the advantages of either submarine or airplane deployment. Ships cannot easily replenish the minefield without great risk and are not capable of the secrecy provided by submarines. They do have the advantage, however, of being able to hold large quantities of mines.

International treaty

It is estimated that around 26,000 people are killed or maimed by land mines every year. Once land mines are laid, safely finding and eliminating them is extremely difficult and costly, and they may remain a danger to civilians long after a war has ended. In 1997, worldwide campaigning against land mines resulted in a treaty banning the use, stockpiling, production, and transfer of antipersonnel land mines. This treaty has since been ratified by 111 countries and signed by 139.

SEE ALSO: AMMUNITION • BOMB AND MINE DISPOSAL • EXPLOSIVE • METAL DETECTOR • MISSILE

Mining Techniques

In common with many other heavy engineering activities, mining is essentially a large-scale exercise in materials handling, although of a complexity and scale much greater than in any other industry. For example, in underground mining, not only must large tonnages of mineral and ore be moved distances of up to 10 miles (16 km) or more underground, the necessary circulation of ventilating air or the pumping of water can entail a further considerable mass movement. Indeed, there are some mines where, for every ton of mineral or ore brought to the surface, up to 20 tons (18 tonnes) of air have been circulated or up to 100 tons (90 tonnes) of water pumped out of the mine. The cost of such ventilation and drainage facilities, in addition to the expense of providing electric lighting, can be a major part of the cost of the mining operation.

Similarly, with surface mines there is often a considerable quantity of overburden that has to be removed before the ore or mineral layer is reached. Even if it is going to be used to refill the mine when operations are completed, the overburden has to be moved away from the working area for storage. In some areas, the sheer scale of material movement is such as to transform the landscape. Restoration or reclamation of the land once mining is completed is a major consideration with modern mining, often enforced by legislation.

Mining development

The earliest known examples of mining date from the Stone Age, when Neolithic people exploited flint deposits, first on the surface and then underground. Some of the early flint mines consisted of

▲ Minerals found near the surface can be mined by opencast methods. Once the overlying earth or rock is removed, the ore can then be dredged out, as in this Australian uranium mine.

vertical shafts up to 6 ft. (1.8 m) in diameter sunk into the ground to a depth of 30 ft. (9 m). Tunnels were driven out from the foot of the shaft to extract the flints, extending to the limits of natural ventilation. Tools used in these mines included deer horn picks and shovels made from the shoulder blades of various large animals.

These flint mines were highly organized with as many surface as underground workers, but the first records of mining are those of the Egyptians from around 3000 B.C.E. Mining for gold, silver, copper, and turquoise was carried out on a large scale, although most of these operations were confined to surface deposits. As the early miners followed a seam farther underground, deeper pits were required to reach the seam. Eventually, bell pits that opened out underground and so into shaft mines were developed.

Gradually, bone tools were replaced by metal ones on wood handles, while deposits of other metals such as copper were gradually exploited. The technique of fire setting was used to drive tunnels. Fires were lit against the rock face to heat it, and cold water was then thrown against the hot rock to rapidly cool it and cause cracking, allowing the use of picks and wedges to break the stone up. Deep mining was seldom attempted owing to the problems of draining water from the workings, though in some cases, it was possible to use narrow drainage tunnels, or adits, to carry the water away. Much the same techniques were used by the Romans, though on a large and highly organized scale, while surface mining continued to be a major source of minerals.

Development of deep mining depended on the introduction of pumping and ventilation sys-

▲ When a mineral lies deep below the surface, special underground mining techniques have to be used. Here, a prospecting drill is in operation in an underground mine in Coventry, England. As it advances, it shoots out low-pressure water jets, which form a fine rain. The rain catches the dust in the air and prevents its buildup, so it cannot cause visibility difficulties and fire problems.

tems and the use of water wheels and horse gins to supplement human power. Power systems were also applied to lifting materials up the mine shafts. Gunpowder was introduced for blasting toward the end of the 17th century.

However, it was the introduction of steam power that enabled the greatest advances in mining technique to be made. The early devices, as produced by the British engineer Thomas Savery for Cornish tin mines around 1700, used the vacuum produced by rapidly condensing steam to draw the water up directly. Since atmospheric pressure will only support a 32 ft. (9.7 m) head of water, the pumps based on this system had only limited application. The next step was taken by a British engineer, Thomas Newcomen, who built his first beam engine in 1712 for a coal mine. This engine used a rocking beam to transfer the piston movement to a pump shaft that extended down into the mine. Further development of this beam-type of steam engine was made by the Scottish inventor James Watt, resulting in a design that remained in use until the early years of the 20th century. Other designs producing rotary motion allowed steam engines to be used for hoisting, and deep mining was rapidly developed. The availability of more movable power sources, such as compressed air, internal combustion engines, and electricity, led to increasing mechanization, although many mines still make extensive use of hand labor.

Modern techniques

Modern mining techniques can be divided into four main types: surface, or opencast, or strip; underground; fluid—mining of natural liquids or by using solvents; and marine—mining of seabed deposits. These techniques are applied on a large scale; for example, world production of coal at the start of the 21st century was around four billion tons (3.6 billion tonnes) and U.S. production around 1 billion tons (0.9 billion tonnes). World production of iron ore is around 1 billion tons (0.9 billion tonnes), while some 20 million tons (18 million tonnes) of kaolin (china clay) are produced.

Surface mining

When the mineral to be mined lies relatively close to the surface, various forms of surface mining are employed, with the overburden, or waste material, being removed first to give access to the mineral. The simplest approach is the open pit, in which the mineral is simply dug out, and the pit gets deeper and deeper as more material is removed. As the depth increases, the pit widens out and is formed into a series of terraces that are worked at the same time and also give the pit sides the slope required for stability.

Most ores are fairly hard and are broken up by the use of explosives. Rotary or percussion drills are used to produce holes in the rock for filling with explosive, which is then detonated in a controlled sequence to shatter the rock. Power shovels and front loaders with capacities of up to 10 cubic yards (7.6 m³) are used to transfer the broken rock to dump trucks that can carry loads of up to 400 tons (360 tonnes) out of the pit. Heavy-duty conveyor systems may be used to transfer the rock, while railway transportation is employed in situations where the ore has to be moved longer distances. Draglines are also used for loading, especially with softer ores that do not require blasting and can simply be scooped out. Open pit mines can reach considerable depths; the Bingham Canyon copper mine in Utah (one of the most productive mines in the world) has a depth of 2,500 ft. (760 m).

Strip mining is carried out when the mineral layer, or seam, to be exploited is comparatively thin but extends for a considerable distance beneath the surface. Once the seam to be exploited has been identified and its extent established (usually by test borings), the overburden from an initial strip is removed using bulldozers and scrapers or power shovels and off-road trucks and stacked back away from the working area. The mineral layer is then broken up (if necessary), stripped, and removed. The process is then repeated by taking another strip along the seam, with the overburden being deposited in the space left by mining the first strip. In hilly country, this technique is not always possible.

▼ Underground mining is an expensive undertaking and requires meticulous planning to work a seam safely and economically.

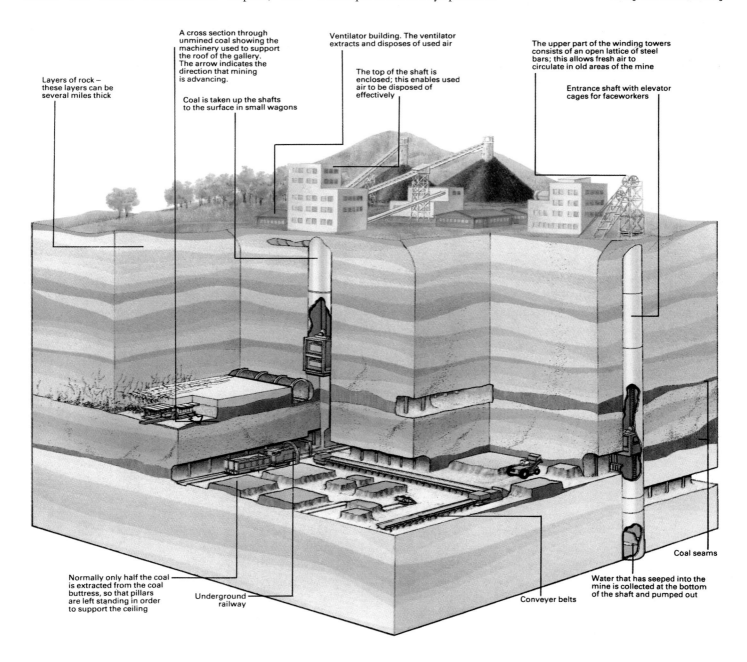

Layers of rock – these layers can be several miles thick

A cross section through unmined coal showing the machinery used to support the roof of the gallery. The arrow indicates the direction that mining is advancing.

Coal is taken up the shafts to the surface in small wagons

Ventilator building. The ventilator extracts and disposes of used air

The top of the shaft is enclosed; this enables used air to be disposed of effectively

The upper part of the winding towers consists of an open lattice of steel bars; this allows fresh air to circulate in old areas of the mine

Entrance shaft with elevator cages for faceworkers

Normally only half the coal is extracted from the coal buttress, so that pillars are left standing in order to support the ceiling

Underground railway

Conveyer belts

Coal seams

Water that has seeped into the mine is collected at the bottom of the shaft and pumped out

◄ Opencast coal mining in Siberia. This exploitive technique can ruin fragile environments.

In cases where an outcropping seam of coal is covered by a thick overburden that cannot be economically removed, the coal is sometimes extracted by the use of augers. These are essentially large screws with cutting heads that are rotated (by a diesel engine power system) to drill into the seam to a depth of up to 200 ft. (60 m), and the cut coal is thus screwed out of the hole.

Placer mining is another surface mining technique, used to extract ore from alluvial deposits in rivers or streams. Currently, the most common method of placer mining is by dredging using a bucket-ladder dredge. A long chain of buckets is conveyed around a rigid frame called a ladder, which can be adjusted to enable the buckets to dredge the deposits.

Underground mining

Opencast mining can be used where the overburden is up to around 100 ft. (30 m) thick, depending on its nature, but when the mineral to be exploited lies deeper, underground mining methods have to be used. The simplest type of underground mine is the drift mine, which is driven into the side of a hill to follow an outcropping seam, often sloping down as it follows the seam. Tunnels known as adits may also be driven horizontally to reach a seam and are often used to provide water drainage from the workings. More frequently, a vertical shaft is sunk into the ground, and galleries are dug out at levels where there are mineral deposits to be extracted.

Underground mines can extend to considerable depths with, for example, some of the South African gold mines being more than 12,000 ft. (3,650 m) deep. At such depths, Earth's heat can raise the temperature in the mine tunnels to over 122°F (50°C), and cooling systems have to be employed to give bearable working conditions.

Excavation of the levels can be carried out in two main ways: room and pillar and longwall. In the room (or stope) and pillar system, parallel roads are driven into the seam from the main galleries, and then the ore (coal) is extracted from a series of working areas (rooms or stopes) mined between a pair of roads. Unmined pillars of ore may be left between the rooms to support the roof or may be mined out and the roof allowed to collapse. Where such a collapse could lead to surface subsidence, the original rooms are filled with waste rock to support the roof before the pillars are mined.

With the longwall system (which is the main method used for coal mining in Europe) extraction is carried out on a face, up to 600 ft. (180 m) or more long, between a pair of roads. The face is advanced in a line with all the material along the face being removed. Supports hold the roof up in the area immediately adjacent to the face, and the roof farther back is allowed to collapse. Along the line of the roads, the rock of the roof is generally ripped back to give increased height. Supporting walls are built along the sides of the roads using the ripped rock with additional roof support provided by props. The need to support the roof over the roads can be eliminated by first driving the roads to their full extent and then retreating the face back along the roads so that the roof is allowed to collapse behind the face working area. Generally, the longwall system is used in deeper mines, where surface subsidence is unlikely to prove a problem.

Manual labor is still used to extract the ore in some mines, but mechanization has been widely applied to modern mining. The main operations that have to be carried out are cutting or breaking the ore away from the face and transporting it to the surface. Where the material to be mined is hard, such as rock, it is normally broken up by the use of explosives, with special types of explosives being used in coal and other mines where there is a risk of fire or gas explosion. Holes, generally 1 to 2 in. (2.5–5 cm) in diameter, are bored in the rock face to a depth of 6 to 10 ft. (1.8–3 m), the holes being arranged in a specific pattern. Explosive charges are loaded into the holes and fired in sequence to shatter the rock into small fragments. The other main method of breaking the face material up is by mechanical cutting or shearing, a method commonly used for coal.

Once the material has been broken away from the face, the fragments are picked up using power shovels, scrapers, or conveyor loaders ready for removal. In some cases the material is loaded into haulage trucks or rail cars that run along the underground roads, while in others conveyor systems are employed. In a drift mine the material can be transported directly to the surface, but in shaft mines, the material has to be lifted out on a hoist system. With coal mining equipment, the

◄ Tunnel-boring machines can weigh up to 900 tons (810 tonnes) and dig holes 33 ft. (10 m) in diameter. Here a Demag borer is completing a Penstock shaft at a hydroelectric power plant in Switzerland.

cutting head may be arranged to work in conjunction with a face conveyor so that the cut coal falls directly onto the conveyor and is carried away.

Fluid mining

Fluid mining generally involves the drilling of boreholes from the surface to gain access to the material to be extracted. In the Frasch process for the mining of sulfur, boiling water is pumped down pipes installed in the borehole to melt the sulfur deposits, which are then pumped to the surface as a liquid. Hot water and steam at high pressure are also used to extract the oil contained in bitumen tar sands. In the "huff and puff" mine at Cold Lake in Alberta, Canada, the steam is injected continuously for a period of several

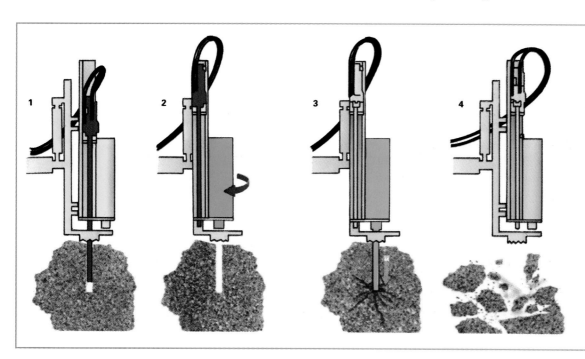

WATER CANNON

An alternative to using explosives in mining is to use a water cannon. The tensile strength of rock is one-tenth its compressive strength, so the cannon fragments the rock easily from within. A hole is drilled in the rock (1), and a water cylinder is swiveled into position (2). Water is blasted into the hole, causing the rock to crack (3), and then to break (4).

weeks to soften the bitumen so that it can be pumped out from a series of collection wells surrounding the injection well. Another approach involves setting the bitumen on fire, with combustion air being supplied through the well along with water, which is converted into steam. Although some of the bitumen is consumed by the fire, the majority is softened by the heat of combustion and the steam generated so that it can be pumped out.

Solvents can be pumped down boreholes to dissolve the required material so that it can be pumped up. This technique is commonly used in salt mining, with the salt being dissolved in water and pumped out as brine, while natural brine occurrences are also exploited by pumping. Selective solution mining can be used to recover materials such as potash.

A related process is leaching, which involves passing a weak acid over underground broken ore deposits. The acid dissolves the metal from the broken rock and is then pumped back to the surface for recovery of the metal. Tailored bacteria may also be used as the leaching agent. The main difference from the other borehole techniques lies in the fact that the metal content extracted represents only a small fraction of 1 percent of the mass of the ore. A major difficulty with leaching is that the ore rock has to be broken up to let the

acid or bacteria get to the ore. Conventional mining methods can be used to break up the rock or explosives introduced down the borehole.

In the mining of some relatively soft surface deposits such as kaolin, high-pressure water jets are used to dislodge the clay and wash it down to the treatment plant. This technique is known as hydraulic mining. The same principles have been applied to borehole mining to wash insoluble material free so as to create a slurry, which can then be pumped to the surface.

Marine mining

The alluvial mining of tin deposits by dredging offshore sands has been carried out for over a century, but the general principle of recovering mineral deposits from the seafloor has undergone considerable development following the discovery of rich deposits. Marine mining is carried out using bucket-wheel, grab, or suction-pump dredgers to recover a variety of minerals ranging from diamonds to metal ores and sand and gravel. Although most commercial marine mining operations are confined to a maximum water depth of around 200 ft. (60 m), systems have been developed for working at much greater depths. For example, airlift pumps have been used to recover manganese nodules from the bottom of the Pacific Ocean at depths of 3,000 ft. (900 m). Some authorities believe that economic mining of the seabed is possible down to 12,000 ft. (3,600 m) deep and that the tonnage of metals that can be recovered is greater than the land reserves. However, full exploitation is being hindered by political arguments over the ownership of deep-sea deposits.

▲ The best-known use of uranium is as a nuclear fuel, although it has other uses: its components have been used in photography for toning and as a dye in the wool industry. Mining uranium is an expensive and highly technical job, requiring mechanized systems and careful monitoring.

FACT FILE

- *In the Serra Pelada mountain district of Brazil, 10,000 self-employed miners work shoulder to shoulder, using only shovels, picks, and bare hands to mine gold. These "garimpeiros" have taken part in violent riots to exclude the mining companies, and the police have declared the area off-limits to women, alcohol, and gambling.*

- *In the alluvial tin mines of Malaysia, the ore-bearing land is torn apart with the aid of high-power water jets. The resulting tin-rich gravel is gathered by means of huge suction pumps.*

- *Metal-bearing nodules of manganese, iron, copper, and nickel discovered on ocean floors beneath the Atlantic, Pacific, and Indian Oceans would need to be mined by unusual techniques, including giant suction pipes and remote-controlled sledges, which would scoop up the nodules by the ton.*

SEE ALSO: COAL MINING • CONVEYOR • COPPER • EARTHMOVING MACHINERY • EXPLOSIVE • QUARRYING • SULFUR • TIN • TUNNELING

Mirror

All materials reflect some of the light that falls on them. A mirror is special because it reflects close to 100 percent of that light and it reflects it specularly. Specular reflection occurs at a surface that is smooth, possessing no pits or bumps as large as the wavelength of the light. Such a surface redirects an incident ray along one direction, enabling the formation of a clear image of an object. A rough surface, on the other hand, scatters incident light in all directions, creating a diffuse reflection.

Light rays from a point object spread out in all directions. After being reflected by a mirror, they continue to diverge. The new point from which they appear to diverge is called the image point. The condition that an extended object forms an image is that every point on the object forms just one image point. The image of such an object can be located behind or in front of the mirror surface.

The normal domestic mirror is flat and consists of a thin film of silver, coated on the back of a sheet of glass. It forms images that are identical in appearance to their objects except that they are laterally inverted—the mirror-image of a left hand, for example, is a right hand. Other mirrors, such as car rearview mirrors, are convex and form reduced images that are also laterally inverted. Concave mirrors, such as shaving mirrors, form enlarged laterally inverted images of objects that are close to them. The distorting mirrors of a fairground are concave in parts and convex in others, thus stretching and squeezing different parts of the image.

Images can be formed by multiple reflection: double reflection removes inversion. Using two ordinary mirrors, it is easy to make a mirror that forms a correct or noninverted image. So-called one-way mirrors consist of glass that has been coated with a layer of silver thinner than normal. This half-silvering reflects most of the light that falls on it (from either side) but permits some to pass through. On the observer's side of the mirror is a darkened room while on the other is a normally lit room. Most of the light from this side is reflected to form a bright image that masks the small amount passing through from the other side. Enough light passes through the mirror from the normally lit room to give the observer a clear view of it.

Mirror production

Metals have always been favored for mirrors because they are highly reflective, able to be cast and polished to a high degree of smoothness, and

▲ The silver coating on these mirrored lenses reflects most light away and reduces glare.

hard wearing. Bronze hand mirrors, often highly ornate, were made by the Egyptians, Etruscans, Greeks, and Romans in the centuries before Christ. Luxury mirrors were made of a highly polished silver.

The Roman writer Pliny reports the existence of mirrors made of glass coated with tin or silver, but this principle was not in common use until the Middle Ages. It was first used on a large scale by Venetian craftsman in the 16th century. They would lay a large sheet of tinfoil flat and coat it with mercury (which is liquid at normal temperatures), squeezing out excess mercury by laying a sheet of paper on top of this surface. Then a sheet of glass was gently laid on the paper and the paper withdrawn. An amalgam, a chemical combination of tin and mercury, would then remain as a coating on the lower surface of the glass.

This craft was supplanted in the 19th century by a chemical process invented by the German chemist Justus von Liebig, who discovered how to deposit silver onto glass from the solution of a silver salt. This process is used today to make mirrors for everyday purposes. To prevent the delicate silver layer from being scratched, a coating of copper sulfate and other chemicals is added, finished with a layer of paint. One-way mirrors dispense with this step, and use transparent lacquer instead.

The glass of an ordinary mirror serves the purpose of providing a very flat surface and of protecting the reflective silvering. It has the disadvantage of absorbing some of the light that passes through it, giving rise to multiple reflection, which in turn creates multiple images. These images are too faint to be troublesome in everyday use, but in scientific work, mirrors are frequently front-silvered to avoid multiple images.

Astronomical telescopes use concave mirrors, which are really shallow paraboloids. The parabola has the property that all light that strikes it and is parallel to its axis (in the case of a telescope, therefore, all light from the sky) ends up focused at one point. This property may be used in reverse. If a bright light is placed at the focus of a parabolic mirror, it will emerge as a parallel beam. This is exactly the principle used in a car headlight.

The mirror of a telescope consists of an aluminum or chromium-plus-aluminum film coated onto the accurately shaped glass or ceramic surface. The coating is formed by vacuum deposition: a small piece of the desired metal is placed on a heating coil in a vacuum chamber. It vaporizes, and the vapor deposits on the uncoated glass, which is also placed in the vacuum chamber. The resulting film is only a few millionths of an inch thick and can easily be removed chemically when necessary. It can then be renewed without disturbing the accurately ground glass surface. It is common to realuminize telescope and similar optics every couple of years

▼ Wavelengths of light striking a rough surface cause scatter—a diffuse reflection.

▲ The mirror of an astronomical telescope is carefully polished by this machine down to a 16 ft. (5 m) width, ensuring a highly reflective surface.

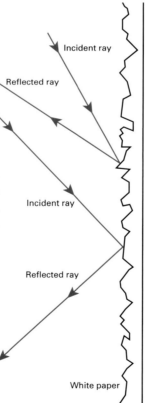

Incident ray

Reflected ray

Incident ray

Reflected ray

White paper

or so, when the surface becomes less reflective, and large telescopes have their own built-in aluminizing plant, close by the observing floor.

Liquid-mercury mirrors

Liquid mercury has been used to provide a mirrored surface for telescopes. Conventional large-scale telescopes cost enormous sums of money to build and consequently must by shared by a number of different research projects. Liquid-mercury telescopes, however, are much cheaper to make. One recent example, the Large Zenith Telescope (LZT) made by scientists at the University of British Columbia in Canada, uses a pool of mercury to create the 13th largest telescope in the world—236 in. (6 m) in diameter—which constantly rotates at about 5 rotations per minute. The spinning action causes the mercury to change its surface contours in such a way that it becomes an ideal shape for a telescope mirror. A conventional mirror on this scale is estimated to cost around $100 million, while the mercury mirror costs only $1 million. The disadvantage of this telescope, however, is that it can only point straight upward, thus limiting its applications.

| SEE ALSO: | GLASS • LIGHT AND OPTICS • MERCURY • REFLECTOR • SILVER • TELESCOPE, OPTICAL |

Missile

A guided missile is a pilotless, self-propelled airborne vehicle or spacecraft that carries a destructive warhead to a preselected target.

There are many different types of missiles, and one way of classifying them is by their application. Strategic missiles can be used to attack an enemy's home territory, while tactical missiles are used during the course of a battle. Developments in the capabilities of modern missiles have tended to blur this distinction though so that, for example, a cruise missile fitted with a nuclear warhead and targeted on an enemy city would be strategic, while the same missile fitted with antitank submunitions can have tactical applications.

Another way of differentiating between missiles is by the way they work; ballistic missiles are fired in a ballistic trajectory with the propulsion system acting during the first boost portion of the flight only. In aerodynamic types, the engines fire throughout the flight. A further classification favored by military analysts, since it provides a good description of the application, is based on the medium (land, sea, or air) from which the missile is launched and at which it is targeted. Thus, there are surface-to-surface missiles, air-to-surface missiles, air-to-air missiles, and so on.

Whatever the type or specific application, a missile consists of an airframe—with or without wings and fins—that houses a propulsion unit, a guidance system, and the warhead.

Airframe and propulsion system

The configuration and size of a missile are determined by its range and the size of the warhead package, since these determine the propulsion thrust and fuel load required. Largest of all are the strategic intercontinental ballistic missiles (ICBMs) with a range of at least 5,000 miles requiring multistage rocket motors, which take them to a height of up to 1,000 miles (1,600 km) during the boost stage. Speed at reentry is on the order of 15,000 mph (24,000 km/h), making interception difficult, while flight time is in the order of 25 minutes or less. The cylindrical fuel tanks for liquid propellant motors or the casings of solid-fuel motors often form the main structure of the missile, being arranged in a series of stages that are jettisoned in turn as the fuel is used

▶ The land-based Peacekeeper missile being launched from its silo. This ICBM, which can carry up to ten independently targeted nuclear warheads, uses silos originally designed for the Minuteman missile system, which it has replaced.

up, leaving the warhead package to complete the trajectory to the target. Wings or fins are not generally fitted because most of the missile's flight is outside Earth's atmosphere, where aerodynamic control surfaces would be ineffective. The earliest successful U.S. ICBM was the Atlas, tested in 1959. It was quickly followed by the Titan and then the Minuteman. Currently, the United States uses Peacekeeper ICBMs, which are capable of carrying ten warheads.

Most of the above types of missiles have rocket motors; both solid- and liquid-fuel motors are used. Solid-fuel designs are generally preferred, since they can more readily be prepared for firing.

Other types of missiles have a cylindrical body fitted with cruciform wings and either cruciform tail fins or nose-mounted foreplanes. Cruise missiles, such as the Tomahawk, are air breathing with ramjet or turbojet engines and are designed to travel within Earth's atmosphere. They tend to resemble piloted aircraft, with air intakes for the engines and wings or fins to sustain them in flight.

Control system

Missiles that operate within Earth's atmosphere are able to use control surfaces moved by electric, hydraulic, or pneumatic actuators. Either the cruciform wings or the tail surfaces may be pivoted for this purpose. Less frequently, the use of wing-mounted ailerons or elevons or pivoted vertical and horizontal tail surfaces, or a combination of both, provides an even closer similarity to the control surfaces of a piloted aircraft.

An alternative to aerodynamic control is some form of vectored thrust, which is effective in both atmosphere and space. In large missiles, such as ICBMs, it is usual to gimbal the nozzles of the rocket motors—or even the motors themselves—thus steering the missiles by changing the direction of thrust. A similar deflection of thrust can be achieved by liquid injection on one inner wall of the nozzle or by blanking off part of the nozzle. This last technique, employing pivoted semaphores, is particularly suitable for close-range air-launched antiaircraft missiles, which must have high maneuverability to match that of the target.

Guidance system

The most important component of a missile is the system that ensures that it hits the correct target. Some guidance systems are self-contained within the missile, using devices such as gyroscopes: these systems often have the advantage of being less susceptible to enemy electronic countermeasures (ECM) or jamming. Others involve continuous monitoring of the missile's position and course corrections during flight. The U.S. tactical missile system (TACMS), for example, uses the global positioning system (GPS) to guide the missile to its target.

One of the simplest forms of guidance for short-range missiles, such as antiarmor weapons, is wire guidance. As the missile travels toward its target, it trails one or two fine wires that unwind from bobbins and continue to link with the operator's controls. The operator can steer it into the

▼ The antiship version of the BGM-109 Tomahawk cruise missile with the land-attack warhead (11) below. A submarine launch begins with the flooding of the torpedo tube. The tube is then opened and the cruise missile ejected from its protective capsule. The booster rocket (8) fires about 30 ft. (10 m) out and its four jet tabs (9) vector the thrust to steer Tomahawk out of the sea. The missile surfaces at an angle of 55 degrees with a speed of 55 mph (88 km/h), and the tail fins (7) spring out to roll the missile the right way up. After 6 to 7 seconds, the booster burns up and is jettisoned while the wings (4) extend. The air scoop (10) deploys and the turbofan engine (6), spun up to 20,000 rpm by hot gas from a starter cartridge, begins the cruise flight at about 1,000 ft. (300 m).

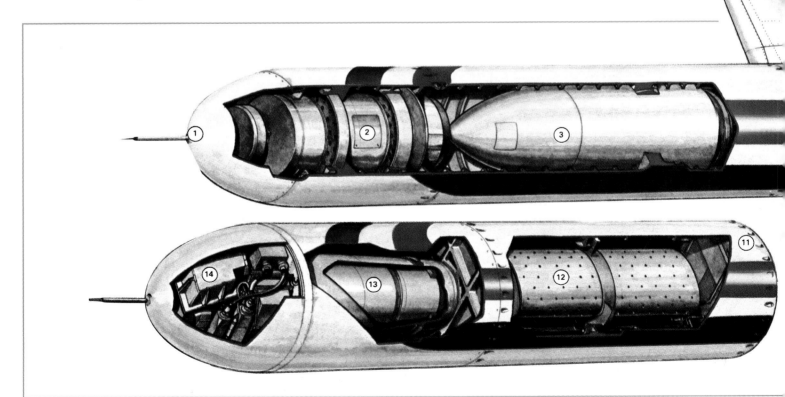

target using a thumbstick or miniature aircraft type of joystick to generate electric signals, which are transmitted over the wires to the missile's control system. The weight of the wires limits range to about two miles, and both target and missile must be visible to the operator. Tracking flares attached to the missile help the operator follow its path as distance from the launcher increases, especially in poor light conditions.

If the missile is to be fired against a target beyond visual range, a cathode-ray viewer rather like a TV screen is used. The precise position of the target, if fixed and known, can be set up on the screen. The missile can then be tracked by radar in flight and its blip steered into the target. Greater accuracy can be achieved by fitting a small TV camera into the nose of the missile. Then, as it approaches the target, the controller receives a TV picture of the target area and can steer the missile to a precisely chosen pinpoint. Such techniques have enabled controllers in aircraft to hit a particular bridge support or part of a ship beyond visual range.

Smart missiles

Improved technology has led to the development of "smart missiles" that use a variety of techniques to assist the missile in reaching its target. More sophisticated TV guidance systems, for example, enable the camera to be locked onto the target before launching; the missile then homes automatically on where the camera is aimed, by means of onboard electronics.

Radar tracking is used widely for surface-launched antiaircraft missiles, the advantages being that it can, if required, eliminate the need for manual steering and it is fully effective in bad weather or at night. The automatic system

▲ Launching a cruise missile from an armored box launcher installed on the deck of the USS *Merrill*. The box launcher is designed for use on certain U.S. Navy surface ships and can carry up to four cruise missiles, which would be used primarily against enemy ships.

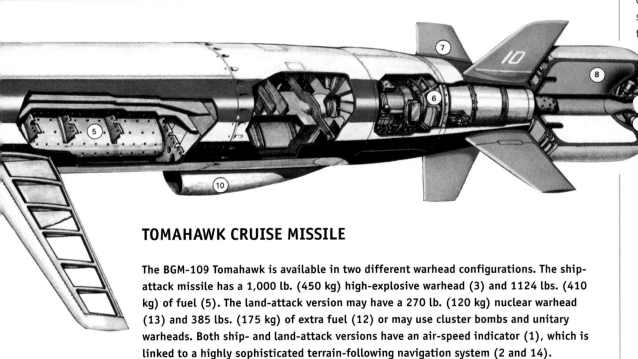

TOMAHAWK CRUISE MISSILE

The BGM-109 Tomahawk is available in two different warhead configurations. The ship-attack missile has a 1,000 lb. (450 kg) high-explosive warhead (3) and 1124 lbs. (410 kg) of fuel (5). The land-attack version may have a 270 lb. (120 kg) nuclear warhead (13) and 385 lbs. (175 kg) of extra fuel (12) or may use cluster bombs and unitary warheads. Both ship- and land-attack versions have an air-speed indicator (1), which is linked to a highly sophisticated terrain-following navigation system (2 and 14).

requires two radars, to track the target and missile, respectively. Radar information is fed into a computer, causing signals to be transmitted to the missile so that it will intercept the target. This system is called radar command guidance.

Only one radar is needed for beam-riding guidance. After the radar has been locked onto the target, a missile is launched and guided into the radar beam. It locks onto the beam and flies along it to the target. Semiactive homing is somewhat similar. This system involves illuminating the target with a radar, causing radar signals to be reflected back from it. The missile then homes onto the source of the reflected signals. Active homing differs in that the missile both transmits and receives the signals, making it independent of radar transmitters on the ground or in the launch aircraft. Such independent guidance systems have the advantage that the launch aircraft can then turn its attention to another target or break off the engagement, thus minimizing the risks of being attacked itself.

Active homing missiles tend to be comparatively large and complex. By comparison, those that employ passive homing are among the simplest of all, requiring no transmitters of any kind although they are self-contained. Typical are missiles fitted with an infrared heat-seeking head. This locates any source of heat emission, such as the exhaust of an aircraft jet engine or the motors of ground vehicles, and homes in on it. Heat-seeking missiles, however, can be made to miss their targets through the use of decoy jamming signals emitted from the threatened aircraft. The infrared countermeasure (IRCM) system confuses the missile with a plethora of signals, causing it to fly harmlessly off course.

Another homing technique uses laser designators to achieve high effectiveness even in a rapidly changing combat environment. A controller on the ground or in an aircraft locates a target and directs a laser beam onto it. The missile then picks up the reflected laser beam and homes in on the source of the reflections.

Ballistic missiles generally use inertial guidance systems, though satellite navigation techniques using GPS can also be used, with high levels of accuracy being possible. On current models of cruise missiles, a combination of guidance systems is used, including an inertial guidance and a terrain-matching system.

Newer navigational techniques include the McDonnell-Douglas terrain-contour matching system (TERCOM). This system compares pre-programmed digital information on the terrain the missile will cross on its way to the target with information recorded by the missile while in flight. A further refinement of this technology is the digital scene-matching area correlator (DSMAC), which uses digital representations of the target area taken from many different angles during different weather conditions. The onboard computer system in the missile compares this store of digital maps with the scene below as it nears its target. Both TERMAC and DSMAC are used in Tomahawk missiles along with GPS, resulting in a high-precision weapon capable of striking within 33 ft. (10 m) of the target area. The first operational use of this missile was made during the Gulf War in Operation Desert Storm in 1991, where it achieved a direct-hit accuracy of almost 85 percent.

Warheads

Missiles can carry almost any kind of military warheads, including those for chemical or biological warfare, though high-explosive and nuclear types are most common. For example, some anti-tank missiles can be fitted with interchangeable armor-piercing warheads capable of piercing 24 in. (60 cm) of steel, high-explosive, and antipersonnel fragmentation warheads. Small nuclear warheads with explosive powers as low as 1,000 tons (900 tonnes) of TNT can be fitted to almost any class of missile. With high-explosive warheads, both contact and proximity fuses can be employed. An increasing trend is the use of submunitions that are released by the missile as it approaches the target area. Such submunitions may consist of antipersonnel blast bombs or mines or terminally guided units designed to home in on and destroy vehicles and armor.

Strategic intercontinental missiles are generally equipped with nuclear warheads, which can have explosive powers of several tens of megatons—1,000,000 tons (900,000 tonnes) TNT equivalent—though increasing accuracy has encouraged the adoption of smaller-yield warheads. The effectiveness of ICBMs is increased by the use of multiple reentry vehicles (MRVs) and multiple independently targetable reentry vehicles (MIRVs). MRVs have several physically small warheads (but of high-explosive power) that are released following the initial boost stage to continue to the target as individual units, thus increasing the difficulty of defense and spreading the damage over a wider area. MIRVS take this concept a stage further by ejecting the warheads along a number of different reentry trajectories.

SEE ALSO: Ammunition • Ballistics • Global positioning system • Laser and maser • Nuclear weapon • Pilotless aircraft • Radar • Rocket and space propulsion • Torpedo

Mobility Aid

◀ This yacht has been extensively altered to make it accessible to a wheelchair user. Many mobility aids are available that can improve accessibility for people with disabilities.

Environments constructed for the able-bodied can present overwhelming obstacles to people with physical disabilities, forcing them into seclusion and isolation. However, applications of new technology have led not only to voice-controlled wheelchairs but also to an array of other sophisticated devices that aid mobility and independence.

Motor-driven wheelchairs

Several types of powered wheelchair, such as the Jazzy range produced by Pride Mobility Corp, have a curb-climbing facility, which, on some models, enables the wheelchair to climb up curbs as high as 6 in. (15 cm). Several methods may be used to achieve this goal, such as designing chairs with six rather than four wheels, the extra pair of wheels providing stability as the wheelchair negotiates the curb.

Many different models of motorized three- or four-wheel scooters are available with handlebar steering and a swiveling seats. Often they are narrow enough to pass through doorways and can be dismantled to fit in the trunk of an automobile. Looking more like a sidewalk scooter than a wheelchair, these mobility aids offer disabled people who can sit upright unaided a new mobility in the home, at work, in shops, and in other public places. They are operated by rechargable battery and can be driven by the light touch of a finger over a range commonly up to 25 miles (40 km).

Many wheelchair users are unable to stand up by themselves to reach high cupboards, filing cabinets, shelves, or windows. The Levo Stand-up wheelchair—an ingeniously designed appliance developed in collaboration with the medical team of the Swiss Paraplegic Center in Basel, Switzerland and subsidized by the Swiss Foundation in Aid of Spastic Children—solves this problem by raising and lowering the user's body at the touch of a switch.

Powered by a dry battery, the lifting movement of the Levo wheelchair can be interrupted at any desired point and continued or reversed at will. Padded safety straps secure the upper part of the user's body and the legs, while nonslip rubber pads beneath the footrests make toppling impossible—even if the occupant wriggles around. By enabling wheelchair users to stand, the Levo wheelchair helps to improve blood circulation and the functioning of the intestine and bladder.

Currently under clinical trials and awaiting approval by the Federal Drug Administration is a completely new design of wheelchair called the iBOT. Designed by the U.S. inventor Dean Kamen, this revolutionary wheelchair uses a complex system of gyroscopes coordinated by microprocessors and software to maintain balance when climbing curbs or even stairs. Unlike a conventional wheelchair, this design uses four swivelling wheels and is capable of balancing on only two of the wheels. When climbing stairs, the pairs of wheels rotate around each other to move the chair upwards or downwards, while the gyroscopes keep the chair stable. The ability to balance on two wheels also enables the iBOT to rise vertically so that the user is able to achieve the same eye-level as a standing person and also reach objects placed at a height that would normally make them inaccessible to a wheelchair user. In addition, the iBOT is designed so that during all of the above activities the seat remains level.

Remote-control wheelchairs

People with quadriplegia are totally unable to control the movements of their arms and legs and, therefore, cannot operate a conventional wheelchair. However, they can control an electric chair with their mouth by operating a suck-and-puff switch. The mouthpiece is connected to the wheelchair's automatic controls by a flexible tube. When the

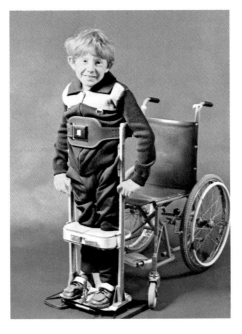

▼ The ORLAU swivel walker enables people with paraplegia to move around without a wheelchair. The walker consists of a rigid body frame that holds the user upright. By rocking from side to side, the user is carried along by two interlocking footplates.

user exhales strongly, the chair goes forward; when the user inhales, the chair reverses. Lighter inhaling or blowing on the mouthpiece turns the chair to either the right or the left.

Eye-controlled wheelchairs for people with quadriplegia have evolved from switches activated only by eye movements. Developed for the National Aeronautics and Space Administration by a company in Alabama, eye-controlled switches have been used by astronauts in situations where high gravitational forces make arm and leg movements impossible.

Light sources, mounted at either side of a pair of eye glasses, bounce light into the wearer's eyes and detect the differences between the reflection from the whites and darker pupils. Whenever the pupil moves across the path of the light beam, the reduced reflection activates an electric switch. Adapted to a motorized wheelchair, the switch enables users to control their progress solely with their eyes. The switch can also be adapted to turn the pages of a book and operate electric appliances, industrial machinery, electric typewriter keyboards, and other devices.

The voice-controlled wheelchair is another NASA-sponsored device based on teleoperator and robot technology for space-related programs. Developed by the Jet Propulsion Laboratory, the wheelchair can pick up packages, open doors and windows, turn a television knob, and perform a variety of other everyday functions for the disabled occupant. Another voice-controlled chair is capable of responding to 35 one-word voice commands, such as go, stop, up, down, right, left, forward, and backward. The device contains a voice-command analyzer, which uses a computer. The user repeats commands into the computer until the analyzer recognizes them. Then the computer translates the commands into electric signals, and these signals activate appropriate motors to move the chair.

Related devices

People paralyzed from the waist down with spina bifida or severely disabled by muscular dystrophy and cerebral palsy can be enabled to walk with the aid of a swivel walker. Designed by Gordon Rose, the orthopedic surgeon at the Orthotic Research and Locomotor Assessment Unit in Britain, the walker consists of a rigid body frame, which supports the body, and two swiveling footplates.

The users—adults and children as young as 15 months—stand upright supported by the frame and rock from side to side so that the interlocking footplates carry them along. Most people can slide unaided from wheelchair to walker frame, thereby achieving a degree of independence and

The Commodore hoist can be operated independently by a series of pull cords. It has a motor to lift the person up and down through openings between floors and a transverse unit to move the person across a room. Both the motor and the transverse unit are attached to tracking, which can be either portable or fixed to the ceiling. Again, the user is carried in a sling.

Not only can a hoist allow a disabled person to move about independently, it may also, for example, help a mother with diminished muscle power and poor coordination by lifting her baby from bassinet to buggy, high chair, and changing table in a specially designed baby harness. A hoist can also be used to transfer a disabled person from a wheelchair to a car seat. Some models clamp onto the automobile roof and are hydraulically operated by an attendant. The user is secured in slings attached to a spreader bar and moved clear of the wheelchair using a pump; then the lifting arm is swiveled and pushed in toward the automobile. As the pump valve is released, the person is lowered into the seat. Afterward, the lifting unit can be detached and stowed in the trunk of the automobile until needed.

Driving aids

Whatever method of transfer is chosen, once inside the automobile, even people with severe disabilities—such as malformation caused by thalidomide—can become mobile drivers by using lever-control steering, which can be fitted to standard automobiles. The lever control, which is operated instead of the steering wheel, is mounted wherever convenient—on either the dashboard or the car floor—so that the automobile can be driven by hands or feet.

For safety reasons, the control system is in triplicate. The lever control has potentiometers that convert its position into voltages and two electronic channels that drive motors to turn the wheel as instructed by the lever. There are three other potentiometers, turned by the gearing, which also turns the wheel.

If one of these circuits becomes faulty, its motor is disconnected automatically and an alarm sounds. The driver can still pull over to the side of the road, because the remaining motor is designed to be capable of moving the wheel on its own. Once the vehicle has stopped, the driver presses a reset button, the system resets, and the alarm stops.

In addition to the automobile's standard battery, smaller batteries provide the power to turn the wheel. Because the lever control can be switched on or off, an able-bodied person can also drive the automobile in the normal way.

mobility. The swivel walker is mass-produced from industrial components, so it is inexpensive; it is available in several countries.

Some disabilities, such as those related to certain cases of multiple sclerosis or a high-level lesion of the spinal cord, may prevent a person from being able to move his or her own body weight unaided. A fairly light person can be lifted by a strong helper, but constantly lifting a heavy person may well damage an assistant's back. To solve this problem, a range of manual and electrically operated hoists have been designed.

The Mecalift, a small and mobile attendant-operated hoist, consists of a mast made from cold-drawn seamless steel that slots into a chassis of high-tensile steel tubing. Four heavy-duty nylon wheels allow the hoist to be moved backward and forward, and a swivel castor at the rear of the mast allows the hoist to be pivoted for turning. The mechanism consists of a screw-jack with automatic load-sustaining clutch and winding handle. The winding handle, situated at the top of the mast and operated by the helper, raises and lowers the jib and hanger bar from which the disabled person is suspended by means of slings.

In some instances—for example, when an aging couple can no longer manage the strain of lifting and lowering a severely disabled offspring from bed to wheelchair, bath, or toilet—an attendant-operated hoist can be a great benefit. Its installation may make it unnecessary for a disabled person to be taken into residential care.

▲ The Vessa Power Chair has two curved climber arms fixed above the two front wheels. When the wheels touch a curb, the climber arms pivot and raise the wheels over the curb, then roll the chair forward, providing the direct-drive rear wheels with enough power to lift the chair up a 5 in. (12.5 cm) step. The chair's direction and speed are controlled by small levers located on the arm rests.

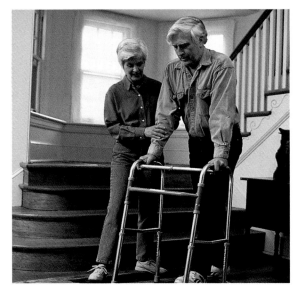

◀ This Zimmer walking frame enables people whose balance has become impaired to walk without fear of falling. It also allows the user to rest some of their weight on their arms rather than supporting themselves completely with their legs.

For children whose mobility is severely impaired, possibly due to spasticity, a firm based in Britain and the United States has designed the Ortho Kinetics Travel Chair. Its frame consists of upper and lower parts pivoted at the front and tensioned with a spring between them. At the rear of the chair is a telescopic tube assembly, complete with a latch pin and release lever. By releasing the lever and moving the chair up and down, a range of functions is possible. It can be used as a high chair for eating at the table, a stroller, a reclining chair, or a car seat.

To convert the chair into a car seat, the chair's front wheels are cantilevered into the floor of the car and the telescopic tube mechanisms are fully released so that the undercarriage retracts up to the base of the travel chair. The chair is then swung across into the car seat, and the normal seat belt is attached. Very little effort is involved in this procedure, and thus the strain of lifting a severely handicapped child into a car is eliminated.

Bathing aids

One of the most difficult activities for people who have had strokes or who have joint-related disorders, such as rheumatoid arthritis or osteoarthritis, is bathing. For those who can get into a bath unaided, there is a range of inexpensive bathing aids, such as bath boards and liners, that fit into a standard bath.

For people who cannot lower themselves into a bath without assistance, Mecanaids has produced the Autolift, a self-operated or attendant-operated bath seat, which is mounted on a pillar bolted to the floor. The bather remains in the seat while it is raised, lowered, and swung through an arc of 180 degrees, in and out of the bath.

A firm specializing in marine products also produces a bath for the elderly and disabled—the

Parker bath—based on the concept of moving the bath and water to the user, rather than the reverse. This goal is achieved by the use of a simple pivot principle. The bath is mounted on a pedestal base of adjustable height, so it can be raised or lowered by hydraulic jack for direct access even from a wheelchair or a bed. When tilted to an upright position, the bath forms a seat. Once the footwell is filled with water, the bather slides onto the seat from the side. Then the counterbalanced watertight door is closed over the side by light hand control. With the hydraulic release valve in the locked position, either the pump handle in the bath or the pedal beneath it is gently pumped. The bath slowly reclines and water flows up around the bather's body. On release of the hydraulic valve mechanism, the bath returns to the upright position.

The incidence of physical handicap is often linked to the effects of poverty. Yet in poorer countries, where the proportion of disabled to able-bodied people rises dramatically, expensive technological aids are unobtainable.

Instead, the Appropriate Health Resources and Technologies Action Group (AHRTAG) has been designing low-cost aids that can easily be made from materials readily available in developing nations—such as string and wood. Simple walking and climbing frames, back supports, and seats have enabled children who had never risen from their backs to sit up and even move about.

Walking frames

Walking frames are simple mobility aids that consist of U- or V-shaped lightweight metal frames with three or four rubber feet to prevent slippage. Some models may be easily folded to allow for car transportation, while others may include wheels, which permit even greater ease of use. Currently under development by Eldercare Robotics is a mobility aid for walking that consists of a frame with motorized wheels. The inventors of this device intend it to be able to respond to verbal requests to take the user to particular locations, such as the supermarket or the kitchen. The users simply hold on to the handles of the frame, while the motorized wheels guide them to their destination. Sensors and actuators will enable the mobility aid to negotiate difficult terrain, while manual breaks on the handles will be supplemented by automatic safety breaks that cut in when the sensors detect a dangerous situation.

SEE ALSO: Accessibility aid • Automobile • Battery • Bioengineering • Computer • Electric motor • Hydraulics • Voice recognition and synthesis

Modem and ISDN

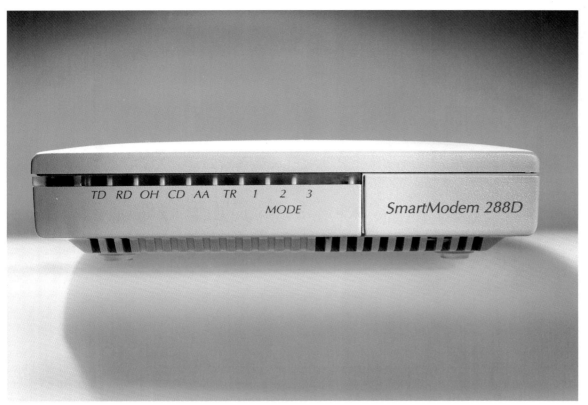

◀ Early modems were housed in separate boxes like the one shown here, and connected with wires to ports on a computer. Modern modems are now fitted internally as cards that slot into housings inside the computer.

The personal computer revolution that has changed all our lives has depended heavily on the modem and, for many of us, on ISDN. Today, there are almost as many modems in use as there are PCs, and it is primarily because of the modem and ISDN that the current popularity and usefulness of personal computers has come about.

What is a modem?

The term modem is an acronym—a new word derived from some of the letters of other words. Modem is made from the letters "mod" taken from modulator and "dem" taken from demodulator. Modulation is an important principle in radio, television, and communications generally. It is the process in which, by modifying in various ways some characteristic of a radio wave, beam of light, or electric current flowing in a wire, information is carried. In this context, the term information means any kind of code or data, that can be reproduced in any form, and includes text, the spoken word, music, graphics, video, and so on.

In the earliest days of radio transmission, modulation was achieved by switching the wave on and off with a Morse key. Later, amplitude modulation (AM) of the radio wave was developed so that speech and music could be transmitted. In this method, the size (amplitude) of the high-frequency radio wave was varied in accordance with the rapidly-changing electrical signal from a microphone. That system was soon followed by an improved method called frequency modulation (FM), in which the amplitude remains constant but the number of cycles per second of the radio wave is varied in accordance with the sound signal. In both systems, the receiver equipment, whether radio or television, removes the high-frequency carrier wave leaving the audible signal. This process is called demodulation.

Conventional telephone lines are designed to carry a simple amplitude-modulated signal and can do so over long distances. Computers, however, carry information in the form of a rapid stream of digital signals in the form of square electrical pulses representing 1s and 0s. Regular telephone lines are quite unsuitable for the transmission over long distances of such rapidly-altering digital signals, which would suffer such severe electrical losses that in a short distance the pulses would be reduced to virtually nothing. So some way of converting them into a form transmissible by simple wires is necessary. The modem is used for this purpose.

Modem operation

Telephone lines do not actually carry sounds; they carry the electrical equivalent of sounds. So the function of the modem is to generate the electri-

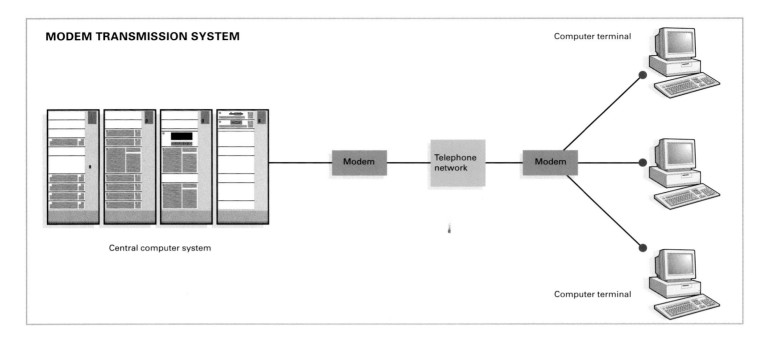

MODEM TRANSMISSION SYSTEM

Computer terminal

Central computer system

Modem

Telephone network

Modem

Computer terminal

cal signal for a particular audible tone to represent a digital 1, and another electrical signal for a different audible tone to represent a digital 0. One tone is higher in pitch than the other, and the signals switch rapidly from one to the other. When these electrical signals are converted to sound, they produce a characteristic warbling noise that will be familiar to many personal computer users, as it can often be heard soon after the phone number of the Internet service provider (ISP) is dialed. This method of modulation is known as frequency shift keying, and the sound it produces can also be heard on short-wave radio.

The tones are generated by simple electronic oscillators and are switched electronically. In present-day modems, it is unnecessary for the tones to be converted to actual audible sound. Modems must, of course, work in both directions, so they have to convert digital signals into electrical "tones" for outgoing information and convert "tones" into digital signals for incoming information. It is important to note that modems do not directly convert the electrical pulses of the computer into "sound" pulses for the phone lines.

Computers can move single streams of binary digits (bits) around at a rate of over a million per second, but because they move bits along parallel tracks of 8, 16, 32, or more conductors, the real rate is much faster. The fastest modems, however, are limited to a rate of about 56,000 bits per second (56 kbps) and must work with a single stream only. Computers are parallel devices handling 8, 16, 32, or 63 bits simultaneously; modems are known as serial devices, that is, the binary digits are sent one at a time. So the modem has to handle information a little at a time. A 10 megabyte file (80 million bits) that can

▲ Modems act as a linking device between computers separated over a distance. The modem converts digital data from a computer into analog signals that can travel down a telephone line, then reconverts them back to digital when it reaches the receiving computer.

be moved about within a computer in a few seconds will take 24 minutes to download via a fast modem.

Early modems

The first modem was a crude device with a microphone and a small loudspeaker onto which the telephone receiver had to be placed. It was necessary to ensure that the mouthpiece was lying on the modem loudspeaker and the earpiece on the modem microphone. This design was dictated by the fact that, at that time, phone companies objected strongly to direct connections being made to their wiring. These modems were slow and were able to transmit data at a rate of about 300 binary digits (bits) per second. This is known as the baud rate, after the French engineer Jean-Maurice-Emile Baudot, who invented a method of sending five messages simultaneously over a single telegraph line and who, in 1874, patented a five-bit code with equal on and off intervals that could send all the letters of the alphabet and a range of punctuation signs. In the case of a binary channel, the baud rate is equal to the bit rate—the number of bits transmitted in a second.

These early modems were, necessarily, external to the computer with which they were used. And for a time, even after direct electrical connections were allowed, most modems were in the form of boxes external to the computer. These modems had indicator lights (light-emitting diodes, or LEDs) to show the state of reception or transmission. Although external modems are still available and can be connected very easily to a universal serial bus (USB) socket on a computer, most PC modems are now internal and come already installed in the machine. Internal modems take the form of plug-in cards that are inserted into multiconnection slots in the main board (motherboard) of the computer but with a narrow panel that appears in a slot at the back of the PC. This panel carries the socket for the phone line. All the internal connections to the computer, including those for the power supply for the modem, are made when the modem board is plugged in.

The third development in the history of the modem is the PCMCIA modem. This is a credit card-sized device used with laptop computers, and the name is an acronym of PC Memory Card International Associates. This very compact type of modem fits into a flat, 68-pin connector slot originally intended for adding memory cards.

Improving modem speeds

The commonest complaint of Internet users is the lack of speed, especially when waiting for connections and downloading software. The fastest current modems, theoretically capable of working at a speed of 56 kbps, seldom if ever actually reach this speed. The difference between bits and bytes (groups of 8 bits) and their relationship to computer alphanumeric characters must also be remembered. One character requires one byte. Thus, the theoretical maximum speed of transmission of characters is only about 6,000 per second. In real life, the actual speed may be much lower.

One way of improving modem speed is to abandon the two-tone idea and modulate a simple electrical wave by a process known as phase-shift keying (PSK). The phase of a regularly changing quantity, such as an alternating electric current, is the stage, or state, of the quantity at any particular moment during the cycle. Such a wave can be modified so that the phase no longer changes smoothly in a sine-wave manner but makes a sudden change in direction. This change of phase can represent a binary digit. The phase is shifted one way for binary 1 and the opposite way for binary 0. Quadrature amplitude modulation, used in some higher-speed modems, involves two simultaneous carrier waves that are 90 degrees out of phase with each other, allowing more information to be transmitted in the same time.

Modem protocols

Data transmission in both directions between two or more points can be conducted only if an agreement has been reached between all participants as to how the communication is to be conducted. There must be agreement on the digital code to be used; on how each letter sent is checked and, if wrong, automatically corrected; on the speed of transmission; on how the machine at each end of the line knows that a message has been started and stopped; and so on. These agreements are called protocols, and until standard protocols were designed and universal agreement obtained for them, the kind of universal two-way Internet communication we now enjoy was impossible.

Internet Service Providers (ISPs), such as Compuserve, Microsoft Network, America OnLine, and hundreds of others, use agreed-upon protocols to connect the user to the Internet. The most popular of these are point-to-point protocol (PPP) and Serial Line Internet Protocol (SLIP). PPP is the more recent and better protocol, but popular browsing software, such as Internet Explorer and Netscape Navigator, are designed to work with both of them.

The PC user need not be much concerned with protocols because these are usually built into the software, known as the operating systems, required by all personal computers. Windows 95, 98, NT, ME, and 2000 all incorporate a dial-up networking program that is PPP and SLIP compatible so that any ISP account using these

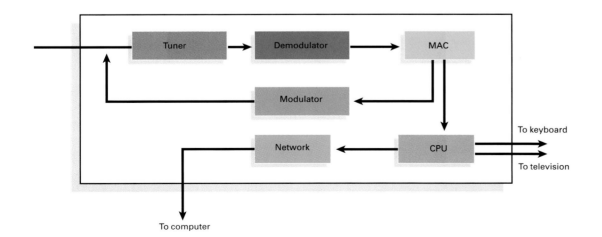

To computer

◀ Cable modems are proving to be a popular way to connect to online digital services because of their fast transmission speeds. The tuner connects to the cable outlet and passes the analog signal to the demodulator, which converts it to a digital format. A media access controller (MAC) acts as the interface between the hardware and software portions of the network protocols.

protocols can be used. Similarly, users with machines with a Linux operating system can sign up with these ISPs.

What is ISDN?

The real answer to speed of data transfer is not to try to design faster or more efficient modems but to do away with modems altogether and to arrange a system that conveys data in digital form. Integrated Services Digital Network (ISDN) is such a system. ISDN is more expensive than modem systems, because for its highest speed links, it does not use regular copper wire. ISDN is capable of carrying digital signals at a speed that calls for quite different kinds of conductors—fiber-optic cabling with modulated light beams over land and satellite communication for longer distances. The higher the frequency of the carrier wave, the more information it can carry in a given time. A light beam in an optical fiber is an electromagnetic wave of the highest possible frequency and has an enormous capacity.

People occasionally talk of ISDN modems. The confusion arises because ISDN requires a device that may appear similar to a modem but is actually a terminal adapter that links the serial output from the computer to the special network.

The name Integrated Services Digital Network refers to the fact that the system was designed as a single service, involving various parts, that can carry all forms of digitally encoded traffic—for speech, data, music, and video. Regular ISDN offers a range of data rates ranging from 64 kbps to nearly 2 million bits per second (2 Mbps). Broadband ISDN is offered in a variety of formats in different countries, providing transmission rates up to tens or hundreds of Mbps.

For the PC user, installation of an ISDN line means that the phone company must upgrade the regular phone line to the home or office to a type that will carry the higher-speed transmission. Upgrading may be expensive, and the price will vary widely, depending on the degree of existing local usage of ISDN. Domestic ISDN on the basic rate interface (BRI) usually provides three channels, two of which can be combined to give a 128 kbps connection to the Internet. If the phone or fax is used at the same time, one of these fast channels is used, and the Internet connection drops in speed to 64 kbps. The third channel is much slower and is used for other administrative tasks such as signalling that the line is busy.

Digital subscriber lines

ISDN is not the only high-speed connection available to users of personal computers. An alternative is the asymmetric digital cable line (ADSL). It too requires an upgraded phone line because it is an all-digital system. The adjective "asymmetric" is used because the system has a much greater capacity for downloading than it has for outgoing data. This makes sense because most outgoing data, such as for e-mail, shopping, and browsing, involves much shorter messages than those involved in downloading software, music, graphics, video, and so on. The downloading speed of an ADSL will put a web page on your screen 25 times faster than the fastest existing analog modem. Uploading speeds are much slower, but, in practice, speed usually makes little difference to the performance.

Cable modems

Cable modem services are available, in theory, to people who already have a cable TV system installed. It must be remembered, however, that cable TV is a one-way—downstream—system, and the cable TV company may not yet be equipped to handle upstream traffic properly. In some cases, cable modem systems use the regular phone line for upstream transmission. The rate at which TV cable systems can download information is impressive—it has to be, because of the huge data demands of television. So there is no problem in that direction, and data can, in theory, be supplied faster than the PC can use it. For adequate upstream data transfer rates, however, special hybrid cabling is necessary, and it is being installed in many areas. One limiting factor with cable modems is that the service is shared between groups of neighbors. This means that the greater the simultaneous usage, the lower the performance.

Future developments

Developments in cell-phone technology have demonstrated to millions that Internet access can be achieved with neither modems nor cables. The principal advance—the replacement of the modem and other digital networks with wireless links—is already well under way and may be expected to expand rapidly. It is inevitable that this development will spread to the regular domestic desktop, laptop, and palm computer.

It also seems likely that the modem is now obsolescent. No doubt modems will continue to be used for a number of years, but the device was always a compromise solution and, although immensely important in the development of the Internet, has now outlived its potential for significant further development.

SEE ALSO: Cable network • Computer • Computer network • Fiber optics • Internet • Telecommunications

Molecular Biology

Since the 1990s, molecular biology has become one of the most exciting fields of life science. Many experts see it as the route to major discoveries that will have applications in medicine, industry, and farming.

During the 1950s, molecular biologists studied the biochemistry of large molecules, such as enzymes, in living cells. These were mainly proteins, and the building blocks they are made of, known as amino acids.

Nowadays, molecular biology is more concerned with another group of molecules in living cells—the nucleic acids, such as DNA (deoxyribonucleic acid), the "blueprint for life." Genetic engineering and genetics both involve the nature of genes and manipulating DNA.

Most living things use DNA as the carrier of their genetic information. This huge molecule is a double helix, shaped like two intertwined spiral staircases. The information in the genes tells the cell how to make various proteins. Proteins are the molecules that build the structure of the cell and also, in the form of enzymes, control the hundreds of biochemical reactions happening inside each cell.

The genetic information is coded as a string of chemical subunits along the DNA molecule. The subunits are known as nucleotide bases or, more simply, bases. They are like letters in a sentence of instructions. However, in the case of DNA, there are only four different "letters." They are adenine (A), guanine (G), thymine (T), and cytosine (C). There may be hundreds of thousands of bases along one strand of DNA. The bases are arranged in linked pairs with those in the other strand, like steps on the staircase of DNA.

A gene is a sequence of pairs of bases that makes up one unit of genetic information. A simple organism, such as the virus lambda, has relatively few genes. A complex organism such as a mammal has many thousands. In molecular biology, each gene is a sequence of bases that represents the code for making a structural or enzyme protein. (*Gene* is a term with different meanings, depending on the branch of science.)

Making a protein from its gene is known as protein synthesis. It involves intermediate molecules that translate the genetic code—the ribonucleic acids, or RNAs.

Making proteins from genes

In a DNA molecule, each base on one helical strand links, or pairs, with a base in the opposite strand. However, of the four bases, adenine can

◀ A scientist examining an autoradiogram of a DNA sequence. Each group of four strips represent a sequence of the nucleotide bases adenine, guanine, cytosine, and thymine in the DNA of the worm *Ophocera volvulus*, a parasite responsible for diseases like river blindness in tropical countries. The proportion and sequence of the bases determines the genetic properties of the organism.

pair only with thymine, and guanine pairs only with cytosine. Therefore, when the two strands in a double helix of DNA are separated, each forms a template or "mirror image" from which the other can be constructed. If two DNA strands fit together with the correct bases cross linking, they are known as complementary.

The first stage of protein synthesis involves separating the two DNA strands. Then a long strandlike molecule of messenger RNA, mRNA, is assembled, using one DNA strand as a template. The mRNA is also made of nucleotide bases. These are put together by the enzyme RNA polymerase according to the coded message in the DNA. This part of the replication process is termed transcription.

The mRNA carries a complementary copy of the coded base sequence to which a specialized cellular subunit, the ribosome, can attach. The ribosome tracks along the mRNA; each RNA molecule may have several ribosomes tracking along it in parallel. At the front of the mRNA, or "upstream," is a ribosome-binding site so that the mRNA can link to the ribosome. Then comes an initiation site, or promoter (the "go" switch) and the coded protein-building sequence. They are followed "downstream" by a terminator site where the coded sequence ends and the mRNA detaches from the ribosome.

There are 20 main kinds of amino acid subunits available for building proteins. Some proteins have relatively few amino acids, others have many thousands. Assembling them involves transfer RNAs or tRNAs. On the mRNA, three nucleotide bases, or "letters," code for one amino acid. This three-letter code is known as a codon. Each tRNA has a corresponding complementary code, the anticodon. Within the ribosome, each tRNA is bound whenever its three-letter sequence is matched in the mRNA passing through the ribosome. Attached to each tRNA is its specific amino acid. In this way, the amino acids are lined up in the right order and joined to make the protein. This step of the process is called translation.

Manipulating genes

Modern genetic engineering techniques allow the isolation and detailed study of single genes. The entire set of DNA in an organism can be purified and cut at specific sites by enzymes called restriction endonucleases. For example, the restriction enzyme known as *Eco*RI cuts DNA wherever there is a base sequence GAATTC. The HindIII enzyme cuts at AAGCTT. The resulting set of small DNA fragments, when cloned to a plasmid or phage vector, is known as a library and can then be further manipulated.

Redundant and junk DNA

An organism's entire set of DNA is called its genome. Much of the genome, particularly in more complicated organisms, may not code for protein synthesis. Its function is often a mystery. It may divide the rest of the DNA into gene units or be redundant and unused.

To get rid of this "junk" DNA when making gene libraries for analysis, molecular biologists reverse part of the protein synthesis process. The starting point is the total mRNA in a cell. This has come only from sequences of DNA intended for protein synthesis. An enzyme called reverse transcriptase makes a single strand of DNA from the mRNA code. This complementary DNA is then made into normal double-stranded DNA by another enzyme, DNA polymerase. In this way, only DNA sequences that are active genes, coding for protein synthesis, are represented in the library.

Many similar or identical genes appear in widely differing organisms and code for building similar or identical proteins, presumably because they come from the same evolutionary ancestors. The degree of similarity is known as sequence homology, and it varies according to the evolutionary relationships between the organisms.

◀ An automated DNA synthesizer, capable of producing lengths of high-purity DNA. The bottles at the bottom contain reagents needed for the synthesis.

Many of the essential proteins in ourselves, for example, show a high degree of homology with those of apes and monkeys but less homology with other mammals.

Sequence homology can be used by the molecular biologist to isolate genes. First, the desired DNA sequence is purified and labeled by radioactive marker substances. This radio-labeled sequence is used as a probe to screen a DNA library from another species. The library DNA is multiplied in bacteria, and the bacteria are stuck to a special membrane and treated to expose their DNA in a single-stranded form. The membrane is then flooded with the radio-labeled probe DNA. The bases of the probe DNA pair to those of the library DNA where there is greatest homology (similarity).

The ability to determine the individual sequences of bases in a strand of DNA now allows molecular biologists to study the anatomy of genes in great detail. The technique involves taking a single-stranded DNA template and synthesizing a double strand from it using the enzyme DNA polymerase. In separate reactions, the synthesis is terminated by special dideoxynucleotide forms of each of the four bases, adenine, cytosine, thymine, or guanine. These act as stop switches, or "terminators." Using radioactive labels, the resulting "ladder" of randomly terminated fragments can be analyzed by the common laboratory method of electrophoresis and compared directly to known sequences. A map of the nucleotide bases in the DNA is gradually built up.

Gene banks

A great many genes from a wide variety of organisms have been isolated and sequenced in this manner. The huge amounts of information being produced by molecular biologists are stored in computerized databases known as gene banks. The information is widely used by researchers who wish to compare unknown and new DNA sequences with those from other sources. The use of computers to compare sequences has speeded the progress of molecular biology considerably.

Known DNA sequences may be used as a starting point for isolating homologous genes from other species of organisms. For example, a number of human genes have been isolated using an unlikely intermediary, the microscopic yeast *Schizosaccharomyces pombe*.

Short synthetic pieces of DNA, called oligonucleotides, are designed by genetic engineers and molecular biologists to be used as primers in a useful and very important technique, the polymerase chain reaction, or PCR. PCR-synthesized fragments of DNA can in turn be used as probes for library screening, ultimately to identify and isolate a whole gene.

Many diseases have their roots in gene mutations or changes to the DNA sequence. A change in just one nucleotide base of the DNA can instruct the mRNA and tRNAs to build a completely different amino acid into the protein, thereby producing abnormal results. In deletion mutations, whole lengths of DNA are changed or lost, causing genes to disappear completely. These mutations may be detected using restriction endonucleases and restriction fragment length polymorphisms, or RFLPs.

Genetic changes and mutations can have particularly important implications if they arise in genes that control cell multiplication. Mutations arise naturally when DNA copies itself and also more frequently under the influence of environmental agents, such as ultraviolet radiation from the Sun, other radiations, or certain chemicals in the surroundings. In an organism such as the human being, the cells can normally deal efficiently with these changes as they arise. "Housekeeping" genes detect and repair the damaged DNA. Current research is concerned with how these housekeeping genes work. Defects in these genes have been implicated in the development of cancers, when cells multiply out of control.

The human gene map

In higher organisms, the huge lengths of DNA that represent genes are not floating around each cell. They are coiled and packed into structures called chromosomes. Each human body cell has 46 chromosomes in 23 pairs.

One of the most ambitious of all scientific projects has been a multinational effort to make a chromosome map, a gene map, and ultimately a nucleotide base sequence map (it is estimated that there are 3 billion such base pairs in human DNA) of the entire set of human genetic material—the human genome. Despite the large size of the human genome, between 40,000 and 100,000 genes, the draft structure was determined in 2001, and it is expected that the complete sequence will be available in 2003.

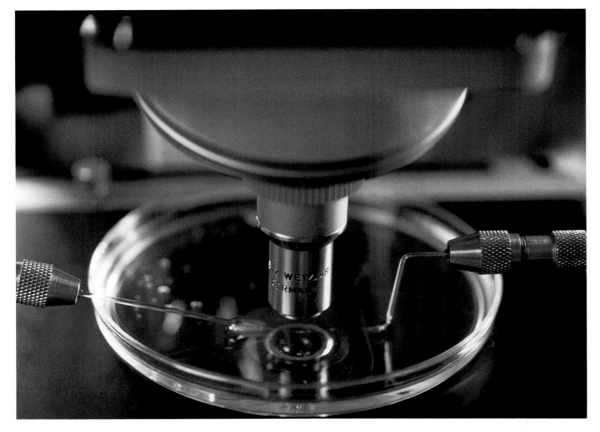

◀ A light microscope being used to view lengths of DNA in the petri dish while they are being manipulated.

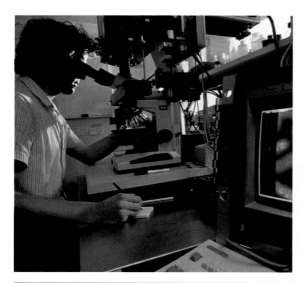

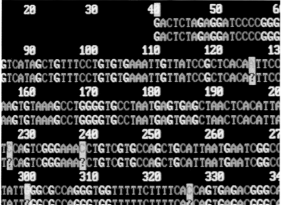

◀ Top left: a researcher uses a light microscope to map long fragments on human chromosomes. The researcher is using a method known as radioactive in-situ hybridization. The chromosomes appear in red on the monitor screen while the DNA fragments (called probes) appear in yellow-green. The process involves a physical survey of each chromosome to find the location of genes and other markers. Bottom left: a computer analysis of the DNA sequence of a human chromosome. The screen shows the amount and sequence in which the four nucleotide bases appear in a gene complex called HL-A, which has been implicated in transplant rejection. Right: DNA sequencing using gel electrophoresis, a technique used to examine the nucleotide base sequence of DNA. The fragments, contained in an algarose gel, are viewed under an ultraviolet light.

The first organism to have its entire DNA sequence determined was a type of virus, lambda. This virus infects bacteria, such as *E. coli*, and is a useful tool for molecular biological research. It provides a relatively simple model for the coordinated action of several genes.

The end product of the Human Genome Project should be a picture of the entire genetic make-up of a typical human individual. A vast database of information should result, providing a standard against which to compare the genes of individuals suffering from genetic disorders. The great hope is that by understanding the organization of the human being at the level of molecules such as proteins and DNA, we might better understand the mechanisms of inherited diseases and how to treat them.

Exploring the genome

Determination of the genome of some simpler organisms such as yeast and a nematode worm, *Caenorhabditis elegans*, has shown molecular biologists that there is much about the natural world that they still do not understand. Yeast has over 6,000 genes, and as yet, scientists can only guess the function of a quarter of them. To explore them fully will require the development of new analytic techniques capable of processing millions of gene sequences at a time.

One new tool is the DNA microarray. Microarrays are manufactured in the same way as microchips but contain thousands of distinct DNA probes placed precisely onto a grid of spots on a glass slide. A computer keeps track of where each probe is located. Messenger RNA is extracted from a sample, replicated millions of times, tagged with fluorescent dye, and then split into fragments. The fragments are then washed over the slide where they randomly bump into the probes until they find their exact match. The dye ensures that the spot lights up only if enough complementary mRNA is present.

Microarrays offer biologists the ability to discover the purpose of genes more quickly than ever before. One test using the yeast genome confirmed the seven genes known to control production of one protein in a matter of weeks rather than the 30 years it had taken by conventional means. Knowing how such genes are turned on or off will aid medical research considerably.

SEE ALSO: Cancer treatment • Cell biology • Forensic science • Life • Surgery • Transplant

Monorail System

Monorail systems, railways with only one rail instead of two, have been built experimentally for more than 100 years. They would seem to have an advantage in that one rail and its tie would occupy less space than two, but in practice, monorail construction has tended to be complicated and unsightly on account of the necessity of keeping the cars upright. There is also the problem of switching the cars from one line to another.

Early systems

The first monorails used an elevated rail with the cars hanging down on both sides, like pannier bags (saddlebags) on a pony or a bicycle. A monorail was patented in 1821 by Henry Robinson Palmer, engineer to the London Dock Company, and the first line was built in 1824 to run between the Royal Victualling Yard and the Thames. The elevated wooden rail was a plank on edge bridging strong wooden supports, into which it was set, with an iron bar on top to take the wear from the double-flanged wheels of the cars. A similar monorail was built in 1825 to carry bricks to barges on the Lea River from a brickworks at Cheshunt, Britain. The cars, pulled by a horse and a tow rope, were in two parts, one on each side of the rail, hanging from a framework that carried the wheels.

Later, monorails on this principle were built by a Frenchman, C. F. M. T. Lartigue. He put his single rail on top of a series of triangular trestles with their bases on the ground; he also put a guide rail on each side of the trestles on which ran horizontal wheels attached to the cars. The cars thus had both vertical and sideways support and were suitable for higher speeds than the earlier type.

An electric Lartigue line was opened in central France in 1894, and there were proposals to build a network of them on Long Island, radiating from Brooklyn. There was a demonstration in London in 1886 on a short line; trains were hauled by a two-boiler Mallet steam locomotive. It had two double-flanged driving wheels running on the raised center rail and guiding wheels running on tracks on each side of the trestle. Trains were switched from one track to another by moving a whole section of track sideways to line up with another section. In 1888, a line on this principle opened in Ireland linking the towns of Listowel and Ballybunion, a distance of 9½ miles (15 km); it ran until 1924. There were three locomotives, each with two horizontal boilers hanging one on either side of the center wheels. They were capable of going 27 mph (43.5 km/h); the carriages

were built with the lower parts in two sections, between which were the wheels.

The Lartigue design was adapted further by F. B. Behr, who built a 3 mile (4.8 km) electric line near Brussels in 1897. The monorail itself was again at the top of an A-shaped trestle, but there were two balancing and guiding rails on each side so that, although the weight of the car was carried by one rail, there were really five rails in all. The car weighed 55 tons (50 tonnes) and had two four-wheeled undercarriages, four wheels in line on each undercarriage. It was built in Britain and had motors providing a total of 600 horsepower. The car ran at 83 mph (134 km/h) and was said to have reached 100 mph (161 km/h) in private trials. It was extensively tested by representatives of the Belgian, French, and Russian governments, and Behr came near to success in achieving widespread application of his design.

Gyroscopic monorails

An attempt to build a monorail with one rail laid on the ground to save space led to the use of a gyroscope to keep the train upright. A gyroscope is a spinning flywheel that resists any attempt to

▲ An elevated monorail provides rapid passenger transit at this holiday camp in Britain. In addition, by elevating the monorail above the ground, pedestrians are able to walk around the site unrestricted.

alter the angle of the axis on which it spins. A true monorail, running on a single rail, was built for military purposes by Louis Brennan, an Irishman who also invented a steerable torpedo. Brennan applied for monorail patents in 1903 and exhibited a large working model in 1907 and a full-size 22-ton (20 tonne) car in the early part of 1910. It was held upright by two gyroscopes, spinning in opposite directions, and carried 50 people or ten tons (0.9 tonnes) of freight.

A similar car carrying only six passengers and a driver was demonstrated in Berlin in 1909 by a German inventor, August Scherl, who had taken out a patent in 1908 and later came to an agreement with Brennan to use his patents also. Both systems allowed the cars to lean over, like bicycles, on curves. Scherl's was an electric car; Brennan's was powered by gasoline rather than steam so as not to show any telltale smoke when used by the military.

The disadvantage with gyroscopic monorail systems was that they required power to drive the gyroscope to keep the train upright even when it was not moving.

ALWEG systems

The most successful modern monorails have been the invention of Dr. Axel L. Wenner-Gren, an industrialist born in Sweden. ALWEG (*A*xel *L*ennart *We*nner-Gren) lines use a concrete beam carried on concrete supports; the beam can be high in the air, at ground level, or in a tunnel, as required. The cars straddle the beam, supported by rubber-tired wheels on top of the beam; underneath, there are also horizontal wheels in two rows on each side, bearing on the sides of the beam near the top and bottom of it.

▲ Top: the most successful monorails have been the ALWEG systems, designed by the Swede Axel Wenner-Gren. This is the Tokyo installation, which runs from Haneda Airport to the city center. Electric power is picked up from cables on the side of the beam. Above: a monorail in an amusement park in Blackpool, England, built by Habegger Thun of Switzerland.

Thus, there are five bearing surfaces, as in the Behr system, but combined to use a single beam instead of a massive trestle framework. The carrying wheels come up into the center line of the cars, suitably enclosed. Electric current is picked up from power lines at the side of the beam. A number of successful lines have been built on the ALWEG system, including a line 8¼ miles (13 km) long between Tokyo and its Haneda airport.

There are several other saddle-type systems on the same principle as the ALWEG, including a small industrial system, used on building sites and for agricultural purposes, that can run without a driver. With all these systems, trains are diverted from one track to another by moving pieces of track sideways to bring in another piece of track to form a new link or by using a flexible section of track to give the same result.

Other systems

Another monorail system suspends the car beneath an overhead carrying rail. The wheels must be over the center line of the car, so the support connected between rail and car is to one side, or offset. This design allows the rail to be supported from the other side. Such a system was built between the towns of Barmen and Elberfeld (now Wuppertal) in Germany in 1898–1901 and was extended in 1903 to a length of 8.2 miles (13 km). New stations were added in 1926 and 1967, bringing the total number of stations to 19. Designed by Eugen Langen, a German civil engi-

FACT FILE

■ The French Aerotrain is a monorail hovertrain powered by gas turbines that drive a rear-mounted propeller. The Aerotrain has reached 233 mph (375 km/h) in tests but is too noisy for public use.

■ The Listowel and Ballybunion monorail, designed by the Frenchman Charles Lartigue to straddle an A-shaped rail section, had to be load balanced. A farmer taking a cow to market balanced it with two calves, the calves then balanced each other on the way home.

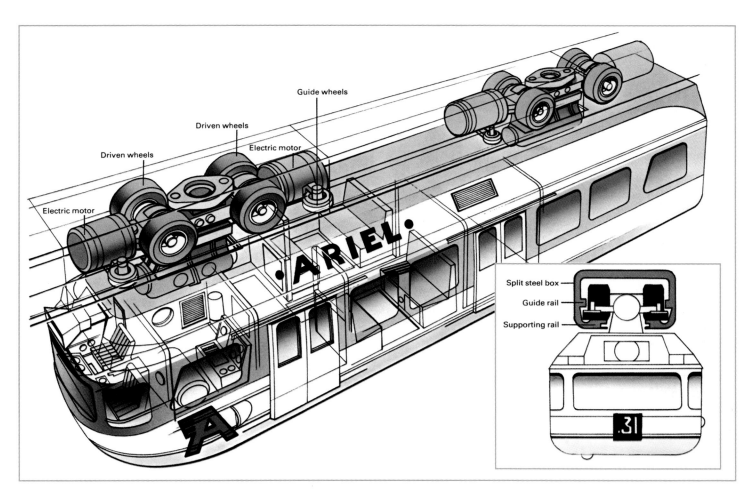

Guide wheels

Driven wheels

Driven wheels

Electric motor

Electric motor

ARIEL

Split steel box

Guide rail

Supporting rail

neer, this monorail has run successfully ever since, with a remarkable safety record. Tests in the river valley between the towns showed that a monorail would be more suitable than a conventional railroad in the restricted space available, because monorail cars are able to take sharp curves in comfort. The rail is suspended on a steel structure, mostly over the Wupper River itself. The switches, or points, on the line are in the form of a switch tongue forming an inclined plane, which is placed over the rail; the car wheels rise on this plane and are thus led onto the siding.

Another system, the SAFEGE (Société Anonyme Française d'Etude de Gestion et d'Entreprises) developed in France, has suspended cars but with the rail in the form of a steel box section split on the underside to allow the car supports to pass through it. There are two rails inside the box, one on each side of the slot, and the cars are actually suspended from four-wheeled axles running on the two rails.

Recent monorails

In Germany, a half-mile (1 km) suspended monorail called the H-Bahn was opened in 1983 at the University of Dortmund. Driverless cars shuttle to and fro at a top speed of 40 mph (65 km/h) under a box-section guideway inside which run small rubber-tired wheels; the guideway beams are supported by hook-shaped masts.

In 1985, the 5.3-mile (8.6 km) Kokura monorail opened in the city of Kita-Kyushu. This ALWEG system was followed by monorail developments throughout Japan, making this country the world's leading user of monorails.

Several new monorail systems are in development throughout the world. They include two new lines in Japan: the Naha monorail on the island of Okinawa and a new monorail at Tokyo Disneyland. The Naha monorail is scheduled for opening in 2003 and, like the German monorail in Wuppertal, will travel part of its route along a river channel. The Tokyo Disneyland line is built on a straddle system derived from the original ALWEG designs. This monorail will connect four stations along 3 miles (5 km) of track. In the United States, a new system is due to go into operation in Las Vegas in 2004. Based on the Mark VI ALWEG monorail in use at Walt Disney World Resort in Florida, the Las Vegas monorail will link seven stations, giving rapid access to eight resorts and the Las Vegas Convention Center.

▲ The French SAFEGE monorail system. The car is suspended from a box made of steel and split on its underside. Each car has two four-wheeled axles; the wheels support the car on the inside of the split box. Each axle carries two electric traction motors that drive two wheels; there are also four small horizontal guiding wheels on each axle.

SEE ALSO: AIR-CUSHION VEHICLE • LINEAR MOTOR • MAGNETISM • MASS TRANSIT AND SUBWAY • RAILROAD SYSTEM

Mortar, Bazooka, and Recoilless Gun

A mortar is a high-trajectory fire weapon in which the recoil force is passed directly to the ground by means of a base plate. The conventional mortar, as used by the armies of most countries, is muzzle loading and has a smooth bore. It fires a fin-stabilized projectile at subsonic velocity and establishes zones of fire by variation of the charge weight. Range is adjusted by altering the elevation. The high trajectory of a mortar allows the weapon to be placed behind hills, in valleys, or in small steep-sided pits and to engage troops in trenches, sunken roads, or behind cover.

The mortar was one of the earliest forms of artillery and is known to have been used by Mohammed II at the time of the siege of Constantinople in 1453. Known in Europe as the bombard, it consisted of a metal pot secured to a timber base. It was used for attacking fortresses and cities under siege and also for action against ships close to shore. There was also a naval equivalent. The bombard fell out of favor as other forms of artillery developed and did not come into prominence again until World War I, when a British inventor, Sir Wilfred Stokes, produced a mortar 3 in. (76 mm) in diameter, a caliber that is still in favor today. Probably the largest mortar ever produced was the Little David mortar, which was built in 1944 for the U.S. Army. It had a 36 in. (914 mm) caliber and fired a massive projectile weighing 3,700 lbs. (1,678 kg).

Construction

The great majority of mortars have four main parts: the barrel, the base plate, the mount, and the sight. The barrel is a smooth-bore steel tube, and the exterior is also usually smooth, although some mortars incorporate radial finning to assist cooling. The firing mechanism is incorporated in a breech piece, which is usually screwed into the base of the barrel. In many cases, the firing mechanism is a simple stud, which sets off the propellant charge of the mortar bomb by impact as soon as the latter has fallen to the lower end of the barrel after loading. In some mortars, however, the firing mechanism is a spring-operated device controlled by an external trigger. The base plate is designed to distribute the downward force of the propellant explosion over as large an area as possible to prevent the mortar from being driven downward into the ground. The mounting is normally a bipod, but occasionally, a tripod is used. The mounting supports the barrel and carries the elevating and traversing mechanisms, which are used for aiming. In many mortars, a shock

absorber is incorporated in the mounting; it usually consists of one or two cylinders containing springs, although in some heavier mortars a hydraulic system may be employed. These cylinders are interposed between the barrel collar and the bipod, and after the barrel has recoiled and been pushed back by the reaction of the baseplate, the springs ensure that the barrel returns.

The bipod carries a cross-leveling device that enables the sights to be kept upright regardless of the slope of the ground on which the mortar is situated. Mortar sights have increased in complexity as the years have passed. Initially, they were very simple and consisted of an aiming tube and a flat plate, which allowed the gunner to relate the direction in which the mortar was pointing to some arbitrarily selected reference point. The modern mortar sight allows the target bearing to be determined and also allows the range and bearing to be recorded so that once a target has been attacked, it can be reengaged without going through the entire process again.

In today's armies, handheld computers give the mortar an impressive ability to hit a target

▲ A 4¾ in. (120 mm) mortar of the Argentine army. On the battlefield, the mortar is more feared and disliked than conventional artillery, because of its high-capacity bomb and high trajectory. A mortar fires at between 45 degrees and 70 degrees elevation, and so the bomb arches high into the sky and descends steeply. This technique ensures that fragments are distributed more lethally than those of an artillery shell, which arrives at a shallow angle. Artillery fragments either bury themselves in the ground or fly into the air only to return to the ground with little force.

after a single ranging shot. Speed has become of great importance, as modern mortar-locating radars can detect a mortar's position after a few rounds, so it can then be put under attack itself.

Characteristics

Mortars range in caliber from less than 2.4 in. (60 mm) for light mortars to above 3.9 in. (100 mm) for heavy mortars. A light mortar fires a projectile weighing from 1 to 3 lbs. (0.45–1.36 kg) to a maximum range of between 1,500 and 6,000 ft. (450–1,800 m). Heavy mortars have a maximum range of about 30,000 ft. (9,000 m) and fire a projectile weighing 15 lbs. (6.8 kg) or more.

The limited number of components and the relative simplicity of the fire-control system make the mortar easy to handle and reduce training time. Mortars are cheap and easy to produce. The simple design of the mortar and its sight allows rapid switching of targets anywhere within a 360 degree arc, and the low pressure within the mortar chamber allows a thin-walled bomb with a relatively large high-explosive content to be used. This characteristic, combined with the near-vertical angle of projectile descent, provides a good all-round fragmentation and makes the mortar more effective than the artillery gun against troops in the open. The advantages are, however, offset to some extent by the fact that mortars are less accurate than guns.

Mortars have been developed that are lighter and have smaller calibers, making them more mobile and easily portable. One example of this type is the U.S. Army's 2.7 in. (60 mm) light-weight company mortar designated the M224 for use with its most mobile units. The M224 is almost as lethal as the heavier 3.2 in. (81 mm) M29, because its ammunition uses a system called proximity-fusing. This fusing is expensive, but it ensures that much less of the mortar bomb's explosive energy is absorbed by soft ground, and because it bursts in the air, it is very much more dangerous to troops who are dug in but without overhead protection.

Recoilless gun

Conventional guns suffer from the disadvantage that when they fire a projectile, the gun recoils, that is, it moves backward rapidly. The bigger the projectile and the faster it is fired, the greater the recoil. The explanation is contained in Newton's Third Law of Motion, which states that for every action there is an equal and opposite reaction. Thus, as the projectile is accelerated toward the

▼ The Swedish Carl Gustav M2 recoilless antitank gun. It has a caliber of 3.3 in. (84 mm).

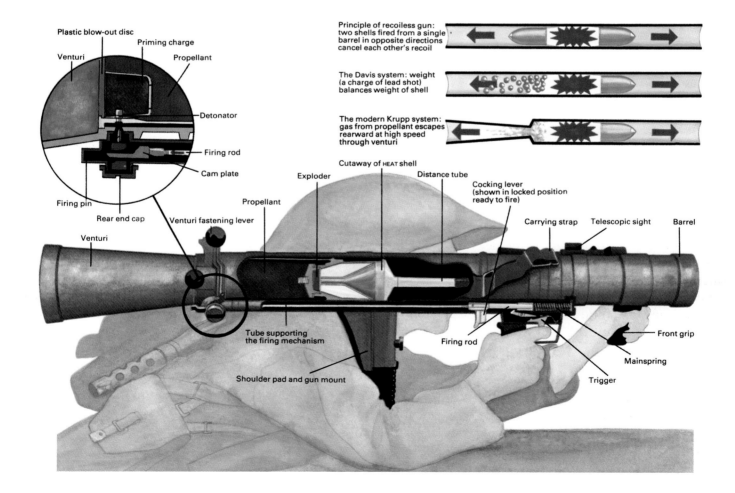

muzzle, the gun is pushed backward by an equal force. Early guns had no means of absorbing this force, and every time they were fired, they jumped back several feet.

The search for a means of reducing recoil began with the first guns, but the only practical answer was to take it up with springs and buffers, which are expensive. Modern guns have highly developed recoil systems that weigh many times more than the basic barrel and breech and add enormously to the manufacturing cost and time.

The simplest way to eliminate recoil is to put two identical guns back-to-back and fire them at the same moment. The recoil of one will exactly balance that of the other. Unfortunately, the idea is scarcely practical for other than a laboratory experiment, but the principle is the key to present-day recoilless guns. The idea was first expanded by an American naval officer, Commander Davis. In 1910, he merged the back-to-back guns into one with a central breech, which was loaded by separating the two barrels. He used one charge of propellant and fired a shell out of one barrel and an equal weight of lead shot out of the other. The lead shot, which balanced the shell momentum, traveled only a short distance before it fell to the ground. It was not an ideal arrangement, but it was used on a few aircraft in World War I. However, the idea was dropped after 1918.

The idea was secretly revived in Germany in the 1930s, when a light field gun was required for mountain and airborne troops. Krupp, the German armaments firm, experimented with

◄ The British Milan antitank system fitted with a Weston Simfire SIMLAN, which simulates the firing of the tank-stopping rocket.

guns that fired a variety of different substances to the rear of the gun. It was soon found that the counterbalance could be something as light as a mass of gas, provided that it was given sufficient velocity. By putting a venturi, or rocket nozzle, at the back of the gun, the speed of the gas was enormously increased and could then balance quite a heavy shell. The brilliance of the Krupp design, however, was the fact that it used gas generated by the burning propellant; it is this system that is used today. The gas may flow through one large venturi or several small ones. The variations stem from different manufacturing techniques for the breech and the ammunition, but most modern designs use a single nozzle.

In the Davis gun, the propellant charge had to be almost twice the usual size, but in the Krupp design, the amount of propellant has to be five times the normal. The extra four parts burn up into the gas, which is forced out of the nozzle to balance the recoil. Naturally, the cartridge case is very much larger and heavier as a result.

The design of the breech is critical, and it requires much care to ensure that the venturi remains closed for about half a millisecond after ignition, to allow a proper start to the burning propellant. A closing disk is then blown out, and burning continues very rapidly as the gas begins to flow rearward and the shell begins to move forward. The gun does not move at all.

Weight

Since there is no recoil to be absorbed, the recoilless gun is much lighter than a conventional type. The 25-pounder of World War II weighed 4,300 lbs. (1,950 kg). The Wombat recoilless gun weighs only 600 lbs. (270 kg), yet it fires a slightly heavier shell at the same muzzle velocity as the 25-pounder. However, the Wombat shell and case weigh 60 lbs. (27 kg)—because of the large cartridge case—whereas the 25-pounder shell and case together weighed less than 30 lbs. (14 kg). If the Wombat were required to fire a barrage of shells for a long time, the difference in ammunition weight would soon become apparent to the gun crew concerned.

Back blast

Another difficulty with the recoilless gun is the back blast. It limits the range of the gun, since if the barrel is tilted to give a high trajectory, the back blast gouges a hole in the ground below the breech. The blast is also hard to conceal, as it is powerful enough to blow down vegetation and light structures and gives off a brilliant flash and some smoke behind the gun. For these reasons, almost all recoilless guns are now used only for short-range antitank defense, when the barrel can be pointed directly at the target and the large shell is an advantage in penetrating the armor. The bigger recoilless guns are dying out, mainly because their comparatively low muzzle velocities make it difficult to hit a moving target at long range, and the majority of use is now with small, shoulder-controlled guns called bazookas.

Bazooka

Bazooka has become the generic name for shoulder-launched, portable antitank rocket systems after the first weapon that came into service with the U.S. Army in 1941. The name came from the musical horn used by the American comedian Bob Burns, but the weapon itself was an extremely serious addition to the infantryman's capacity to destroy armor. The loaded launcher weighed only 16¼ lbs. (7.6 kg), but it could fire a warhead as far as 2,100 ft. (640 m) to detonate a charge shaped so that it could penetrate up to 5 in. (127 mm) of armor plating.

Although rockets have been used for centuries, the bazooka introduced new principles of safety and accuracy that have made it the ancestor of a host of modern battlefield weapons. The rocket was battery fired, and there was no recoil, because the force of the propellant gases blasting from the rear of the tube equaled the force of the rocket being launched from the muzzle at 265 ft. per sec. (80 m/s). The important thing was that the propellant was fast burning so that it would all be consumed before the rocket left the tube. Therefore, there was a dangerous area of blast and flame immediately behind the tube, but in most cases, there was no flashback to injure the firer as the rocket left the tube. Unfortunately, in the original version, cold weather retarded the burning of the propellant, and thus made the weapon dangerous to use.

Advances in rocket technology have made great strides in solving the problem of launching without inducing a flashback. In the original bazooka, the rocket was not powered once it left the mouth of the launch tube, as its propellant had been completely expended, and the rocket itself then became a mere projectile. In order to increase range and shorten the time of flight, there was an inevitable demand for an increased thrust. In addition, shoulder-launched rockets were seen to have a role as antiaircraft weapons, so they obviously needed great speed to catch and strike targets traveling at supersonic speed. The answer was found in a two-stage rocket round. It is typical for modern shoulder-launched rockets to have an initial eject motor, which propels the rocket to a safe distance in front of the firer

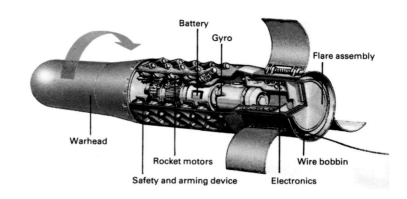

before the main rocket motor cuts in to take the missile on to its target. The U.S. Army's Stinger missile has a separable booster launcher that takes it more than 40 ft. (12 m) from the operator before its main motors fire and take it to supersonic speed to engage aircraft targets. The main motors can carry the Stinger missile to a maximum distance of 4.8 miles (8 km) with a ceiling of 10,000 ft. (3,046 m). The Stinger is a guided missile, and change of direction is effected by altering the rocket thrust by blanking off part of one of the two exhaust nozzles. Guidance is provided by an automatic heat-seeking device and a proportional navigation system. In other guided systems, fins or wings spring from the sides of the rocket after launch, and they can be manipulated by command to alter flight course.

In addition, the Stinger is a throwaway round. The original bazooka tube had to be loaded with a rocket and delicately fused warhead in an anxious and lengthy operation. A lot of its modern descendants are throwaway and simply have to be clipped to an initiator mechanism for use. Each disposable launch tube contains a single rocket and is delivered to the operator as a certifiable round. In the case of the Stinger, each round is clipped to a grip stock that will effect the cycle of prelaunch functions and then the launch itself.

The numbers and variety of small rockets in military use are now very great indeed. The antiarmor weapons can be used very effectively against concrete emplacements as well as armored vehicles. Besides their high explosive warheads, they can also carry incendiary, smoke, or chemical gas warheads. Some types are used as fast moving targets, and others are mounted in aircraft. They have also long had a civilian use as distress signals at sea and similar danger areas.

▲ The U.S. Dragon XM47 TOW (tube launched, optically tracked, wire commanded) system launches its antitank missile by means of a gas generator.

SEE ALSO: AMMUNITION • ANTIAIRCRAFT GUN • BALLISTICS • BOMB • BOMB-AIMING DEVICE • DYNAMICS • EXPLOSIVE • GUN • NEWTON'S LAWS • VENTURI EFFECT

Motorcycle

The first commercial motorcycles, built at the beginning of the 20th century, were usually heavy pedal cycles to which crude internal combustion engines had been added. The tradition persisted through to mopeds, which today are no longer required to be fitted with pedals.

Before World War I, motorcycles were capable of modest speeds and were fairly reliable because of intensive racing development. The frames became heavier and lower, sprung front forks were adopted to protect the rider from road shocks, and crude rear-wheel rim brakes were standard. The friction clutch was made reliable, and this development transformed motorcycling from the pastime of enthusiasts into a utilitarian mode of transport. The use of a clutch made starting simple (by either hand or foot lever) and gear-changing convenient through three ratios, ensuring progress up the steepest hills for the first time. The chain drive and shaft drive were not uncommon in the early development of motorbikes, but V-belt drive gained popularity because of its low cost and simplicity and because it absorbed the coarse action of the often crude engines.

Development

World War I spurred development, so the 1920s models were infinitely more robust, reliable, and convenient to ride. Powerful, high-tension magnetos, sophisticated jet-metered carburetors, efficient drum brakes on both wheels, dynamo lighting, and automatic lubrication systems had become commonplace. By the mid-1920s, the foot-change gear selection had been perfected, and the motorcycle achieved the basic performance and form it was to keep for the next 60 years.

Germany, Italy, and Britain rivaled each other for racing and commercial supremacy until the outbreak of World War II. Significantly, this war contributed nothing to the development of the motorcycle, largely because the importance of the dispatch rider had declined in favor of enormously improved radio communications. For two decades following the war, the European factories achieved high sales to a public eager for any form of inexpensive personal transportation. In the main, however, the postwar motorcycles were little more than cheaply improved prewar models, and sales declined. Designs improved in the 1960s with the introduction of new technology by Japanese manufacturers such as Honda.

Modern motorcycles

Motorcycles are built in sizes ranging from 50 to 1,300 cc (cubic centimeters). Most small machines (under 250 cc) have one or two cylinders, and most large machines (over 250 cc) have two or four. There are also six-cylinder engines, and the rotary (Wankel) engine.

Although most manufacturers employ the bicycle-chassis configuration, a car-type chassis design incorporating hub-center steering, load-bearing bodywork, and single-arm air suspension has been fully developed for both racing and on the road. Tubeless tires on cast aluminum wheels carrying hydraulic disk brakes are now commonplace. Off-road motorbikes with smaller engines may be supplied with kick-starters, while road bikes and larger off-road bikes use electric ignition controlled by an ignition key and a starter switch. Lighting and instrumentation are similar to those of cars.

The cost of buying and running a modern, big motorcycle now exceeds that of a small automobile, but no car can compare with the overall economies of a small motorcycle. The fastest motorbikes have a power development of close to 140 horsepower, providing a top speed in excess of 160 mph (255 km/h) and quarter-mile (0.4 km) standing start times of little more than 10 seconds.

Transmission design is peculiar to motorcycles. Five gears are normal and six are common on sports machines. The rapid and simple gear change possible with the positive-stop system, which incorporates an inertia-absorbing false neutral between each gear, has made the development of automatic gear changing unnecessary. Moto Guzzi and Honda developed a successful

▼ The Moto Guzzi Le Mans Mark III was produced during the early 1980s. This Italian motorbike was designed with an easily accessible engine, making it simple to service.

variable-slip torque converter in place of automatic gear changing for two big models, and similar systems have been employed on some models of scooter and moped.

Scooters and mopeds

Mopeds are lighter in weight than motorbikes and have smaller engines and a much lower top speed—about 30 to 35 mph (48–56 km/h). Mopeds developed in the 1950s from motorized bicycles and are very economical to run, achieving around 100 miles per gallon (42 km/l).

Scooters also usually have smaller engines than motorbikes and lower top speeds but are bigger and faster than mopeds. The scooter frame is constructed in such a way that the rider can easily step on and off the bike, and a horizontal running board allows a more upright posture than on motorbikes or mopeds.

Engines

Four-stroke engines employ a recirculatory lubrication system identical to a car's, but two-stroke systems meter the oil via injection pumps directly into the crankcase and from there into the combustion chamber, where it is burned. The fastest racing machines are 500 and 750 cc four-cylinder,

▶ The exhaust from the six cylinders of the Honda CBX is led into two branching pipes. These are usually situated low on a bike, to avoid burning the rider's legs.

two-stroke engines, and sports roadsters are generally of similar size. These engines are sophisticated and water cooled but use about 30 percent more fuel than four-stroke engines.

Turbocharging is generally unpopular on motorcycles, because of its bulk and complexity. Performance increases have come mainly from improved electronic ignition accuracy, the adoption of fuel injection engines, sophisticated carburetors, and attention to gas flow within the engine.

Controls

Motorcycle controls have become standardized. Speed is varied through an axially rotating twist-grip on the right handlebar called the throttle, which also incorporates the front-brake lever in such a way that the rider must release the speed control to apply the brake. The clutch, often hydraulic, is operated by a similar lever on the left handlebar. Gear change is by the left foot, and rear brake by the right foot. One company, Moto Guzzi, has for many years specialized in successful coupled brakes. Hydraulic disk brakes are standard equipment today, and switchgear is designed for thumb activation on miniature consoles.

FACT FILE

- The Copeland steam-driven motorcycle made its first appearance in 1885. It was of high-wheeler bicycle shape with the small wheel at the front and the engine mounted on a central steering column. A twisted rawhide belt transferred power to the larger rear wheel. A total of 200 were built.

- The Excelsior Welbike was made in Britain during World War II for use by airborne troops. Weighing 70 lbs. and with a 98 cc engine, the Welbike had tiny wheels and folding handlebar and saddle pillars. It was designed to be parachuted into combat areas packed in a crate but proved to be too small for use.

- One of the most unorthodox of early motorcycles was the Megola. The number produced between 1922 and 1925 was 2,000. The Megola had a five-cylinder rotary engine fitted into the front wheel hub, an armchairlike bucket seat, running boards, and leaf springs at the rear.

SEE ALSO: Automobile • Bicycle • Braking system • Clutch • Friction • Gear • Hydraulics • Internal combustion engine • Transmission, automobile

Mouse and Pointing Device

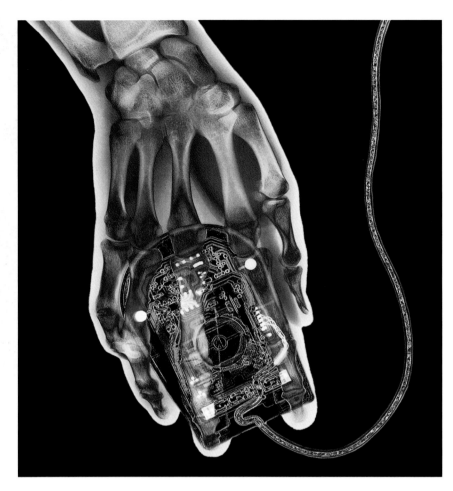

A computer mouse or other pointing device eases the use of computers, often by interpreting an operator's hand or finger actions as movements of a pointer within the on-screen image. That pointer may take the form of a cursor that marks the insertion point in a word-processing document, it may be the sight of a weapon in a computer game, or it may be the tip of a virtual pen in a drawing program. In some cases, instructions from the pointing device govern the movements of a figure within a virtual landscape.

Apart from mice, pointing devices include trackballs, joysticks, light pens, touch screens, and graphics tablets, or digitizers. The best choice of pointing device for a given type of software depends on the nature of the tasks inherent in the operation of that software. In some cases, more than one pointing device is used at the same time.

Pointing devices work in conjunction with graphical user interfaces (GUIs). GUIs, whose development started in the 1960s, replace lines of often-complex program instruction with graphical representations, called icons. The computer user gives instructions by using the pointing device to place the cursor over the appropriate

▲ Colored X ray of a computer mouse being held in a human hand. The mouse (green outline) contains a small rubber ball that spins as the mouse slides over a flat surface. Sensors detect the movements of the ball and translate them into movements of a pointer or icon on a screen.

icon and then pressing once or twice on a button to select that icon. In this way, a few hand and finger movements initiate an operation that would otherwise require programming knowledge and meticulous keyboard entries.

Mouse

Computer mice are the most ubiquitous pointing devices, preferred by more than 80 percent of computer users. A typical mouse has an approximately rectangular, round, or teardrop-shaped casing whose underside has low-friction pads that allow it to move freely over flat surfaces. Most computer mice communicate with their computers through flexible cables—their "tails."

Almost all mice detect their motion using an optomechanical mechanism. At the core of such a mechanism is a ball that sits in a cradle inside the mouse and protrudes through a hole in the underside of the casing. The ball is usually around 0.8 in. (2 cm) in diameter and made of rubber, which gives it reasonable grip on most surfaces and particularly good grip on specially-made rubber or felt-covered "mouse pads."

The ball rolls freely as the mouse moves, turning two rollers that rest on its surface within the mouse casing as it rolls. One roller responds to left-to-right mouse movements; the other responds to back-and-forth movements.

Each roller connects to a disk that has evenly spaced open slots around its edge. Each roller has two sets of infrared light-emitting diodes (LEDs) and infrared light sensors that are so arranged that infrared light passes through the disk between the LED and sensor of one set shortly before it passes between similar components of the other. Each sensor emits an electrical signal while it is exposed to light, so the frequency of signal pulses from each sensor indicates the rate at which the attached roller turns.

The spacing between the pulses from the two sensors indicates the direction of rotation of the rollers. In the time taken for a pair of slots to pass one of the sensors, that sensor will emit two electrical pulses; in the same time, the other sensor will emit one pulse. The direction of rotation determines whether the midpoint of that pulse is closer in time to the first or second pulse from the other sensor, so there is a means of decoding the pulses to ascertain the direction of rotation of the roller that is in contact with the rolling ball.

Circuitry within the mouse decodes the pulses and converts them into a signal that a piece of software in the computer called a driver interprets as an indication of the speed and direction of motion of the mouse in two dimensions. Left-to-right movements of the mouse cause left-to-right movements of the cursor; back-and-forth movements cause up-and-down cursor movements.

The drivers of many mice offer various options for how the motion of the mouse influences the motion of the cursor on the screen. In the most straightforward case, the cursor moves at a rate proportional to the rate of movement of the mouse; the rate at which the cursor moves for a given mouse speed can be increased or decreased, however, thus having the effect of changing the sensitivity of the mouse.

In more advanced options, the cursor accelerates as the mouse continues to move. This advance has the benefit that short mouse strokes are more precise—the cursor moves little in comparison to the mouse—while longer mouse strokes shift the cursor over great distances without requiring excessively long strokes of the mouse.

Apart from the cursor-positioning function, a mouse has one or more buttons that can be pressed to send signals to the software in use. In word-processing software, for example, a single click—press and release—selects a word, a second click selects a sentence, a third selects a paragraph, and so on. Once an area of text has been selected, the mouse can be used to select an option from an on-screen menu that caters for editing or changing typefaces, for example.

Different menu options appear if the mouse button is pressed and held down (rather than clicked), or used in conjunction with "shift," "alt," "option," or "control" keys. Alternatively, a second button on the mouse can offer different menu options. For right-handed users, the principal button is on the left of the top surface of the mouse, where the index finger can operate it without the hand having to move. A driver option can reverse the positions of the principal and secondary buttons for left-handed users.

In the case of a mouse that has three buttons, the third button—between the other two—can be custom programmed to perform tasks. The user then has the option of "training" the mouse to give commands that are not in the menus of the two main buttons but that are frequently used in that particular operator's work.

Nonstandard mice

One of the main drawbacks of a conventional mouse stems from its reliance for power and communication on the cable that connects it to the keyboard or to the main processor casing. This cable can clutter the operator's work space, or it can become tangled and impede the motion of the mouse. Some mice overcome this problem by using an infrared beacon to transmit signals to the computer, which receives the signals through an infrared sensor. There must be a direct path for light to travel from mouse to sensor for such a mouse to function well. Power is supplied by batteries housed within the mouse casing.

Hand-steered mice have also been criticized for promoting the onset of repetitive-strain injury (RSI) in some computer operators. Foot-operated "mice," which in fact consist of two rocking pedals, have been offered as a means of avoiding RSI of the wrist and forearm.

Trackball

The workings of a trackball are essentially the same as those of a mouse: the movements of a rolling ball translate into cursor movements on the screen. The main difference is that the trackball generally protrudes through the upper surface of the keyboard rather than from the bottom of a mouse. Also, the trackball is moved directly by the user's fingers, rather than by the user moving a mouse across a mouse pad.

Trackballs have the advantages over mice that they are integrated in a larger unit and so are less easy to lose or damage when in transit; they also dispense with cumbersome cables. These benefits led to trackballs being used as the pointing devices of some portable computers and games

▼ Small handheld notebook computers have no room for a keypad. Instead they use a stylus to input information directly onto the screen using pressure sensors.

consoles. Click bars on the keyboard perform the functions of a mouse's buttons. Trackballs have the disadvantage that they are awkward and tiring to use in comparison to mice owing to the repetitive sweeping motions necessary to move the cursor over great distances across the screen.

Joystick and track-point stick

A mouse alternative that is particularly popular for use with computer games is the joystick, so named for its resemblance to the steering columns of some light aircraft. A typical joystick is a vertical handle with a molded plastic handle so shaped as to accommodate the fingers of a clenched hand. The rod sits in a sprung pivot and can be moved in any direction away from vertical by applying light pressure. When the pressure is released, the stick returns to the vertical.

Some portable computers have trackpoint sticks rather than trackballs. A track-point stick is a small joystick built into the keyboard of the computer. The main advantage of the track-point stick over a trackball is that the cursor continues to move as long as the stick is tilted, so fewer finger motions are necessary for long cursor sweeps.

Track pad

The track pad is also well suited for use as the pointing device of a portable computer. A track pad has a smooth upper surface over which the operator's finger glides to direct cursor movements. The position of a fingertip in contact with the pad is detected by two perpendicular layers of parallel conducting strips under the pad. The electrodes are electrically insulated one from another, so each point where one electrode crosses another is effectively a capacitor.

Minute electrical charges on an operator's fingertips change the properties of the underlying capacitors, and these changes are detected and interpreted as a finger position by the track-pad circuitry. Unfortunately, droplets of water on the track pad confuse the finger-locating process, so the track pad must be kept clean and dry.

Graphics tablets

The cursor motions produced by mice and most other pointing devices are too imprecise for certain applications, notably for freehand drawing directly into graphics documents. Graphics tablets—also called digitizers—are used for more precise or natural drawing or for handwriting.

A graphics tablet is a flat bed with a smooth surface. A grid of pressure sensors under the surface detect the position of a stylus that is used to draw or write on the input bed. Since there is no need for electrical contact between the stylus and

the bed, images can be traced from documents by placing the document on the bed and following its lines with the stylus.

Apart from detecting the position of the stylus, a graphics tablet detects variations in the pressure applied to the stylus. Software translates these variations into differences in line thickness, just as would happen with a pen on paper.

Light pens

A light pen combines some of the features of mice and graphics tablets. Light pens have they same shape as ordinary pens, but they are connected to the processor unit by a lead. A light sensor in the tip of the pen detects the time at which the scanning electron beam of a cathode-ray-tube monitor passes the position of the pen's tip on the screen. Software then calculates the position of the pen on the screen from that time.

Light pens can draw directly into the screen image or they can be used to select and drag on-screen items. Their drawback is the uncomfortable work position when using a vertical screen.

Touch screens

Touch screens have a grid of light beams that cross the screen. When an operator touches an on-screen "button," for example, the broken light beams indicate the point where the finger touches the screen. Such screens are used in automatic cash tills and interactive information displays.

▲ Light pens are widely used by designers, although they are prone to a number of minor handling problems—for example, any dirt on the pen or screen can interfere with the low-intensity light signal.

SEE ALSO: CAPACITOR • CATHODE-RAY TUBE • COMPUTER • COMPUTER GRAPHICS • OPTICAL SCANNER • TRANSDUCER AND SENSOR

Movie Camera

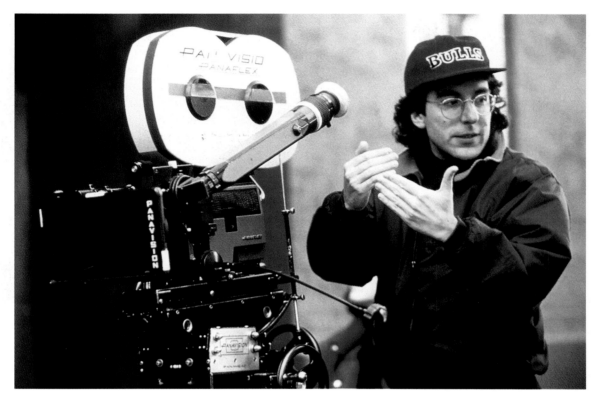

A movie camera—also called a motion picture camera—records a rapid succession of still images on a strip of photographic film. When that film has been chemically processed to form permanent positive images, its images can be projected onto a screen at the same rate that the movie camera recorded them. Objects that were moving at the time of filming then appear to move naturally in the projected image on the screen.

Motion pictures rely on an optical effect called persistence of vision. When a human eye views an object flashed on a screen before it, the image remains "visible" for a fraction of a second after projection stops. Provided that images are flashed on a screen at rates greater than 12 images per second, the brain manages to fuse a series of flashed images into a single continuous image without perceiving flicker.

In practice, motion picture cameras record 24 or 30 frames per second, and projectors function at the same rate. An object that moves during filming occupies a slightly different position in each frame. The brain interpolates between consecutive images and perceives a smooth motion, provided the filmed object moved smoothly.

Basic components and operation

Movie cameras vary in shape, complexity, and the number of facilities they offer. Certain elements, however, are common to them all: lightproof con-

tainers that protect the film before and after exposure; a transport mechanism that advances the film frame by frame between exposures and holds it still during exposures; an exposure mechanism that lets light reach the film only when it is stationary (to prevent blurring); a photographic lens that focuses images on the film; a viewfinder, which provides the camera operator with an image of the area being filmed; and a counter that indicates either the amount of film already exposed or the amount remaining to be exposed.

The lightproof film container or containers may be an integral part of the camera body, or they may be mounted on the main body along with other components. Unexposed film is tightly wound on reels that have close-fitting edges that allow the reels to be loaded in subdued daylight without risk of premature exposure. A small length of film is unwound from the full supply reel and its leading edge attached to the center of an empty take-up reel. The two reels are placed on their respective spindles, and the stretch of film between them is laced through the camera mechanism. The camera is then closed, and the initial stretch of film, fogged by exposure to light, is run through the camera. Filming can then begin.

Nearly all current amateur cameras use cartridges of film wound on spools in lightproof packages that provide protection from accidental exposure and reduce loading time. Professional

TYPES OF FILM

Films are often classified by their gauge, which is the total width of the film expressed in millimeters. The standard film for professional use is 35 mm (1.4 in.). When the U.S. inventor Thomas Edison pioneered the use of 35 mm film in 1889, each frame was 1 in. x 0.8 in. (24 mm x 18 mm), almost filling the area between the perforations. The shooting speed was 16 frames per second.

When sound was introduced in the late 1920s, the frame size was reduced to 0.9 in. x 0.7 in. (22 mm x 16 mm) to enable the frames to fit between a 0.1 in. (2.5 mm) wide soundtrack and a single row of perforations. At the same time, the shooting rate was increased to 24 frames per second; this combination of frame and soundtrack layout and shooting speed is still the most widely used. Studio cameras typically have a capacity for 1,000 ft. (305 m) of film, which runs for 11 minutes; portable cameras carry 400 ft. (122 m), which runs for just over four minutes.

Wider films, such as 65 mm (2.6 in.) or 70 mm (2.8 in.), are sometimes used for shooting and projecting spectaculars; they have the advantages of giving finer

grain and brighter pictures when projected. Some popular movies originally made in 35 mm have been transferred to 70 mm simply to give a brighter image in large movie theaters.

The 16 mm (0.6 in.) and 8 mm (0.3 in.) film gauges were designed for amateur use, although 16 mm was the favorite medium for documentaries, television news, and scientific records for many years. Such film gauges ran at 18 frames per second. Video cameras and recorders have now almost completely replaced movie cameras for the applications of 16 mm and 8 mm film.

The 8 mm gauge was originally a 16 mm wide film but with double the number of perforations. The film ran twice through the camera, exposing half the width on each pass. In processing, the film would be split into two 8 mm strands, each 25 ft. (7.6 m) long, which were then joined end to end to give a film that had a running time of four minutes.

In 1965, Super 8 was introduced using much narrower perforations, which allowed a 43 percent greater picture area on the same film width. The film is supplied in easily loaded lightproof cartridges.

Single 8 film has the same dimensions but uses a different cartridge. Both types hold 50 ft. (15.2 m) of film, giving a running time of 3 minutes 20 seconds at the standard speed of 18 frames per second.

The aspect ratio—or width-to-height ratio—of frames has varied during the history of film. Early films generally used an aspect ratio of 4:3, or 1.33:1, although some feature films were made with greater aspect ratios. Since the 1950s, the various standards for aspect ratios have settled around 1.66:1 to 1.85:1, the wider field of vision contributing to a superior illusion of reality. In some cases, notably the CinemaScope system, increased aspect ratios were achieved by using lenses to squash the image horizontally on filming and restore it on projection. More usually, aspect ratios are determined by the shape of the aperture in the camera.

▼ Common film gauges. Left to right: standard 8 mm; Super 8, with smaller sprocket holes and larger frame area; 16 mm film with optical sound track; 35 mm CinemaScope or Panavision film showing the image before it is "unsqueezed"; Cinerama 70 mm film with magnetic sound tracks.

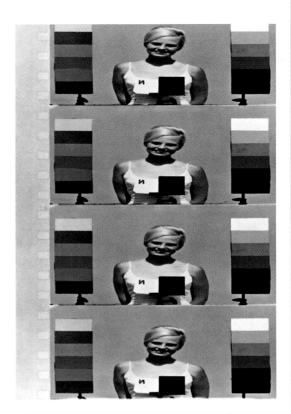

motion picture cameras often house the film in external magazines, which are simple to fix onto the camera body but must be loaded in the dark.

Lenses

The photographic lenses of professional movie cameras are interchangeable so that different focal lengths can be used to vary the scale of the image and, as a result, alter composition and apparent perspective from a given viewpoint. Most lenses in fact are compounds of several lens elements, sometimes fused together, designed to reduce distortion by chromatic and spherical aberrations. Nonreflective lens coatings prevent stray reflected images and loss of light—and therefore image intensity—through reflection.

One type of lens is the zoom lens, whose focal length can be adjusted continuously over a wide range, so a shot can start with a close-up of a principal performer, for example, and then zoom out to a wide-angle view of his or her surroundings. Another popular zoom technique starts with a sweeping landscape view before zooming in to a close-up view of the center of the action. Early zoom lenses had manual focal-length adjustment; modern versions have motorized zooms.

In some cases, several lenses are mounted on a rotating turret that allows quick lens changes to be made. Each lens can be focused separately and incorporates an iris diaphragm to control the amount of light that enters the lens. The setting of the iris diaphragm is chosen according to the brightness of the subject, the sensitivity of the film, and the intended effect in the finished film.

Certain filming techniques use anamorphic lenses that squeeze widescreen images onto standard film by virtue of having different magnifications along their vertical and horizontal axes. Images filmed in this way must be projected through further anamorphic lenses, which restore the original ratio of horizontal and vertical magnifications and produce wider-than-usual images.

Most movie cameras for amateur use have a single lens that is built into the body and therefore is not interchangeable. In all but the simplest models, a zoom lens is fitted so as to provide a degree of flexibility. Most amateur movie cameras incorporate an automatic exposure mechanism that regulates the iris diaphragm to suit the lighting conditions and the sensitivity of the film.

Film-transport mechanism

Scenes are filmed frame by frame by alternately advancing the film by the length of a frame and exposing that frame through a rectangular aperture in a gate that holds the film at a fixed distance behind the camera lens. Evenly spaced sprocket

◀ A Hycam high-speed camera, which can shoot 10,000 frames per second.

holes along one or both edges of the film provide the means by which a claw mechanism can drag the film forward by a constant distance between frames. The claw enters one or two perforations and pulls the film down one frame at a time. The mechanism that engages the claw in the sprocket holes, draws the film down, and then withdraws and returns the claw is called the intermittent.

In many professional cameras, one or two register pins engage with the perforations to hold the film absolutely steady during exposure; they are then withdrawn (or the film is lifted off) during pull down. In less elaborate cameras, including all amateur types, friction from a sprung pressure-plate stops and holds the film during exposure.

The film transport and other mechanisms of early movie cameras were driven by hand cranks; the constancy of frame rates therefore depended on the skill of the camera operator. When sound films were introduced in the late 1920s, speed variations became more noticeable, and constant shooting and projection speeds became necessary. Studio cameras had electrical motors that took power from the public supply; amateur and portable cameras were at first spring driven, but developments in compact electrical motors and batteries made motor-driven cameras both smaller and cheaper than the spring-driven types.

The camera motor also drives the exposure mechanism and turns the take-up spool by means of a slipping clutch so that film is wound on under a gentle tension. Some cameras have a rewind facility that returns exposed film to the supply reel after filming; a mechanism withdraws the pull-down claws during this operation.

Motor noise must be absorbed to prevent it from reaching the soundtrack microphones. To this end, early cameras were enclosed in sound-absorbing hoods called blimps; modern cameras have sound insulation in their casings.

Exposure

To avoid blurring, light from the lens must be cut off while the film is in motion between frames. This end is normally achieved by a use of a rotating-disk shutter, placed between the lens and the exposure gate, into which sectors have been cut. Open sectors allow light to reach the static film for frame exposure, while the closed sectors cut off all light while the film moves from frame to frame. A mechanism ensures that the shutter is always closed at the end of filming.

In some cameras it is possible to vary the size of the open sectors of the shutter so as to vary exposure. At typical maximum exposure, 170 to 180 degrees of the total 360 are open—in some cases, the maximum is as much as 220 degrees of the full circle. The open sectors can be gradually closed to zero during filming, having the effect of fading the scene. One scene can be dissolved into another by then rewinding the film to the start of the fade and then gradually opening the shutter as the film rolls. In general, however, effects such as scene dissolves are achieved in the editing process using two strips of film, thus allowing freedom in choosing the dissolve timing.

Reduced open sectors minimize blurring when filming fast-moving objects or performing rapid camera movements. Panning, when the camera is swept around a scene, is an example of such a movement. The exposure time for each frame is reduced from the usual $\frac{1}{30}$ second to $\frac{1}{50}$ second or so, and the amount of motion within each frame reduces accordingly. The iris diaphragm must be opened to provide greater light intensity for each exposure so as to compensate for the shorter exposure of each frame.

Soundtracks

Some cameras record the soundtrack as strips of magnetized or opaque dots along one edge of the film. The usual method is to record sound on a separate tape recorder while recording synchronization signals on the film.

Viewfinders

The simplest viewfinders are separate optical systems that may be coupled with a zoom lens or the lenses of a rotating turret to match the focal length of the lens used for filming. The view obtained is similar to, but not exactly, the view that is filmed. Differences occur because the viewpoint of the viewfinder is slightly different from that of the main lens and because the focus might not match that of the main lens.

More sophisticated cameras have reflex finders, in which the light that passes through a single lens system is divided between the viewfinder and film exposure. This division is done by either a beam-splitting prism in the lens or a mirror on the rotating shutter. The viewfinder creates an image on a ground-glass screen or other focusing aid and shows the exact view of the lens. Some viewfinders include a small video camera, which allows the director and production crew to preview on screen what is being filmed.

Footage counters

Footage counters show the amount of film used. They can be gear driven from the camera mechanism or connected to a lever that gauges the diameter of the feed or take-up rolls. With Super 8 and Single 8, whose film rolls are inaccessible in cartridges, the counter is usually coupled to the drive for the take-up spool. A few cameras have counters that monitor the number of single frames shot. Such devices are particularly useful for animation and special effects work.

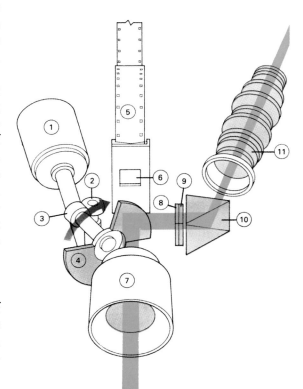

◄ Diagram of the reflex viewfinder of a movie camera, which uses light reflected from the shutter. (1) Shutter motor, (2) vertical drive shaft, (3) helical gear, (4) reflective shutter blade, (5) stock of film, (6) film plane, (7) camera lens, (8) focusing screen, (9) field lens, (10) prism, (11) viewfinder optics.

SEE ALSO: Camera • Lens • Movie production • Photographic film and processing • Shutter • Underwater photography • Video camera

Movie Production

Movie production is the process that creates a motion picture. The term *production* is sometimes confined to the stages that generate film or video and sound recordings; the assembly of these elements into a finished film by editing and sound mixing is then called postproduction.

The filming process often starts with the preparation of a screenplay, which combines a script for the actors' dialogue and actions. In addition, a shooting script is formulated to guide camera and lighting work. The shooting script may include a storyboard, which is a sequence of rough sketches that show the positions and views of actors in each camera shot.

Preparations

Scripts contain information for various members of the production team. Casting directors can deduce which scenes will require extras—nonspeaking or minor-role actors. Location hunters can find appropriate settings and arrange filming permission for scenes that will be filmed out of studio. Set builders can prepare suitable environments for scenes that will be filmed in studio.

Property "buyers" buy, hire, or retrieve from stores items such as clothing and furniture that create an impression of the era and geographical location of the film's plot. Some of these props—short for "properties"—are indicated in the script; others are chosen to reflect the socio-economic status of the characters. In the case of a high-profile film with glamorous stars, it may be possible to tempt fashion designers to contribute garments for the leading roles.

Schedules and continuity

Films are rarely shot according to the sequence of the story. The limited availabilities of principal actors may dictate that all scenes in which they appear be filmed in concentrated blocks that fit those actors' schedules. Block filming is also necessary when a key location is available for filming during a limited period only.

The seasonal variation of foliage also imposes constraints on the filming of outdoor scenes—a summer's day stroll in a park would not be convincing if filmed against a background of bare-branched trees, for example. Furthermore, last-minute schedule changes may be needed to take advantage of specific weather conditions, such as snow flurries or blue skies.

Given the scant correlation between the shooting schedule and the sequence in which the scenes will appear, great care must be taken to avoid continuity problems. Failure to match clothing, hairstyling, and props between consecutive scenes can create bizarre effects—for example, items of clothing that change color on passing from an indoor shot to a street scene, jewelry that appears or vanishes mysteriously during the course of a meal, or hair that grows inches in days. Some critics take great pleasure in spotting these blunders, which can detract from the illusion of reality that the director sets out to create.

The only way to guarantee continuity is by viewing footage from previous scenes and making sure that all details are correct before shooting proceeds. Most movie production teams include a continuity expert who is charged with this responsibility; nevertheless, some blunders of this type can slip through the net in even the most prestigious film productions.

Shooting

Once the actors and props are in place on a film set and the continuity checks have been done, the actual shooting of a scene can begin. The storyboard for that scene indicates the number of shots that the scene will comprise and the different types of shots—long, medium, or close-up static shots, zoom shots, and pans. Long shots take in a wide view of a scene, medium shots close in on more detail, and close-ups fill the screen with a

▲ Getting the right effects for a movie sequence sometimes requires the set builders to go to extreme lengths. This storm scene from the film *Eye of the Needle* had to be created in a watertight sound stage capable of holding thousands of gallons of water. Wind and wave machines were used to make the water appear rough and heavy-duty hoses simulated lashing rain. Scenes like this take a great deal of planning and are expensive to produce, but are easier than trying to film at sea or waiting for the right weather conditions.

◀ Most postproduction of movies is now carried out using computers. Here, Jim Clark is editing scenes from the James Bond film *The World Is Not Enough* using special computer programs that eliminate the need for physical cutting and splicing of film and sound tracks.

small part of the scene, such as a face or hand. Zoom shots provide smooth transitions between static shots of different focal lengths, and pans—short for "panoramic shots"—sweep across a view. In some cases, a camera is mounted on a dolly or truck and pushed along a track to achieve the required motion during shooting. Often, camera aperture and focal-length settings must be changed during the course of such shots.

Specialist engineers consult the requirements of each scene and install microphones and lighting equipment accordingly. Scenery lighting creates a great deal of heat and tends to be switched on just before filming, hence the cry "lights, camera, action!"

Each scene is typically filmed in several "takes" to cater to the different shot types and for actors' mistakes. The start of each take is marked by holding a board in front of the camera. The board carries such information as the scene and take numbers and helps identify the scene in the later editing stages. Older boards were hinged in two parts and would be clapped together at the start of the take to help synchronize the soundtrack with the film, as will be described later.

The footage from a day's filming is developed and printed without fine adjustments to provide "rushes"—rapidly available rough copies of the film. On the basis of the rushes, the director decides which scenes—if any—will have to be scheduled for reshooting. In some cases, video rushes taken from the camera viewfinders provide cheap and easy replacements for film rushes.

Media and synchronization

The most popular medium for motion pictures is 35 mm color film, which has a frame size of 0.87 x 0.63 in. (22 x 16 mm). Some directors choose to use monochrome film to create a moody feel or the impression of old newsreel footage, for example. Others use different film formats or lens systems to create widescreen-format footage. In any case, the camera runs at 24 frames per second.

Images recorded using analog video systems have a graininess that becomes apparent when blown up for a movie theater screen; analog video is also less tolerant than film of variable lighting conditions. These two weaknesses have limited its use to low-budget films and cases where a grainy, home movie effect is desired. Developments in high-resolution digitally recorded video for HDTV (high-definition television) may well cause movie directors to reconsider video as a medium for moving pictures.

Sound is recorded on magnetic audio tape using analog or digital systems. The inputs from microphones are recorded as separate tracks for later mixing as a soundtrack. An additional track records a time code that corresponds to a similar code on the frame, making it possible to synchronize, or "sync," the video and audio elements in the editing suite.

Before the introduction of time-code synchronization, editors had to search through the film for the frame where the two parts of a clapboard just met. The audio tape would then be run back and forth to find the precise start of the clapping sound. That point in the tape would then be matched to the corresponding frame of the film. This system was susceptible to synchronization problems caused by stretched film or audio tape.

Editing

In the modern editing process, filmed images and the associated sound recordings are transferred to magnetic video tape, which is easier to manipulate than the film itself. The editor—usually with input from the director—then assembles each scene using a computerized montage system. Different shots are isolated from their respective takes, and a sequence of cuts is built up.

Once a scene has been made up to the satisfaction of the editor, director, and producer, the montage machine prints out a report of the frame numbers at which the film must be physically cut and spliced together to correspond to the scene as created using the video recording. The soundtrack is still raw at this stage, consisting only of the original recordings from the scene.

The next stage is to unite the scenes to make a film. Certain conventions and clichés help communicate with the movie audience. A slow fade out of one scene and a slow fade into the next hints that a great deal of time passes between the events of the two scenes. This message can be reinforced by including a screen caption with the date or location of the scene that is about to be

▶ Even in sunny climates movies need lighting rigs to guarantee the look of the scene that the director requires. Big-budget films often require the equivalent of a small army of production staff, including carpenters, electricians, continuity, sound engineers, and camera crew. There may be two or three unit crews who shoot scenes in other locations, while the main production crew remains in the place in which the story is being set.

▼ Behind the scenes on one of the studio sets for the film *Brimstone and Treacle*. The scene is being shot from inside the house, but rather than filming on location, painted background scenery is used instead. A wind machine and dead leaves give the impression that there is movement outside the window.

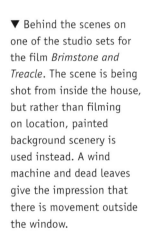

played out. In contrast, a fast dissolve or cut from one scene to another suggests that the events of the two scenes are essentially concurrent.

The equipment used to create dissolves, titles, and similar effects is called an optical printer. It runs two strips of film at the same time: the pair of scenes that are being crossfaded or a scene and a title, for example. Optical systems project and focus the two images frame by frame onto new film so as to expose it. Apertures open and close to control the amount of light that reaches the film from each strip so as to create the fade. Computer-generated images printed on film can also be introduced by this process.

Music and effects

Incidental and theme music are important tools for creating mood and suggesting the location of a scene's events. Custom-written orchestral scores are played out and recorded under a screen onto which the associated footage is projected. The recording is synchronized to the time code of the film. Prerecorded music is matched to the film action by the sound editor.

Sound effects must be created and recorded so as to add realism without dominating the film or drowning out the dialog. Some effects are obvious, such as crashes of thunder; others are more subtle, such as the clinking of cutlery against china at a dinner party. The simulation of such sounds has become a highly specialist skill.

 Digitization has made it much easier to match scenes on film with the soundtrack and to dub special sound effects at appropriate points in the action. This Avid Media Composer system can match background music to spoken dialog and particular scenes in the film so that the final result is a seamless blending of all the processes involved in making a film.

Once incidental music and sound effects have been recorded raw, they have to be mixed and further processed by one or more of the movie theater playback systems, such as surround-sound or simple stereo. After mixing, this recording is known as the M-and-E (music and effects) track. It is used for all versions of the film.

Dubbing

The acoustics of the set or location where a scene is filmed are often far from ideal for recording dialog. For this reason, performers are required to dub in their own words by speaking into a microphone in a recording studio while watching their own performances. Short sections of scenes are repeated and recorded until the recorded speech matches onscreen mouth movements. Offscreen dialog can be recorded directly.

The dialog track is added to the M-and-E track for original-language distribution and for films that will be subtitled for hearing-impaired people or for speakers of other languages. Alternative-language dubbing is often used when distributing the film to speakers of languages other than that of the film. Apart from the language difference, the recording process is identical to that for the original dialog.

In some cases, recordings are made of the director's running comments on the techniques used in each scene. This track is included on DVD releases, where the viewer can select an audio track from a number of options.

Once the film and its soundtrack are ready, the sound is recorded along the edge of a negative copy of the film. This track is called an optical sound negative. In some cases, the soundtrack may be recorded directly onto a magnetic stripe alongside the picture area on positive copies of the film prepared for distribution.

Grading and printing

The picture negative is viewed on a color video analyzer by a grader, who determines the color and density corrections made necessary by factors such as variations in film stock. These changes are made by adjusting the developing conditions of a test print, called the first answer print. Small additional corrections may have to be made before release printing begins.

Once the grading is complete, graded copies of the original negative are made. These copies, called color-reversal intermediates (CRIs), are used to print the positive copies for distribution. The original cut negative is put in storage.

If bulk orders are expected, it may be desirable to print by the Technicolor process. This is not strictly a photographic process but a dye-transfer process that uses three color-separated matrices in the form of monochrome prints. These prints are made by shining light through the color negative and through a different color filter to produce a gelatin record of the cyan, magenta, and yellow content of the original image. Each of the matrices is then saturated with the corresponding color of dye and mechanically printed in turn onto a clear gelatin-coated film.

SEE ALSO: ANIMATION • COMPUTER GRAPHICS • PHOTOGRAPHIC FILM AND PROCESSING • SOUND EFFECTS AND SAMPLING • SOUNDTRACK

Multimedia

The term *multimedia* has its origin in the arts with the desire of artists, actors, and musicians to involve their audience in their work at a number of levels. The German composer Richard Wagner was one exponent of making the audience part of the performance and had the opera house at Bayreuth specially designed to achieve this goal. Today, the term is also used to describe the ability of computer users to access information in a variety of different forms, including text, sound, pictures, graphics, and video, and even to participate in imaginary worlds through interactive game playing and virtual reality.

One of the earliest multimedia products was the flight simulator developed by the aerospace industry to train pilots. Sitting in an exact replica of an airplane cockpit with a video camera projecting real views of landscapes and airports, pilots can experience real-life flight conditions through the use of sophisticated computer software that controls the hydraulic mechanisms of the simulator and the instrument panels. More recently, computer networks have allowed simulators to be linked so that fighter pilots can practice combat missions and evaluate new aircraft before they are built.

Development of multimedia systems

The idea of using computers as more than mere calculating machines began in 1945 with a proposal for a device named the Memex by a U.S. scientist, Vannevar Bush. The aim of the Memex was that it would be able to store a trail of associated information for later use. However, Bush's idea predated the ability to store data digitally and so was never built. Nevertheless, this early notion of "hyperlinking" discrete pieces of information was to play a key role in the future development of the personal computer.

The next step forward came at the end of the 1960s. The U.S. government had set up the Advanced Research Projects Agency (ARPA) early in the decade to fund research into military use of computers. Among the projects sponsored was work being carried out at Stanford Research Institute by Douglas Engelbart. He used Bush's idea of a digital information retrieval system to create the oNLine System (NLS), for which innovative tools such as the mouse, text-editing windows, and e-mail were developed so that the user could manipulate information. Engelbart then took the idea a stage further by wiring computers using the NLS into a local network so that they could pass information between users. By 1969, the NLS had evolved into the Internet.

The first true multimedia computer, the Xerox Alto, arose from a prototype notebook-sized computer called the Dynabook. Although it was never built, research on the Dynabook in the 1970s led to the development of the graphical user interface (GUI), which was incorporated into the Xerox Alto and later into the Apple Macintosh. Multimedia became less of a specialist task at the end of the 1980s with the creation of software tools that could be used by artists and designers on their own computers. These "authoring" systems connected text, sound, animations, graphics, and video by using a special computer language called hypertext markup language, or HTML, to connect the different elements. Products created using these tools were largely closed systems such as CD-ROMs and the type of fixed installation found in museums.

The CD-ROM

The most popular form of multimedia is the CD-ROM (compact disc–read only memory). Each disc can store 650 megabytes of information that can be accessed by inserting it into the CD drive of a personal computer. The computer converts the binary data stored on the disc into text, sound, and pictures as required.

A multimedia CD-ROM is created much as a book is, but the inclusion of sounds, videos, or animations requires a greater degree of planning than when text and images only are used. The content and look of the product are decided by the editorial and design teams, who then choose which elements are to be linked and their potential for illustration using videos or animations. Designs for the appearance of the screens are roughed out so that a prototype can be developed using an authoring software package such as *Director*. Applications like this allow the links to be tested to see how they work. At the same time, software engineers build the "run-time engine,"

an application that will coordinate how the elements of the CD-ROM work together. Finally, the screens are assembled, and the hyperlinks are added so that the product can be tested for bugs. When the production team is satisfied, the CD-ROM is burned onto a master disc, which acts as a template for mass production of the product. Common applications of the CD-ROM include video games, travel guides, electronic encyclopedias, and training programs.

Another form of optical disc, the DVD-ROM can also be used for multimedia applications. A DVD can hold up to 4.7 gigabytes of data, making it ideal for storing movies or complicated interactive games.

Open systems

Open-system multimedia products make use of computer networks to link the user with people and information sources all around the world. That linking is at all possible is due to the efforts of one man, a British scientist called Tim Berners-Lee, the creator of the World Wide Web. His proposal for an in-house document-sharing system for the particle physics laboratory at CERN in Switzerland combined the communications language of the Internet with HTML to create nonlinear links between files so that they could be accessed across a global network. More important, these links could be written by anyone participating in the system rather than just a single author. Because of its nonhierarchical struc-

▼ Many museums are making their exhibits more interesting by using multimedia technology. This boy is learning navigation skills by using an interactive video game at the Nautilus Interactive Sea Museum in Norfolk, Virginia.

ture and open protocols, the Web has become a focus for multimedia applications and a place where people can play interactive games with others anywhere in the world simply by logging on to a website address, participate in a live debate on cable television, access an electronic encyclopedia through their telephone, or see what is happening somewhere else through a video camera linked to a computer.

One game, launched in 2001, has been designed to totally involve participants, even when their computer is turned off. *Majestic* puts players at the heart of a conspiracy in which they are unable to tell whether other participants are real or are characters created by the computer. The game, which uses artificial intelligence, sends the player faxes, e-mails, and even midnight phone calls as the plot develops. Players can search the Internet for clues but may experience unexpected consequences if they do. Unlike other games, the player can progress only when the computer allows. As the computer gathers information about the player's gaming strategy, it tailors the situation and story accordingly. Artificial intelligence is increasingly being used by programmers as a means of providing experienced video games players with an extra dimension to the extent it may become difficult to tell real life from fantasy.

The Internet in 3-D

While the Internet has grown in use enormously since the early 1990s, the way it is seen on screen has not changed from a two-dimensional interface despite improvements in imaging technology. One piece of software that has managed to overcome many of the problems of making the Internet a more interactive environment is the ViOS (visual Internet operating system) browser.

Using ViOS transforms the search for websites into a three-dimensional experience. The system uses a sophisticated rendering engine to create a landscape with mountains, rivers, and cities that the user can move through in real time using a mouse or keyboard. Regions and cities are themed according to type, such as shopping, sports, or travel so that users can access sites of interest through special 3-D portals or maps or by typing in a keyword. For example, typing "shopping" will transport the user to the shopping area of a city, where they can walk past virtual storefronts. Clicking on a store instantly downloads the retailer's home page.

ViOS works through proximity caching, so when the user moves from site to site in a certain area, data is already downloaded when the user clicks on the site. It operates by precaching data from sites nearest the user while deprioritizing

sites farther away and automatically loads data even while the user is doing something else.

One interesting aspect of the ViOS browser is the ability to create 3-D animated representations, or avatars, of the user and his or her friends. People can talk to each other, visit sites together, and meet other people as they travel around the Internet. Entering chat rooms on the Web becomes a more socially interactive experience, as the other people in the room can be seen as avatars rather than just as lines of text.

Virtual reality

Perhaps the most significant computer multimedia experience arrived with the development of virtual reality. Originally developed at the NASA Ames Research Center to make flight simulations more realistic, virtual reality is now finding many diverse applications. By wearing various interactive devices, such as headsets, gloves, goggles, or entire body suits, users can immerse themselves in a 3-D computer-generated environment. Sensors in the devices attached to the user pick up movements and change what the user can see in real time. As a result, users can tour a virtual museum, for example, with the view and perspective changing as they turn to look at different objects or walk through rooms. Data gloves that use force-feedback mechanisms can even allow an object to be picked up and its surface texture felt. A different system called CAVE (cave automatic virtual environment) dispenses with wearable devices that restrict mobility, allowing the user to move freely within the computer-generated environment.

▲ This virtual reality ride at the Galbo amusement park in Japan allows its participants to experience all the ups and downs of a roller coaster ride while remaining indoors.

 SEE ALSO: COMPUTER • COMPUTER GRAPHICS • COMPUTER NETWORK • FLIGHT SIMULATOR • INTERNET • VIRTUAL REALITY

Muscle

Muscles are bundles of contractile fibers arranged in coordinated systems, and muscle contraction is the means by which movement occurs in animals. In invertebrates, the fibers are only loosely bound together, but in vertebrates, the bond is strong, and muscles become much more recognizable as a tissue. Muscles account for a large part of body weight in most animals. In antelope, for example, around 40 to 50 percent of the animal's weight consists of muscle.

Worms are the simplest animals that have muscular fibers, which pass through loose tissues within the worm's body, forming layers in the body wall. The result is often a circular layer around the body and a longitudinally arranged layer along the main axis of the body. Muscles are attached to the body wall at points called origins, and they are located in every part of the body that moves.

Muscles cause a large range of movements in animals. Physiologists have characterized these movements as extensions of jointed appendages—flexion, retraction, rotation—and movements brought about by opposing muscle systems. All movements are caused by the contraction of a muscle or group of muscles. A muscle cannot push; it can only relax. So a part of the body can return from where a muscle contraction has moved it either by gravity or by an opposing muscle or muscles.

◀ Even seemingly simple movements require the fine coordination of many muscles.

▶ The structure of the cardiac muscles is different from those elsewhere in the body.

Vertebrate muscles

A typical vertebrate muscle is surrounded by the external perimysium—a sheath of connective tissues. Beneath the external perimysium is the internal perimysium.

There are just three kinds of muscles in higher animals—skeletal, cardiac, and smooth. Skeletal muscles are usually under voluntary control of the animal; cardiac and smooth muscles are not. In higher animals, gross movements are caused by muscles contracting against a bony skeleton, causing it to hinge at the joints.

The skeletal muscles and the heart—unique among the muscles not under voluntary control—are striated, that is, they have visible stripes. Smooth muscles, as their name suggests, have no visible striations. Unlike the striated muscles, smooth muscles contract slowly, usually in rhythmic pulses. These muscles comprise the inner wall of the intestines and parts of the viscera—the internal organs.

Striated muscle fibers

Striated muscle fibers are cylindrical in shape and are between 0.02 and 0.08 mm in diameter. Sometimes the fibers extend along the complete length of the muscle. Alternatively, the muscle has a tendon along each edge. Muscle fibers are anchored to the tendon and lie diagonally across the muscle. The exact details of how the fibers are organized vary from muscle to muscle, depending on muscle function.

Each muscle fiber is surrounded by the sarcolemma, which is a complex structure consisting

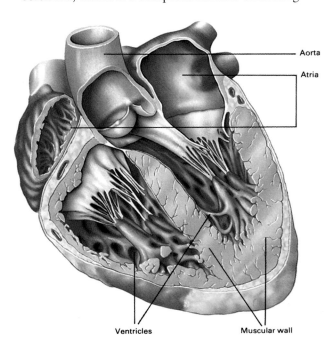

Aorta

Atria

Ventricles

Muscular wall

▶ Voluntary muscles are under the conscious control of the brain. All voluntary muscles are striated muscles—muscles in which the fibers are aligned. In voluntary muscle, the actin and myosin filaments are gathered into bundles called myofibrils, which in turn form bundles of muscle fibers called muscle cells.

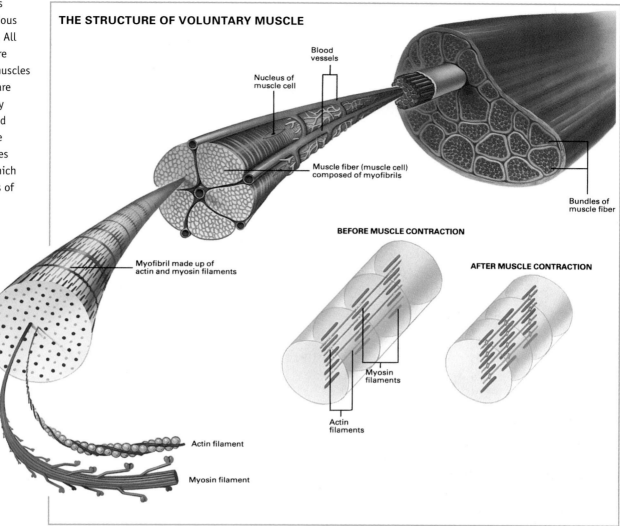

THE STRUCTURE OF VOLUNTARY MUSCLE

of three layers. At the outside is a layer of fine fibrils that, at the muscle ends, form the link with the tendons. A foundation, or basement, membrane is found under the top fibril layer, and next to the fibers is a plasma membrane.

The plasma membrane is more complicated than the other layers. Examined under an electron microscope, it appears as a light layer encased by two dark layers. The layers consist of lipid (fat) and protein, the function of which is to maintain an electric potential—important in muscle contraction.

Muscle fibers consist of two sizes of tiny filaments. Bundles of filaments are called myofibrils and consist of alternating bundles of thick and thin fibers, called myofilaments. Myofibrils are about 0.00006 in. (1.5 μm) in diameter, run along the entire length of the muscle fiber, and at the end are connected to the sarcolemma. Adjacent myofibrils are spaced about 80 nm apart. In this space, there are two membranes, the transverse tubules, which run across the fibers, and the sarcoplasmic reticulum, which forms a series of sacs around each myofibril. The transverse tubules

form a communication link between individual fibers, while the sarcoplasmic reticulum controls the number of calcium ions in the cytoplasm of muscle fibers.

Structurally, the striated muscle cells in the skeletal muscles are different from most cells in the body, including those in cardiac and smooth muscles. They are formed during development of the embryo, when cells with single nuclei fuse to make highly unusual cells with many nuclei.

Cardiac muscle fibers

Mammalian hearts consist of two atria and two ventricles, chambers with walls almost entirely of muscle fiber. Atria receive blood into the heart, and ventricles pump it out of the heart.

The structure of the cardiac muscles is different from those elsewhere in the body. In the ventricles, the myocardial cells are arranged in a complex pattern of sheets, or bands. Myocardial cells are around 110 μm long and 15 μm wide and are branched, forming a netlike pattern. In part of the heart, the cells are highly folded, having large areas of contact, and this structure adds to the great strength of cardiac muscle tissue. Elsewhere in the heart, cells fuse to present lower electric resistance than separate cells.

Smooth muscle structure

In vertebrates, smooth muscle occurs in the stomach, intestines, bile ducts, uterus, blood vessels, bladder, and urinary tracts. Smooth muscles are also known as involuntary muscles because they are controlled by the autonomous nervous system. Examining smooth muscle under an electron microscope shows that the cellular structures are less organized than those in the striated muscles.

Smooth muscles are divided into two main subgroups—visceral and multiunit. Visceral muscles have a pacemaker or are self-stimulated. They work as a syncitium—a functional unit. A multiunit muscle has each of its cells under nervous control, much as individual fibers are under nervous control in skeletal muscles. Some smooth muscles fall between the two subgroups.

Visceral muscle cells, such as those in the intestine, are roughly spindle shaped—wide in the middle, tapering toward the ends. Others are ribbon or rod shaped. The thickest sections of visceral muscles are ten to twenty times smaller than skeletal muscle cells, at about 5 to 10 μm in diameter. The cells are about 50 to 250 μm long, their density of packing depending on the exact function of the muscle.

In the syncytial cells in the intestine walls, the cells are arranged in groups of a few hundred, separated by layers of elastin and collagen fibrils. Thick and thin filaments occur in smooth muscle, but the arrangement is practically random.

In multiunit muscles, such as those in the vasa deferentia (ducts leading from the testes to the penis), activation depends solely on nerves that lie in depressions in the muscle. To each muscle cell is connected at least one nerve.

When smooth muscle cells contract, they do so in a way that makes them spiral like a corkscrew. One hypothesis regarding this behavior is that the proteins responsible for muscle contraction are themselves corkscrew shaped.

Nervous control of muscles

Nerve fibers terminate on the muscle fibers at synapses to form a neuromuscular junction. The part of the muscle fiber at the synapse is called the end plate and is arranged as a folded pattern. One long fold, running parallel to the muscle fiber axis, contains the nerve terminal. In the nerve terminal are mitochondria, which govern the energy conversions in muscle cells, and acetylcholine, which is a chemical transmitter substance.

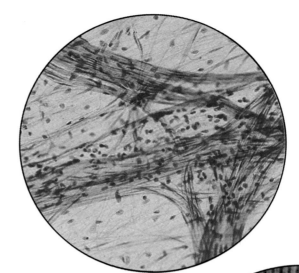

◀ Involuntary, or smooth, muscle is composed of many long, spindly cells. Smooth muscle is not under the conscious control of the brain.

▼ The actin and myosin fibers in voluntary muscle meet together like the teeth of two combs.

Acetylcholine—and sometimes other neurotransmitter substances —passes on the nerve impulse to the muscle fibers, which produce an end plate potential. In turn, the electric impulse fades from the end plate, becomes what is termed an action potential, and travels on the surface of the muscle, causing the muscle to contract.

Contraction of cardiac muscles depends on a different mechanism from that which governs the skeletal muscle system. The main characteristic of cardiac contraction is its rhythm, which depends on pacemaking areas. Pacemaking areas contain cells with few myofibrils.

In human beings, a group of cells called the sinoatrial node acts as pacemaker. Located on the inner wall of the right atrium, the node uses a special excitatory system consisting of Purkinje fibers to conduct messages along the inner walls of the ventricles to the different parts of the heart.

Control of smooth muscles is also different. The contraction of muscles in organs, such as the intestines, is in the form of peristaltic waves in which a ring of contraction appears to move slowly along the organ. Contraction is controlled by a slowly fluctuating membrane potential. There are no specific pacemaker cells or areas in smooth-muscled organs. Instead, pacemaker activity appears to move around different muscle cells.

SEE ALSO: CELL BIOLOGY • DIGESTIVE SYSTEM • FAT • PROTEIN

Musical Scale

Musical tones are sounds with a definite pitch, a quality dependent on the rate of acoustical vibration, or frequency. Low-frequency sounds are low pitched, or bass, notes, whereas high-frequency sounds are treble, or high, notes. When the notes are tabulated in ascending or descending order of pitch, they make a musical scale. The intervals, or leaps, of pitch between successive notes vary in different musical systems, and it is primarily these relationships between pitches that characterize a type of music, not the specific underlying frequencies.

The octave

There are many scale systems or modes, including some, such as in Arab, Indian, and microtonal music, with notes more closely spaced than in conventional Western music. Most scales, however, share certain basic intervals, the most important of which is the octave. The octave is the pitch span produced by halving or doubling of frequency. For each leap of one octave, the ear seems to hear the same note again—of higher or lower pitch but nevertheless merging perfectly with the original note spaced an octave away. This fusion of tones whenever the frequency is doubled or halved has ensured that in all musical systems, the pattern of intervals comprising a particular mode is accommodated within an octave, any such scheme being repeated identically within adjacent octaves, just as the seven white notes and five black notes are repeated along the familiar piano keyboard.

Pentatonic scale

The blending of tones spaced by octaves is an example of consonance, a psychological effect repeated in rather less definite form with some other pairs of notes. An octave corresponds to a frequency ratio of 2:1, but notes with a ratio of 3:2 or 4:3 also blend very pleasingly to form simple chords, and these two intervals coexist with the octave in most scale systems. In fact, the three together provide a complete set of notes for the common pentatonic scale, used in the East and found in much surviving Western folk music. This scale can be plotted onto the modern staff (or stave), where the intervals are given as frequency ratios of the higher to the lower note.

As such ratios are difficult for nonmathematical people to remember, pitch intervals are usually named in terms of their spacing on the staff. Thus, the interval of 3:2 occurs over a span of five possible note positions (inclusive) and is known as a perfect fifth (or simply fifth), that of 4:3 covers four positions and is a perfect fourth (fourth), while a ratio of 2:1 spans eight note spaces and is therefore an eighth, or octave. These and some other important intervals together with their frequency ratios, musical character, and positions make up modern Western scales. The arithmetically least simple ratios, involving a small step either from unison or from the octave, produce dissonance, an effect opposite to consonance.

In the pentatonic pattern, the group of three notes followed by a gap and then a further pair resembles the layout of black keys on a piano, and

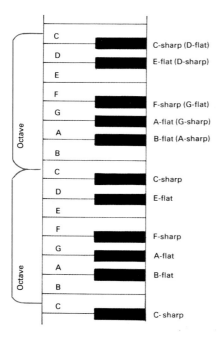

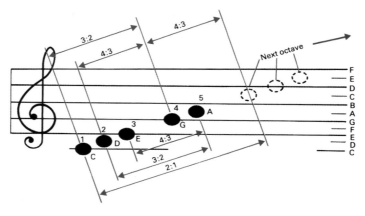

◀ Two octaves of a piano or organ keyboard. The major diatonic scale may be played on white keys starting at C, the basic minor scale on white keys starting at A, and the pentatonic scale on black keys starting at F-sharp.

▼ The common pentatonic scale, as it would appear on a modern stave, starting at middle C.

indeed, the scale CDEGA (which can be played directly on the white notes) may be duplicated on the black notes of a piano starting from F-sharp. The pitches are different, but because the interval relationships are retained, the Chinese musical effect is the same. Much East Asian music uses the pentatonic scale.

Scales such as this were common in the ancient world and provided the foundations on which Western music was built. Pythagoras (sixth century B.C.E.) constructed a scale placing a special emphasis on the interval of a fifth and demonstrated that a step upward of a fifth followed by a fourth equals an octave ($\frac{3}{2} \times \frac{4}{3} = \frac{12}{6} = 2$). This relation may be shown on the staff, where note no. 4 in the pentatone (G) is a fifth up from the first note (C) and a fourth below the octave note (upper C). The same procedure, applied in reverse, moving down in pitch by a fifth and then a fourth from upper to middle C ($\frac{2}{3} \times \frac{3}{4} = \frac{1}{2}$), would fill in the missing note around F. Such maneuvers create note-by-note steps equal to the difference between a fourth and fifth ($\frac{3}{2} \div \frac{4}{3} = \frac{9}{8}$), and this whole-tone ratio of 9:8 was used by Pythagoras to fill in the finer detail of his scales.

Diatonic scales

The apparently unsophisticated pentatonic scale contains not only this collection of fourths, fifths, and whole tones, but also a number of steps between other pairs of notes equivalent to further simple frequency ratios. Important among these are the consonances known as major third and major sixth and also their semiconsonant minor versions. However, these more subtle intervals are only approximated within the pentatone, whose whole-tone steps have to be adjusted slightly, or tempered, to give true thirds and sixths. From such adjustments and because of the needs of an evolving music, today's major and minor eight-note scales slowly emerged as modified versions of the most popular ancient modes.

Just as the fifth followed by a fourth to make an octave was basic to ancient scale building, giving three notes, with a simple 2:3:4 frequency relationship, so an upward step of a major third followed by a minor third to equal a fifth ($\frac{5}{4} \times \frac{6}{5} = \frac{3}{2}$) became an additional vital grouping in modern scales. This set of three notes has a 4:5:6 frequency relationship and is known as a major triad (a triad is a group of three notes), paralleled by the minor triad in which the middle note is moved down (flattened) to make the first step into a minor third (10:12:15 pattern). Interlocking groups of such triads provide a complete framework for the two main diatonic scales, though there are several alternative endings to

the minor scale (diatonic means ranging through the eight conventional tones).

The various consonant and semiconsonant intervals listed in the table appear in these scales not only between the starting note and named note and within the triadic groupings but also at other positions whenever several smaller intervals add together appropriately. Thus, when all the steps in the major scale are set exactly to give just intonation—a system using correct intervals between all notes in the scale—there are 13 consonances and four semiconsonances within the octave. Our feeling for the key, or tonic, note in major-scale melodies is due in some way to this interleaved consonant pattern, an effect less marked with the minor scale and largely lost if too many extra steps are added—as in atonal or 12-tone music. Also, it is because so many of the intervals used in diatonic music have these small-number frequency ratios that brass instruments are able to employ selections of harmonics (simple multiples of a basic note) to make up their scales.

Tones and semitones

The major and minor diatonic scales are composed of a number of small intervals. The two scales employ seven differently mixed steps of two sizes between adjacent notes. The larger step is the familiar whole tone and the smaller one a semitone—of approximately half the size. If a whole tone is labeled T and a semitone S, the sequence of intervals in a major scale is TTSTTTS, which is obtained by playing the white keys on a piano upward from the note C. Western musical instruments and notation happened to evolve with C major as the dominant

▶ This table shows some of the common intervals that are used in building musical scales.

◀ The diatonic scale (diatonic means ranging through the eight conventional tones) can be built by means of an interlinked group of triads. These triads produce a succession of eight notes per octave according to a pattern of intervals. The two main diatonic scales are called the major and minor scales.

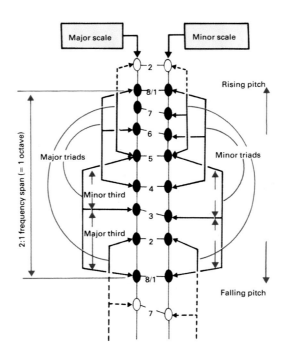

SOME COMMON INTERVALS USED IN SCALE BUILDING (descending order = increasing frequency)			WESTERN SCALE POSITIONS		
MUSICAL NAME	MUSICAL CHARACTER	FREQUENCY RATIO REFERRED TO STARTING NOTE	Major	Minor	Chromatic
Unison	Consonant	1:1	1	1	1
Chromatic semitone	Dissonant	25:24 or 19:18	–	–	2
Minor second (diatonic semitone)	Dissonant	16:15	–	–	2
Lesser whole tone (minor tone)	Semidissonant	10:9	–	–	3
Major second (larger whole tone)	Semidissonant	9:8	2	2	3
Minor third	Semiconsonant	6:5	–	3	4
Major third	Consonant	5:4	3	–	5
Perfect fourth	Consonant	4:3	4	4	6
Augmented fourth (diminished fifth)	Semiconsonant	7:5 or 10:7	–	–	7
Perfect fifth	Consonant	3:2	5	5	8
Minor sixth	Semiconsonant	8:5	–	6	9
Major sixth	Consonant	5:3	6	–	10
Minor seventh	Semiconsonant	7:4 or 9:5	–	7	11
Major seventh	Dissonant	15:8	7	–	12
Octave	Consonant	2:1	8	8	13

tones are joined by two rather smaller steps when chromatic notes (extras outside the immediate scheme) are added by splitting the whole tones. Thus, no one size of whole tone or semitone is correct for filling in the extra five notes, while the addition of such notes creates errors in the existing spacings when these are used as steps in fresh scales.

Various early attempts to deal with this problem led, by the 18th century, to a system of tuning known as equal temperament, in which all notes are spaced by the same size of semitone—equivalent to multiplying the frequency by the twelfth root of two ($2^{1/12}$), which is just under 6 percent of frequency. The regular pattern of frets on a guitar is a good visual example of this tuning method. Equitempered tuning introduces some

scale, and so the above pattern can be repeated from other starting points only by adding further notes to divide the whole-tone intervals into semitones where needed. As latecomers, these accidentals, as they are known, occur either as sharpened versions of the note below or as flattenings of the note above and have no true positions of their own on the keyboard or staff. If the staff is redrawn to represent the real note spacings, the eight plain-letter notes from C to C are now seen to follow the TTSTTTS pattern. It happens that the basic minor-scale scheme (TSTTSTT) can also be played on a keyboard instrument (or drawn on a conventional staff) without using sharps or flats by starting from A, but any other tonic note again demands accidentals for construction of the correct scale sequence.

Chromatic scale

As Western music progressed there was an increasing need to shift between major and minor modes and from key to key and to add extra notes for color and tension, so all five sharps and flats eventually came into general use, giving a total of 12 semitone steps (13 notes) within each octave. With freely intoned instruments, such as the human voice or violin, this shift presents no problems, but devices with fixed tuning—particularly keyboard instruments—raise difficulties because of minor arithmetical irregularities in the just diatonic scales. To achieve its correct overall structure, the major scale incorporates two slightly different sizes of whole tone between its individual notes: Pythagoras's original step of 9:8 and a smaller one of 10:9. In addition, the diatonic semi-

▶ Because the conventional staff distorts true interval relationships between notes, it has been expanded to represent actual frequency spacings. The expanded staff provides for the full chromatic scale of 13 notes by leaving gaps for the five "accidental" notes, the flats or sharps.

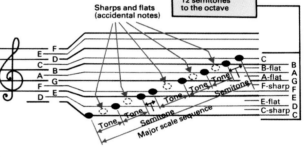

minor errors, which are a matter for continued dispute, though in the worst case, the deviation from just intonation is only slightly over 1 percent. In music not dominated by keyboard or other rigidly tuned instruments, the intervals adopted tend to be those found in the just scales.

Atonal music

The development during the 1920s of a system of music that used all the 12 tones in the octave was partly a progression from the increasingly chromatic music of the 19th century. The Austrian composer Arnold Schoenberg began composing music that dispensed with methods of tonal organization and that has commonly become known as atonal. Schoenberg then further developed this system so that all 12 tones of the octave were arranged in a particular order and then repeated with variation. This system had an enormous influence on the development of 20th century orchestral music.

SEE ALSO: BRASS INSTRUMENT • PIANO • SOUND • SOUND REPRODUCTION • STRINGED INSTRUMENT • WOODWIND INSTRUMENT

Navigation

Navigation is the science of determining location and direction. Originally, the word *navigation* referred to sea travel; from the latin *navis*, meaning boat, and *agere*, meaning guide. Today, however, navigation also refers to direction finding on land, under the sea, in the air, and in space.

History of navigation

Early seafarers used a variety of different means to find their way across seas and oceans. Polynesians, for example, traveled across the vast expanses of the Pacific Ocean by using the stars, the moon, and the motion of the Pacific swells to ascertain their position. Mediterranean sailors tended to rely on the direction and temperature of eight principal winds and a guide on mariners' charts called a wind rose. Then, around 1200 C.E., the magnetic compass was introduced to Europe from China. When exactly the compass evolved and when it was first used for navigation is uncertain. Originally, the Chinese compass was made from a piece of lodestone (magnetic iron oxide), which was hollowed like the bowl of a spoon and floated on water. The lodestone float, acted upon by Earth's magnetic field, would always take up the same orientation along the north-south magnetic axis. Later, it was realized that iron could be magnetized, either by stroking it with lodestone or by heating it and allowing it to remain stationary while it cooled. The first clear reference to the manufacture of a magnetic compass is in a Chinese encyclopedia of 1040 C.E., in which the making of magnetic needles is described. The earliest record of its use at sea by Chinese mariners is in a report of 1115 C.E. By the end of the 13th century, the mariner's compass was widely used in southern Europe, Scandinavia, and Iceland. Also around this time, a major improvement was made to the original form of the magnetic compass. It involved setting the compass in a set of gimbal rings—a series of concentric rings of brass so pivoted that when the ship rolled or tossed, the compass remained upright, thus enabling mariners to use the compass with greater accuracy in rough weather.

Early mariners soon discovered, however, that the direction indicated on a compass was not true north but varies over Earth; the variation is now printed on charts. In addition, when iron and steel ships were built, it was known that these materials could cause deviations in the compass reading, and so compensation for these deviations became necessary. The problems associated with deviation in magnetic compass readings were solved in 1908 with the invention of the gyrocompass, a device that measures the direction of Earth's axis without using magnetism.

Knots

In the Middle Ages, navigators would calculate their speed of travel by casting over the stern a log attached to a rope that was knotted at regular 47 ft. (14 m) intervals. The log would stay more or less stationary on the sea, and as the ship moved,

▼ The visual display unit and the control panel of a computerized navigation instrument. The display combines a bright radar picture with a program written specifically for easy use.

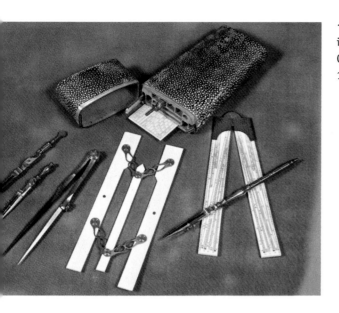

◄ These navigation instruments were owned by Captain Cook during the 18th century.

more of the knotted rope would be payed out. After about 30 seconds, the sailors would drag the log and rope back on board and count how many knots had been payed out. From this number, they could calculate the approximate speed of travel in nautical miles per hour. Modern logs take the form of propellers or use water pressure, the latest types employing electronic principles. However, the word knot, meaning a nautical mile per hour, is also retained. The nautical mile is 6,080 ft. (1,852 m), almost a minute (one-sixtieth of a degree) of latitude.

Dead reckoning

Position finding from course, or direction of travel, and from speed, according to the time since leaving a starting point, is known as dead reckoning, or DR. Were there neither tides nor winds, the navigator at sea could rely on DR, but in practice, fixing or finding position by other means is necessary at intervals. On land, it is possible to pinpoint a position on a map, but at sea, it is a matter of using distant objects, for example, taking bearings on landmarks ashore. At night, these directions may be taken, with the aid of a compass or a lighthouse.

Out of sight of land, dead reckoning checks have traditionally depended on astronavigation. Each point on Earth's surface has a unique vertical and therefore a unique horizontal. The navigator measures the angle above the horizon of Sun, Moon, or stars by means of a sextant. According to where the vessel is thought to be, the navigator then calculates what the angle ought to be at the time. If the sextant altitude is greater than the calculated value, the correction will be toward the star, the distance in nautical miles being the difference of altitude in minutes. A second star's altitude and a second correction will fix position.

Although astronavigation is a worldwide aid, it is not suitable for all weather conditions. Clouds may cover the sky and fog blot out the horizon, which in any event, may not be visible at all during the night, so star observations may have to be restricted to dusk and dawn.

Chronometers

Until the 18th century, a problem for ships' navigators was making accurate measurement of longitude to estimate their position east or west. This problem was solved with the invention in 1761 of a practical marine chronometer—a clock that is capable of working accurately at sea. Mariners were then able to compare the time on the chronometer, which was set to the time at their place of departure, with the time at their current position, calculated from the sun at midday. Using this time difference, it was, for the first time, possible to calculate longitude.

Electronics at sea

In the early 1900s, Guglielmo Marconi successfully demonstrated radio communications, which were used initially to broadcast time signals for checking the chronometers. It was soon found that an antenna wound in a loop could detect the direction from which a radio wave was coming. The navigator could now detect a radio beacon at night or in fog.

A further development in the use of radio waves for navigation occurred shortly before World War II. This technique is similar to that used by bats to find their way around dark caves. Bats produce very-high-pitched sound waves that are reflected off the surfaces of their surroundings. The differences in time taken for the reflected sound waves to reach the bat's ears enables the bat to create an accurate mental image of its surroundings. Similarly, using a directional antenna, generally in the form of a dish, distances and directions of reflected radio waves could be found and the results displayed on the face of a cathode-ray tube. Thus, radar enabled the mariner to see coastlines and other ships at night or in fog.

During World War II, the Loran and Decca Navigator systems came into use. They set up patterns over Earth's surface comparable to the intersecting ripples of water when stones are thrown simultaneously into a pond. More recently, Omega, an ultra-long-range very-low-frequency system was developed. This system was terminated in 1997, when it was superseded by improved methods of electronic navigation.

All these systems work on the same principle, though there are practical differences between them. If two radio transmitters send out the same

◄ This miniature inertial navigation platform weighs only 25 lbs. (11.3 kg) and measures 11 in. (28 cm) long and 8.25 in. (21 cm) wide. It is a precision instrument with applications in rockets, ships, submarines, and aircraft.

signal, say a continuous tone, the two wave motions will coincide with each other—that is, they will be in phase—along certain lines. These lines form a hyperbolic pattern around the transmitters. A ship picking up the signals exactly in phase must therefore be on one of these lines, which are marked on charts. To give a precise fix, signals from another pair of stations must be compared, the hyperbolic lines from which are also marked on charts. Combining the two gives a unique position, once the lines involved are known.

This is the principle of the Decca system, which uses additional lane-identification signals transmitted from the ground stations every minute to give a unique and precise fix. They drive automatic counters on board the ship, so that a continuous readout of position is displayed.

The basic Loran system uses pulses instead of continuous-wave transmissions, giving less information but greater accuracy at long distance; the Loran C system combines both. They are also used by aircraft. A limited system called Consol, giving direction details only, is used on yachts.

Sound waves are also used in modern methods of navigation. The lead line, for example, used to measure depth, has been replaced by the echo sounder, which times the travel of sound waves from the hull of a ship to the seabed and back.

Global positioning system

Electronics systems have largely been superseded by the global positioning system (GPS), which uses satellites orbiting Earth to broadcast details of their orbits by means of a signal code, which is changed by remote control from the ground as the orbit alters. As the satellite moves across the sky, the rate of change of its Doppler shift varies —its distance from the ship varies most rapidly when it is close to the horizon and least when it is overhead. The orbit and Doppler information are fed into a computer on board the ship that calculates the ship's position with great accuracy.

This system has its origins in a decision by the U.S. government in 1973 to create a satellite-based system of beacons that would replace existing techniques. The first of these navigation satellites were called Navstars. They then developed into the current GPS system, which is owned and operated by the Department of Defense. Beginning in 1978, 10 satellites called the Block-I GPS were launched. They were replaced by the 24 Block-II satellites placed in orbit between 1989 and 1993.

The Block-II satellites can provide accurate positioning within 300 ft. (100 m). If a GPS receiver at a known fixed location is also used, then positional accuracy within less than three feet is possible. This remarkable technological development has effectively superseded many conventional methods of navigation and can be used on land, sea, and air or in space. Some cars are now provided with GPS navigation systems, and the next generation of mobile phones will be able to use GPS, giving emergency services instant knowledge of the location of a caller. In addition, if a car or mobile phone with GPS is stolen, it will be possible to easily locate its whereabouts.

Air navigation

At about the same time that Marconi was developing radio, the Wright brothers flew the first piloted heavier-than-air machine. The pilots who tried to navigate these early machines soon discovered some special difficulties. A ship can heave to, but an aircraft must fly on, using up valuable fuel that it needs to keep aloft. Also, at high-speed flying, there is little time for navigating.

Before takeoff, the pilot prepares a complete dead-reckoning picture of the journey, known as a flight plan, which is amended as the journey progresses. Originally, course and speed could be found only relative to the air, which itself travels with the wind. This situation was much improved with the invention of radio Doppler, which can measure speed over the ground. This information is then processed by simple computers, which translate the results into position.

In the air, the pilot needs instruments that provide information not on position but on which direction to take. In the early days, the loop antenna was simply pointed at a beacon on the destination airfield, and the airplane was lined up with the loop. Alternatively, crude beams of radio waves produced by ground stations might be used. Such devices were vulnerable to bad weather, and after World War II, high-frequency directional beacons, known as VOR, and a distance-measuring device, DME, became the standard aids. The Loran and Decca systems are not so useful, because they find positions rather than point the way.

An airplane may also be fitted with an inertial guidance system, consisting of a platform carrying accelerometers that measure the unique vertical with gyroscopes that remember the sky and a computer that gives position continuously. These systems are expensive; only large fast commercial airlines or small military aircraft, where expense is no bar, can afford to be fitted with these devices. Even these precision gyroscopes tend to drift one degree per hour, so positional errors are about one nautical mile for each hour of flight.

An aircraft is much more difficult to control than a ship, for unless kept level, it will not fly straight. The human ear carries balancers, but at high speeds, the accelerations distort the messages. Hence, early pilots restricted their flying to within view of the ground.

At night or in clouds, instruments are essential and the demands on the pilot are severe. Fifty years ago, automatic pilots were being developed and are now standard equipment, except in light aircraft. The autopilot combined with ILS, a precision radio beam, and a radio altimeter to measure clearance above the runway have made automatic landing in fog possible. Indeed, push-button flights are now made in which the pilot hardly touches the control column. All the systems mentioned may be linked to the autopilot through a computer.

Efforts to make air navigation safer have led to the introduction of redundancy, whereby three or more systems operate simultaneously in an aircraft so that, if one disagrees with the other two, it can be disconnected as faulty. For automatic landing, triplicate or quadruplicate autopilots, ILS receivers, and radio altimeters are fitted; in high subsonic or supersonic aircraft, three inertial navigators may be provided if the verticals that they measure are used to level the aircraft. In addition, GPS is now used on military and commercial aircraft, providing rapid and accurate positional information.

The aids employed in airplanes have not greatly affected marine navigation. VOR and DME have insufficient range, and the time taken for a sea voyage is too long for inertial navigation, except for naval submarines, which may use extremely complex systems. Autohelmsmen and computers are, however, provided for many ships.

Collision

A collision at sea does not always involve loss of life. On the other hand, collisions involving airplanes are generally disastrous. The avoidance of collision is the responsibility of air traffic control, a system that specifies flight paths and timings along aerial routes known as airways. A controller covers a certain area, using computerized information entered into the system and frequently updated weeks or months before the actual flight.

Aircraft are separated vertically as well as horizontally, and to help the controller, aircraft automatically signal altitude when picked up by a ground controller's radar.

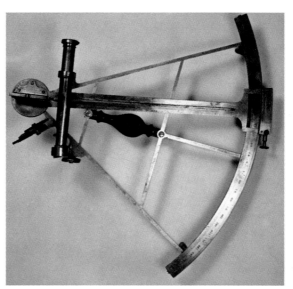

◀ The sextant is a navigational device used to make accurate measurements of the Sun or stars to find the correct latitude.

Shipping traffic generally observes a one-way system of sea lanes, especially in busy channels, such as the Panama Canal. Shipping has also benefited from a worldwide system of buoys and lighthouses to help ships avoid running aground. In open waters, shipborne radar is the main collision-avoidance aid.

The automatic radar-plotting aid (ARPA), manufactured by Marconi International Marine, is one of the latest systems to avoid collisions at sea. Basically, it is a radar with a built-in TV screen and computer that instructs the operator what actions need to be taken.

Special guard bands can be superimposed on the radar screen to warn the operator of any obstruction (ship or land) that comes into a present range. When an object crosses the guard band, its motion is analyzed by ARPA's computer. If it is a closing object, such as an approaching ship, its position is indicated on the radar screen, an audible warning is sounded, and the word "alarm" flashes on the screen—well in time for the ship to take action to avoid a collision.

Lighthouses and buoys may also be provided with a racon, a radar device that transmits a signal only in response to a radar signal from a ship. It can greatly improve the intensity of the echo from an object as small as a buoy.

Space navigation

Journeys into space are based on thorough flight planning so that a Moon landing or a splashdown may be predicted well in advance of the launch. Such planning is possible because there are no winds or tides in space and the gravitational fields of the Sun, planets, and moons are known; thus, the dead reckoning can be remarkably precise.

▲ An early 18th-century mariner's compass with a freely pivoted needle. Early compasses had no lettering, but they incorporated pointers to indicate North and East.

Inertial navigation is used to keep the spacecraft on a steady alignment, which is set according to the brighter stars, while the motors are fired to change the velocity and amend the orbit. The accelerometers then measure the change of velocity, and when the correct value is reached, the thrust is cut off automatically.

Astronavigation on Earth works because the navigator needs only to fix position relative to Earth's surface. In space, there is no such reference, and the stars can give orientation only in two dimensions. The third dimension of position in space is established by radar from Earth supported by computing, though a modified form of astronavigation can be used close to a planet or a moon where a reference surface exists. Doppler from Earth measures velocity with extraordinary accuracy, but the spacecraft is also fitted with Doppler navigation aids for landing purposes. Indeed, its onboard computing makes possible a safe return to Earth should the radio links break down. In the 1980s, the introduction of a satellite navigation system, called the Navstar Global Positioning System, enabled spacecraft to ascertain their position to within a few meters. This system improved and developed into the current global positioning system.

FACT FILE

■ Experiments with migratory birds in a planetarium at Cornell University showed that they used the artificial star patterns to orientate themselves in the direction of their accustomed migratory courses. When the planetarium's sky was turned off, the birds fluttered aimlessly.

■ Early compass needles were magnetized using lodestone (magnetic iron oxide). The method is to stroke the needle in one direction only, using one end of the stone and taking it well away from the needle at the end of each stroke.

SEE ALSO: Doppler effect • Electronics • Global positioning system • Gyrocompass • Inertial guidance • Latitude and longitude • Magnetism • Radar • Radio • Satellite, artificial • Sextant • Telescope, optical

Newspaper Production

Newspapers are essentially daily or weekly publications that provide reports and comments on current events and may be local, national, or international in their coverage.

The modern style of newspaper began as pamphlets and broadsheets in the 17th century. Subsequently, regular weekly and daily publications were introduced. The first newspapers had limited circulation, but improvements in printing, together with the development of popular journalism to widen the readership, resulted in significant growth during the 19th century. This period saw the development of newspapers in much their present form, using techniques that have only recently changed following the introduction of electronic production methods. In countries such as Britain, the availability of good distribution channels covering the whole country led to the establishment of national newspapers as the main source of national and international news, with smaller district newspapers concentrating on covering the local news.

In contrast, because of the great distances in the United States, the district (city) paper took the dominant role, supplying international, national, and local news, along with all sorts of special-interest material. Subareas within the districts, however, often have their own papers covering local affairs in more detail, but the district papers sometimes meet this competition by producing zoned editions for specific distribution areas.

Advertising

Advertising is essential to modern newspapers because the income from sales of copies of the paper is insufficient to cover the heavy cost of gathering the news and production. The revenue from advertising allows papers to be sold at nominal prices. Indeed in some cases, such as the free local papers and shoppers' freesheets, there is no charge for the paper; the wide circulation obtained from free distribution makes the paper more attractive to advertisers and so increases the revenue to a level sufficient to cover the costs and make a sometimes substantial profit.

There are two main categories of newspaper advertising: classified (or linage) and display. Classified advertisements appear under a series of different headings and may be printed in a separate section of the paper, usually at the back. These advertisements are normally sold over the telephone—the sales staff takes down the wording required along with details of the advertiser for billing purposes. Often, such advertisements are

taken on a prepaid basis to reduce administration costs and avoid the risk of advertisers failing to pay. By older production methods, the copy for the advertisements would be sent to the composing room for setting, but with modern systems, it is more likely to be keyed directly into a computer by staff. When required, the production staff assembles the advertisements on an electronic page under a general heading.

Display advertising is generally intermixed with editorial content throughout the newspaper and, as the name suggests, is generally on a larger scale than the classified advertising. It is sold by a display-sales team that may call on advertisers as well as phoning. Papers often have an art department that can prepare illustrations for advertisements, but most display advertising is supplied as finished artwork prepared by specialist agencies.

The number of pages in a newspaper is based on a predetermined ratio of advertising to editorial, with some practical restrictions on the number of pages that can be economically produced by the printing process. The advertising layout can be determined in advance of the news, and much of the display advertising is sold into specific positions in the newspaper, so the advertising content to some extent determines the layout of the rest of the paper.

Editorial

The main function of the editorial department is the gathering, selection, and presentation of the news together with the writing of leaders (editori-

▲ Selecting transparencies at the picture editor's desk. The right picture on the front page can have a huge impact on the sales of a newspaper, and there is often great competition between papers to get the best picture.

◄ The control room of the printing floor. Here, the machines are being monitored for ink density and print quality.

als) and other comment. Some newspapers keep the straight reporting of the news separate from the editorial comment; others have the news stories written with the editorial opinion, in which case the stories often carry a byline of the reporter's name. Bylines are also commonly used by special correspondents even when they are providing a straight news report. In some United States newspaper chains, the main editorial comments are supplied by the head office and reflect the opinion of the chain and are sometimes published without a byline.

The editorial content of a newspaper falls into a number of different areas, such as general news (local, national, and international), business, financial, sports, and the arts. In addition, there may be a number of special-feature sections and supplements. These individual areas—sometimes referred to as desks—are usually under the control of a specialist editor who allocates individual stories to specific reporters and subeditors or copy readers. In turn, section editors report to the editor, though the lines of responsibility may pass through a deputy editor or managing editor. The exact titles and the responsibilities tend to vary.

Whatever the precise title used, it is the editor who is in final charge of the content of the newspaper. Generally, he or she will have a conference each day with senior staff to determine the relative importance of the news coming in, and a rough plan of the day's contents is made and kept under review as the news breaks. The news comes in from various sources, including local reporters (often on special assignments, such as sports reporting or financial news), correspondents, and national and international wire agency services supplying news items gathered and written by their own teams of reporters. News items may be assembled using information from many sources and then extended or shortened to suit the space available. Often the subeditor adds background information to bring the reader up to date on a story. The subeditor is responsible for the accuracy of the items produced and so has to check facts as well as maintain the editorial style and mark up the copy to show the type size in which it is to be printed.

Apart from the mainstream news stories, general articles on a wide range of subjects, often on themes suggested by the news, are prepared by writers in the features department. Similarly, the editorial leaders or opinion columns are normally written to tie in with major news stories. Pictures are widely used to illustrate and emphasize news items, and the taking of photographs and selection of other pictures is organized by the picture editor, using staff or freelance photographers.

The entire process of editorial production is carried out at high speed to meet the deadlines imposed by the need to have the papers printed by a set time for distribution. Careful planning is needed to ensure that all the material needed for an edition or section is ready when required—the editorial process allows flexibility to incorporate developing news stories. Generally, the feature material and any special supplements remain the same for all editions; any changes are restricted to the news pages.

News input

Copy (written news), which is input on computers in the office, is received by e-mail or taken down over the telephone by copytakers, who receive stories from all over the country or even abroad sent by reporters and correspondents. The hub of the news gathering process used to be the wire room, or telegraph room, where a nonstop flow of news and pictures came in through a worldwide communications network. Teletype machines were operated by keyboards at the other end of the wire, using satellite links and submarine cables between the continents. Pictures were sent out by fitting a photograph to the drum of a transmitting machine. The drum rotated and the shades of black and white in the photograph were converted into electronic impulses of varying intensity, which were converted at the receiving end back into a photo by a similar drum holding photosensitive paper. Nowadays, the Internet has substantially changed procedures, with many news agencies having online resources that provide constant updates of breaking news stories. These stories can then be downloaded directly to the newspaper's computer system and followed up. Photographs may arrive by ISDN, a broadband electronic communications system, or the faster ADSL, meaning reproduction quality is much higher.

Production

Production processes on newspapers have changed substantially since the introduction of networked computer systems and lithographic printing. In a traditional operation using hot-metal setting, the edited copy used to be sent to the composing room, where it was set into type.

When the copy was set, a proof sheet was printed and sent to readers so corrections could be made. The corrected type matter was then sent to the stone, or page makeup area, where it was carefully fitted into page formats. Photographs were fitted into the page in the form of zinc halftone blocks, prepared by photoengraving. The process involved the picture being rephotographed through a prism so that the new negative was a mirror image of the picture and then photographed again through a screen divided by a grid of fine lines. The screen breaks up the light into dots of varying intensity according to the light and dark parts of the photograph. Cartoons and line drawings were exposed without the screen, producing a line block.

The negative was placed over a zinc plate coated with photosensitive chemicals. Brilliant light from arc lamps baked the coating on where it passed through the negative; elsewhere it remained soluble. The soluble parts were washed away, and the plate was bitten in a bath of acid. Onto this was pressed a form made of something similar to papier-mâché, known as a flong or

matrix, and this formed the mold from which a semicircular metal plate was created bearing a mirror image of the printed page. This was then attached to the press, along with the plates for the remaining pages in the newspaper.

The rotary letterpress was huge—over 100 ft. (30 m) long, up to three storeys high and weighing more than 300 tons (270 tonnes). Using reels of newsprint weighing a ton and carrying 5 miles (8 km) of paper, a press could print up to 70,000 copies per hour. The system also cut and folded the newspapers, and automatic equipment—which is still used—ties them in bundles or puts them in plastic bags. Most newspapers distribute their own product, but some larger papers use wholesale distributors, who send the papers all over the world.

Cold type

Although the rotary letterpress printing technique was used for more than 50 years without any major changes, it was displaced in the 1980s by methods that allowed faster production and better quality at lower cost. The key to these changes was the introduction of cold-set, or photocomposition, of the text, together with the use of web-offset printing.

The process starts with a photocomposition or photosetting machine, which replaced the entire hot-metal process. Much faster typesetting is possible, and the machine can mix different sizes and styles of type in a single piece of text. The output is in the form of a positive bromide print, which the makeup operator uses to assemble a pasteup of the page. Illustrations are included as screened or line prints, as are the advertisements.

The finished pasteup, a complete representation of the newspaper page, is then photographed, a negative is made, and the page image is transferred to the offset plate, an aluminum plate coated with photosensitive material. This litho plate is not a relief plate but a flat, or planographic, one.

▼ Left: the operating systems, which accept the keying instructions from the control room and change the settings on the printing presses. Right: the floor from which the paper is fed to the presses. Rolls of newsprint are extremely heavy and have to be moved mechanically to where they are needed.

The press applies ink and water to the plate, the image area of the plate accepts the ink but rejects the water, and the image is transferred onto a rubber blanket, which then transfers it to the paper. An additional advantage of the web-offset process is that it is particularly suited to color work, allowing the use of single "spot" colors or full color sections within the main run pages of the newspaper. As computerization has advanced, this process has been further refined in many papers to reduce the role of the compositor and typesetter. In many cases, this part of the process no longer exists, having been replaced by a production department using page-makeup software, such as Quark Xpress or Adobe Pagemaker.

In this system, the production department simply receives a word-processed file electronically from a subeditor, who will have checked the writer's prose. This file is then input in to an electronic version of the newspaper page and set to style (correct type size, type style, column width, and so on). This file is then sent directly to a photocomposing machine, which produces a finished "film" made of transparent plastic onto which the contents of the page is printed. This film is then transferred to the offset plate as before, and the process from then on is much the same. This system is extremely flexible, allowing rapid changes of content as news stories develop or for special local editions.

By the early 1980s, over 95 percent of newspapers in the United States were using photocomposition systems, with over half of the printing carried out on rotary letterpress machines.

The advantage of the latest systems is that copy can be reviewed, corrected, and brought up to date while it is still on the computer. Optical character recognition (OCR) is also sometimes used, in which original documents are scanned on a special machine that interprets the type and translates it into a word-processed document that can be altered on a computer. The new machinery eliminates the need for proofs, retyped corrections, and the hot-metal process, resulting in enormous savings of time and effort.

Computer systems

The introduction of cold-type systems using computers led to a revolution in the way that papers were produced, with the initial keying in of text for setting being undertaken directly by

◀ A high-technology web offset newspaper pressroom. Microwave facsimile transmissions of page films are directly exposed in laser units to produce duplicate films of the pages. The films generate printing plates on the surface of a cylinder, which rotates to form the printed page.

the editorial staff. Editorial staff can also often access the Internet from their own machines to obtain news agency information. The subeditor calls finished stories onto the screen to edit, rewrite if need be, and enter setting instructions.

On more sophisticated systems, a newspaper's database, stored on the central server, can also be accessed by writers at their desk PCs to call up background information and check on facts. Reporters similarly can use the databases while investigating a story and can keep notes and develop articles or stories in password-protected private space either on the server or on their own PCs, often backed up to removable media.

In addition to reducing costs, the direct entry of material by the editorial staff has the particular advantage of reducing the possibility of errors creeping in. With the older systems, repeated rekeying of material inevitably led to mistakes, which were not always corrected before publication. In one case, the introduction of direct entry by a newspaper in the United States was claimed to have reduced the number of errors in the first edition to less than 50, compared with more than 1,000 by the older production methods.

The development of full page makeup on screen, complete with headlines and pictures, went hand in hand with the development of scanners, which convert photographs and illustrations into a digital form that can be processed by the computer. Alternative printing methods, such as laser and ink-jet printers, are becoming increasingly advanced. Although these printers cannot handle the production volumes of most newspapers, they have found application in the printing of low-volume newsletters, particularly with advances in ink-jet technology that enable high-definition full-color pages to be produced. Color laser printers are also capable of producing A3 broadsheet pages, but again the volume is low and cost high compared with offset litho printing.

Digital techniques are also being used to simplify the distribution of newspapers by printing at a number of different locations. ISDN transmission systems are able to send page images from the main editorial center to a series of secondary printing centers around the country, or even around the world. For example, the *Wall Street Journal* produces a string of editions across the United States in which the same main editorial content is combined with local news and advertising for each edition. Similarly, the *Economist* magazine transmits material for its U.S. edition from Britain by satellite link.

Experiments have been carried out with the direct transmission of pages to a subscriber's home, in an effort to replace expensive delivery services, but costs have proved too high with the currently available levels of technology. Electronic newsletters are enjoying some success, sent by e-mail to the reader's PC. However, these seldom carry the sheer variety of information presented in a typical newspaper and for the moment at least printed newspapers remain more popular.

▲ A fleet of trucks ready to start making deliveries of a morning newspaper to wholesalers and newsstands. Sometimes these trucks go hundreds of miles, though new technology has enabled newspapers to send made-up pages electronically to local printers for easier regional distribution.

SEE ALSO: COMPUTER • DESKTOP PUBLISHING • INTERNET • LITHOGRAPHY • MODEM AND ISDN • OPTICAL SCANNER • PRINTING

Newton's Laws

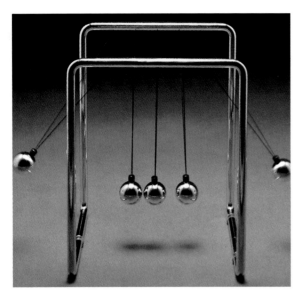

◀ Newton's laws of motion are displayed in this Newton's cradle. When one end ball is swung against the stationary center balls, a ball swings up on the opposite side.

In the course of his pioneering experiments in many branches of science, the English physicist and mathematician Sir Isaac Newton discovered several of the fundamental laws of physics. The basic principles of dynamics (the study of how forces change the motion of objects) are summed up in Newton's three laws of motion, which he formulated towards the end of the 17th century. These laws were published by Newton in 1687 in his *Philosophiae Naturalis Principia Mathematica*, considered to be one of the most important and influential books in the history of science. Newton later applied the laws of motion to astronomical data to prove that the force of gravity between any two bodies obeyed a simple law, now known as the law of universal gravitation. In addition, Newton formulated laws regarding the cooling of matter and the behavior of light, and he also built the first reflecting telescope.

Laws of motion

Newton's First Law states that a body remains at rest or continues to move in a straight line at constant speed unless acted upon by an external force. This concept is not immediately obvious, because on Earth we are used to moving objects eventually stopping, a phenomenon that occurs because outside forces, such as friction and air resistance, act on the body to slow it down.

What happens when, as in most practical cases, an outside force does act on a moving body is covered by the Second Law: the rate of change of momentum of a body is equal to the magnitude of the applied force and takes place in the direction in which the force acts. The momentum is the mass of the body multiplied by its velocity,

▼ Newton stated that the gravitational force between two objects varies with their masses and the distance between them. Because the gravitational force of a large body becomes weaker with distance, the satellites of a planet experience tidal forces that distort their shape. On Io, one of Jupiters moons, tidal effects are great enough to produce volcanic eruptions.

and so another way of stating the Second Law is that the force on a body is equal to the mass of the body multiplied by the acceleration produced by the force: that is, force = mass x acceleration. A consequence of this law is that, if the same force is applied to two objects with different masses, the body of smaller mass will accelerate more than that of larger mass. Because force and acceleration possess both direction and magnitude, they are represented in calculations by arrows, or vectors, where the length of the arrow is proportional to the magnitude of the force or acceleration.

The Third Law states that when a body *A* exerts a force on a body *B*, body *B* exerts an equal and opposite force on body *A*. It is often said that action and reaction are equal and opposite. For example, the weight of a chair standing on a floor must be balanced by an upward reaction force, or else (according to the Second Law) the chair would be accelerated toward the center of Earth.

Anyone who tries to jump off a stationary toboggan notices an effect of the Third Law: the toboggan begins to move in the opposite direction even before the person's feet have touched the ground.

The action of a rocket demonstrates all three laws of motion. A rocket coasting through space with the engine switched off is obeying the First Law. When the engine is on, the force with which the propellant is ejected from the rocket must be balanced by a reaction force of the propellant on the rocket, and it is this reaction force that drives the rocket forward. These two forces must be equal, and act in opposite directions (Third Law). Since the mass of the rocket is much greater than

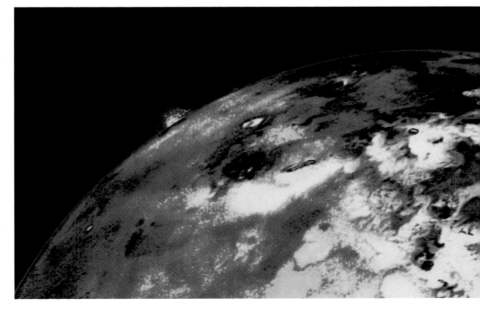

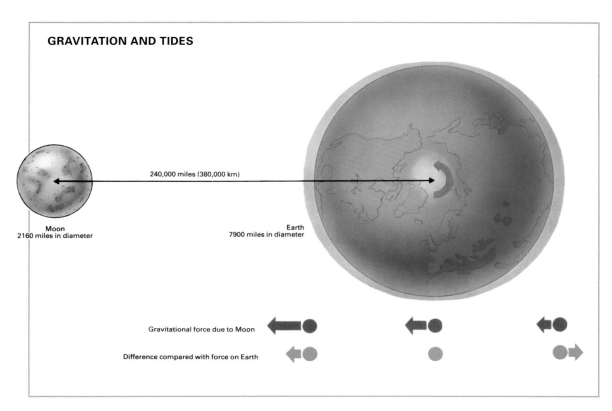

GRAVITATION AND TIDES

240,000 miles (380,000 km)

Moon
2160 miles in diameter

Earth
7900 miles in diameter

Gravitational force due to Moon

Difference compared with force on Earth

◄ Equilibrium tides are created by the influence of gravity. Both Earth and the Moon orbit around their mutual center of gravity, which lies inside Earth. If Earth is regarded as stationary, a centrifugal force is created, which balances the gravitational attraction at the center of Earth. On the side nearer the Moon, however, the gravitational force of the Moon is stronger (red arrows), and anything on Earth's surface feels a slight pull toward it. On the farthest side, the Moon's gravitational force is less than the centrifugal force about the common center, and the resulting force is away from the Moon, that is, upward with regard to the surface of Earth (green arrows). The resulting two bulges are the tides, with the side nearest the Moon having the higher tide.

that of the ejected propellant, the rocket is accelerated at a very much slower velocity than that of the propellant (Second Law).

Gravitation and cooling

Newton's law of gravitation describes how the gravitational force between any two objects varies with their masses and the distance between them. Each body experiences a force equal to the product of the masses of the two bodies multiplied by the universal constant of gravitation, *G*, and divided by the square of their separation. Newton arrived at this law by combining his three laws of motion with the German astronomer Johannes Kepler's third law, which states that the cube of a planet's mean distance from the sun is proportional to the square of the planet's orbital period.

Newton was unable to explain the origin of gravitation, and the German-born physicist Albert Einstein's general theory of relativity (1915) proposed that the geometry of space near massive bodies is altered so that the quickest distance (the geodesic) between two points is not a straight line. By substituting the word geodesic for straight line in Newton's First Law, Einstein was able to incorporate gravity in the First Law of Motion. While relativity requires modifying Newton's laws when high velocities are involved, they still form the basis for much of modern science and engineering.

Newton's investigations of the cooling of a hot body led to his law of cooling: the rate of cooling is proportional to the difference in temperature

between the object and its surroundings. The rate of cooling is measured by the rate at which the temperature of a body falls; so a body at a high temperature relative to its surroundings will initially cool quickly, and its temperature falls rapidly. As its temperature decreases, however, the rate of cooling becomes slower—the temperature of a cooling body falls exponentially. Although the temperature of the body becomes increasingly closer to that of its surroundings, it will never become exactly the same.

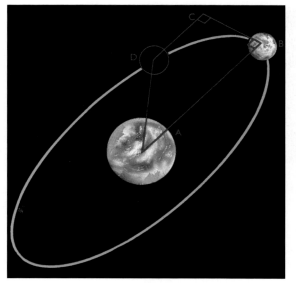

◄ With no outside forces the Moon at point B would move in a straight line (BC). In fact, it follows a curved path (BD) as it falls toward Earth, which also falls away, so the separation is unchanged. The force with which Earth attracts the Moon depends on their masses and separation distance.

SEE ALSO: Dynamics • Energy, mass, and weight • Gravity • Kinetics • Orbit • Relativity • Rocket and space propulsion • Tide

Nickel

Early copper miners in the Harz Mountains in Germany came across an ore that they were unable to smelt successfully, obtaining only a light yellow, brittle, and useless product. They put the blame on the devil and called the ore *Kupfernickel* (Old Nick's copper). When, in 1751, a Swedish chemist and minerologist, Baron Axel Fredrik Cronstedt, first isolated the additional element in the ore that had caused the trouble, he called it nickel. It was not until 150 years later that nickel was first extracted on a commercial scale.

The metal itself (chemical symbol Ni) is silvery white and is noted for its corrosion resistance and its ability to retain good mechanical strength up to temperatures of the order of 1800°F (1000°C). Like iron and cobalt, it is ferromagnetic. More than half of all nickel produced is used for alloying with iron to make steels with superior resistance to high-temperature oxidation and chemical attack or simply having better mechanical properties. The melting point of nickel is about 2651°F (1455°C), and its boiling point is 4946°F (2730°C).

Occurrence and extraction

Nickel constitutes around 0.007 percent of Earth's crust, making it twice as abundant as copper. The largest supplier of nickel is Russia, which produced about 290,000 tons (265,000 tonnes) in 2000, followed by Canada with around 213,000 tons (194,000 tonnes) and Australia with 185,000 tons (168,000 tonnes). In Canada, there is a huge deposit of mixed nickel and copper sulfide at Sudbury, Ontario, and a deposit of similar ore in Manitoba. In total, Canada possesses approximately 16.5 million tons (15 million tonnes) of reserves. Even larger are the reserves in Australia, 20 million tons (18 million tonnes), while the largest reserves known, 25 million tons (23 million tonnes), are in Cuba. The world total is approximately 165 million tons (150 million tonnes). All of these figures, however, include reserves that are not currently economical to extract but that may, with improved techniques, become economical in the future. Currently, reserves that may be mined economically total 54 million tons (49 million tonnes) worldwide.

◀ Inspecting a nickel alloy flange. Designed to be used as a catalyst support grid in a fertilizer plant, its high nickel content (about 50 percent) will ensure a long working life, despite the highly corrosive environment in which it will be placed.

▼ A selection of machined turbine blades, which are checked optically and electronically. The nickel blades are deeply recessed. The big X750 nickel alloy gas turbine blade (back row, right) will be used in the hottest part of the engine.

The first stages of the extraction of nickel from sulfide ores are similar to those used for smelting copper. The ore is first crushed and the sulfides concentrated using the flotation process. The mixed nickel, copper, and iron sulfides are then smelted to form a sulfide matte. It is not possible to produce nickel simply by roasting the matte in air, because much of the nickel would be oxidized before all the sulfur was removed as sulfur dioxide. The matte is partly roasted, however, to oxidize the iron sulfide to iron oxide, which is removed in a silicate slag. The molten matte of mixed nickel and copper sulfides is poured into a mold and slowly cooled to form crystals of the two sulfides, which are then crushed, ground, and separated using a flotation process, and the nickel sulfide, NiS, is sintered to form nickel oxide, NiO.

The nickel oxide sinter is next treated with sulfuric acid to remove the remaining copper sulfate and then reduced to nickel at 662°F (350°C) by a stream of producer gas (a mixture of hydrogen and carbon monoxide). The nickel is refined either electrolytically or by the Mond carbonyl process, in which nickel powder is exposed to producer gas, but this time at 122°F (50°C). The result is the production of volatile nickel carbonyl, $Ni(CO)_4$, which is passed into a decomposition tower where it dissociates at 356°F (180°C) and pure nickel is deposited as pellets.

A hydrometallurgical method for the extraction of nickel from mixed sulfides is also commonly in use. It is based on the ability of the mixed sulfides to dissolve in an ammoniacal solution (a solution containing ammonium ions, NH_4^+) in the presence of air at 125 psi (8.26 bar). The iron sulfide is converted to ferric hydroxide, which is filtered off together with other insoluble solids and the solution boiled to reprecipitate the copper as copper sulfide, which is similarly removed. The nickel itself is precipitated as the metal by treating the solution with hydrogen at 302°F (150°C) and 760 psi (51.7 bar).

Uses of nickel

Japan and the United States are the world's largest individual consumers of nickel, though the European Union and Asia as a whole consume much greater amounts.

Around 8 percent of the world's nickel output is electroplated onto base metals to provide corrosion resistance; it is also sometimes covered with a very thin flash layer of chromium to give a brilliant and tarnish-resistant finish. Vessels that have to resist corrosion over long periods may be made from pure nickel or nickel-clad steel.

Primarily, however, nickel is used as an alloying element, being a component in some 3,000

► The Rolls Royce RB211 is one of many jet engines that rely on nickel-based Nimonic alloys, or superalloys, for high performance at very high temperatures.

different alloys. Historically, the first nickel alloys were the direct result of smelting impure, or mixed, ores. For example, some coins produced in 235 B.C.E. were made from a copper-nickel alloy. Current nickel coinage uses about 25 percent nickel and 75 percent copper. Cupronickels with 20 to 30 percent nickel and sometimes up to 10 percent iron possess a useful combination of strength, ductility, and corrosion resistance.

Nickel silver is an attractive white alloy of copper containing 18 percent nickel and 18 percent zinc. For domestic use, it is often electroplated with a thin layer of pure silver to make the familiar EPNS (electroplated nickel silver) ware.

Around 75 percent of nickel produced is used for improving the properties of steels and cast irons, with the production of stainless steels alone using around 65 percent of the world's supply. Nickel steels contain between 0.5 percent and 10 percent nickel and show superior strength and ductility, because nickel increases the strength of steel, enabling thicker sections to be effectively heat treated and also reducing the necessity for rapid quenching, which can lead to cracking. In cast irons, nickel encourages the precipitation of graphite besides increasing the hardness of the matrix. Nickel is used as a component of stainless steels containing 10 to 12 percent chromium. Its presence in amounts exceeding 8 percent changes

◀ A nickel heat exchanger for process industries. Nickel alloy tubes and tube plates resist corrosion from liquids and gases.

the crystal structure of the steel from body-centered cubic to face-centered cubic and as a result renders it more ductile and easily workable.

FACT FILE

■ *Research has shown that nickel is an essential element for growth in higher plants. Test bean plants grown without nickel produced deformed leaflet tips, because of a buildup of urea. Nickel helps to break down urea at certain stages in the plants' growth cycle. Nevertheless, no soil-grown plant has ever shown evidence of nickel deficiency.*

■ *Canadian nickel deposits were first discovered by railway workers building the Canadian Pacific Railway when they came upon a copper-rich outcrop at Sudbury, Ontario. Hordes of prospectors were attracted, but many abandoned their claims on finding that the copper was heavily contaminated with nickel. The ore is actually extremely rich in a number of valuable elements, including nickel.*

Nickel is widely used as a base metal in alloys that have to resist oxidation and still maintain strength when red hot. The binary alloy nichrome contains 20 percent chromium in nickel and is used for electric-fire heating elements, among other things. Attempts to improve the mechanical strength of nichrome by precipitation hardening have led to the development of the Nimonic alloys, used for components such as turbine blades of jet engines, where the best possible combination of high-temperature strength and oxidation resistance is required. The Nimonic alloys, or superalloys, have additions of titanium and aluminum, which form the strength-giving precipitates.

An alloy of 36 percent nickel in iron is unique in that it has a zero coefficient of thermal expansion; in other words, it does not expand when heated. Under the trade name Invar, it is used for standards of length, measuring tapes, pendulums, and precision machine components. The addition of 12 percent chromium forms another alloy, Elinvar, whose elasticity is independent of temperature. It is used for watch hairsprings and in weighing machines and other measuring devices.

SEE ALSO: ALLOY • CATALYST • COPPER • IRON AND STEEL • METAL • METALWORKING • SURFACE TREATMENTS

Nitrogen

Nitrogen (N_2) is a colorless, odorless gas that forms more than 75 percent of Earth's atmosphere. It was first discovered in 1772 by the Swedish chemist C. W. Scheele, who recognized that air was composed of two different gases, one that would support combustion and respiration (oxygen) and one that would not (nitrogen). He was able to obtain nitrogen by burning a substance in a closed chamber filled with air; the combustion removed the oxygen leaving nitrogen behind. The principal naturally occurring nitrogen compounds are saltpeter (potassium nitrate, KNO_3) found in Spain, Italy, and Egypt and Chile saltpeter (sodium nitrate, $NaNO_3$).

On Earth, nitrogen has two naturally occurring stable isotopes, nitrogen-14 and nitrogen-15, the former being more than 250 times more abundant than the latter. Seven radioisotopes are also known, nitrogen-12, nitrogen-13, nitrogen-16, nitrogen-17, nitrogen-18, nitrogen-19, and nitrogen-20. In 1909, the British physicist Ernest Rutherford produced the first artificial transmutation of one element into another. This transmutation was achieved by bombarding nitrogen-14 with alpha particles, resulting in the formation of oxygen-17 nuclei and protons.

Nitrogen is an important constituent of living tissue, and many agricultural fertilizers—for example, ammonium nitrate (NH_4NO_3)—contain a high proportion of nitrogen.

Production

Because nitrogen has a lower boiling point (–321°F, –196°C) than oxygen (–297°F, –183°C), liquid air can be separated into its components by fractional distillation, and this is the method used to make nitrogen industrially. Small quantities of pure nitrogen can be obtained chemically, for example, by heating sodium azide in a vacuum:

$$2NaN_3 \rightarrow 2Na + 3N_2$$
sodium azide · sodium · nitrogen

Nitrogen for large-scale use, for example, at a rate of several hundred tons per day in large chemical complexes, is supplied as a gas at pressure through pipelines direct from the production plant. For intermediate-scale use, it is delivered by road tanker into insulated storage tanks in liquid form and vaporized into nitrogen gas or drawn off as liquid nitrogen as required and depending upon the end use. Small demands are supplied from steel cylinders containing gaseous nitrogen at a pressure of about 150 atmospheres.

Being very inert, nitrogen gas is used extensively to purge air or dangerous chemicals from process plant and pipelines. It is also used to provide an inert and dry storage atmosphere to maintain the quality of commodities, from chemicals to foodstuffs, which would degrade in contact with the oxygen or water vapor in the atmosphere. In liquid form, nitrogen is used widely as a low-temperature industrial refrigerant.

In certain metallurgical applications, even nitrogen is too reactive, and argon, which is also separated from the air by distillation and is even more inert, has to be employed.

Nitrogen compounds

For many years, the most important nitrogen-containing compounds were potassium nitrate, a component of gunpowder, and sodium nitrate, which both occur naturally. In 1648, a German chemist, Johann Rudolf Glauber, devised a means for preparing nitric acid—a colorless corrosive liquid—by treating sodium nitrate with concentrated sulfuric acid, and this process remained in use for many years until ammonia (NH_3) became a readily available raw material. The modern method of making nitric acid is by oxidizing ammonia in the presence of a platinum–rhodium catalyst. Nitric acid has many different applications, including use in dyes, explosives, drugs, and fertilizers and the manufacture of sulphuric acid.

Most nitrogen-containing compounds derive their nitrogen either directly or indirectly from ammonia, which is made by the Haber-Bosch process. Nitrogen gas reacts directly with hydrogen in the presence of an iron oxide catalyst according to the following equation:

◄ A delivery of liquid nitrogen. In liquid form, nitrogen is widely used as a low-temperature industrial refrigerant, for example, in the food-processing and aerospace industries.

$$N_2 + 3H_2 \rightarrow 2NH_3$$
nitrogen   hydrogen   ammonia

Because at normal temperatures on Earth nitrogen is relatively inert, the reaction must be conducted at relatively high temperatures. Increasing the pressure of the gases, however, reduces the temperature necessary for the reaction to occur. The required pressure also varies with the kind of catalyst used. The industrial production of ammonia takes place at temperatures of about 750 to 900°F (400–500°C) and at 200 to 1,000 times atmospheric pressure. These condi-

tions enable the nitrogen to react with the hydrogen in a way that is efficient and economical.

A major use for ammonia is in the production of ammonium nitrate (for use as a fertilizer) by reaction with nitric acid:

$$NH_3 + HNO_3 \rightarrow NH_4NO_3$$
ammonia   nitric acid   ammonium nitrate

It is also employed as a refrigerator and air-conditioning coolant and is used in the production of urea (for use as a fertilizer or in the production of plastics) by reaction with carbon dioxide:

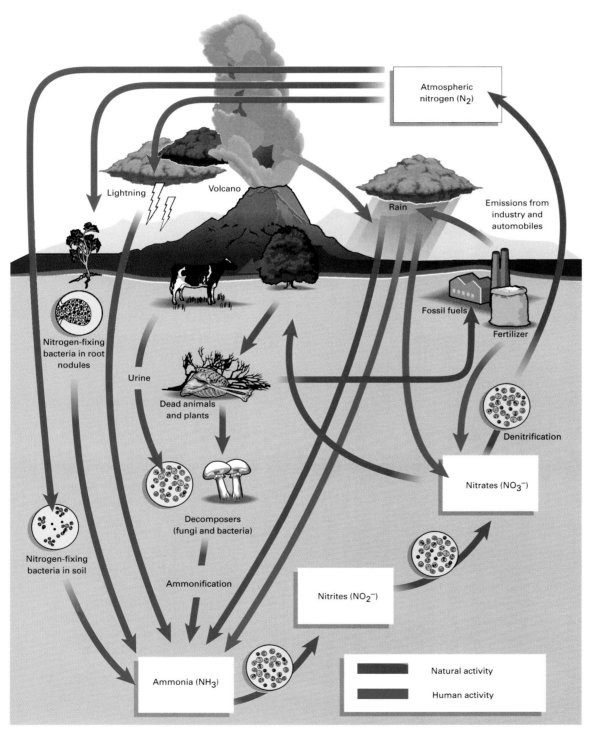

◀ The nitrogen cycle. Nitrogen in the atmosphere may be fixed—converted into nitrogenous compounds—by natural or industrial processes. Leguminous plants carry out this process with the help of symbiotic bacteria in the plant's root nodules. Microorganisms in soil also fix large quantities of nitrogen. The principal artificial method of fixing nitrogen is the Haber-Bosch process, in which nitrogen reacts with hydrogen in the presence of a catalyst to form ammonia.

$$2NH_3 + CO_2 \rightarrow CO(NH_2)_2 + H_2O$$

ammonia   carbon dioxide   urea   water

Ammonia is a gas at room temperature, but it dissolves easily in water to give a mildly alkaline solution containing ammonium ions (NH_4^+) and hydroxide ions (OH^-). Such solutions can be neutralized with acids to give ammonium salts, which are ionic crystalline solids. Neutralization with hydrochloric acid, for example, gives the salt ammonium chloride (NH_4Cl), which is sometimes called sal ammoniac:

$$NH_4OH + HCl \rightarrow NH_4Cl + H_2O$$

ammonium   hydrochloric   ammonium   water
hydroxide   acid   chloride

Ammonium chloride is used as a flux in soldering and galvanizing processes since it reacts at high temperatures with metal-corrosion products, thereby cleaning the surface being soldered or galvanized. It is also used as the electrolyte in batteries of the Leclanché type as well as being a constituent of many cough and cold remedies.

Hydrazine (N_2H_4) and hydrazoic acid (HN_3) are highly reactive compounds containing only nitrogen and hydrogen. Hydrazine may be used in the manufacture of agricultural fungicides but is also used in conjunction with nitrogen tetroxide (N_2O_4) as a rocket propellant, and a fuel of this type was used in both the service module and the lunar excursion module (LEM) of the Apollo Moon program. The chief use of hydrazoic acid is in the preparation of lead azide, $Pb(N_3)_2$, which is a pressure-sensitive compound used in explosive detonators:

$$Pb + 2HN_3 \rightarrow Pb(N_3)_2 + H_2$$

lead   hydrazoic   lead   hydrogen
      acid   azide

Probably the best-known oxide of nitrogen is nitrous oxide (N_2O) which is a widely used anesthetic gas. It is called laughing gas because of the unusual side effects that can sometimes precede anesthesia, and it can be prepared by heating ammonium nitrate:

$$NH_4NO_3 \rightarrow N_2O + 2H_2O$$

ammonium   nitrous   water
nitrate   oxide

Before it can be used as an anesthetic, the gas must be carefully purified to remove traces of other oxides, such as nitric oxide (NO) and nitrogen dioxide (NO_2), which are toxic.

Boron nitride (BN) is a crystalline compound that normally resembles graphite and that can be used as an electrical insulator. It can, however, be converted at very high temperature (3270°F, 1800°C) and pressure (85,000 atmospheres) to a

▲ A windshield for the European Airbus being positioned in a test chamber. Liquid nitrogen is pumped into the chamber to simulate the low temperatures that it will have to withstand when the airplane is flying at very high altitudes.

second crystalline form called borazon, which has the same crystal structure as diamond and nearly the same hardness and is less easily oxidized.

Organic compounds

Nitrogen-containing organic compounds are very common and are classified according to the particular nitrogen-containing groups they contain. Thus, amines contain $-NH_2$ groups, amides contain $-CONH_2$ groups, cyanates contain $-CNO$ groups, cyanides contain $-CN$ groups, isocyanates contain $-NCO$ groups, isocyanides contain $-NC$ groups, and nitro compounds contain $-NO_2$ groups. In addition, azo compounds, used extensively in the production of dyestuffs, contain double bonded nitrogens.

Many explosives, for example, trinitrotoluene (TNT), $C_6H_2(CH_3)(NO_2)_3$, and picric acid, $C_6H_2(OH)(NO_2)_3$, are organic nitro compounds. TNT is prepared by treating the hydrocarbon toluene with a mixture of concentrated nitric and sulfuric acids. During the reaction, nitro groups are introduced into the toluene molecule.

SEE ALSO: AIR • ANILINE AND AZO DYES • CATALYST • CHEMISTRY, INORGANIC • CHEMISTRY, ORGANIC • EXPLOSIVE • FERTILIZER • REFRIGERATION • ROCKET AND SPACE PROPULSION

Noble Gas

The elements helium, neon, argon, krypton, xenon, and radon are all tasteless, odorless, and colorless gases. Together they constitute the eighth group in the periodic table and are called the noble gases, because of their extreme reluctance to form chemical compounds. This reluctance to react with other chemicals results from their outer electron shells being completely filled, and therefore they have nothing to gain in terms of stability by the addition or loss of electrons in compound formation.

Helium

Helium (He) was detected in the Sun's chromosphere before it was discovered on Earth. A bright yellow line, now known to be characteristic of helium, was observed in a spectrum of the chromosphere taken during the total eclipse of 1868 by the French astronomer Pierre Janssen. Helium is a product of radioactive decay, but it was not until 1895 that the British chemist Sir William Ramsay found it on Earth in association with certain radioactive ores. Helium constitutes about 23

percent of the mass of the Universe. On Earth, however, it constitutes only 0.0005 percent of the atmosphere, though in certain natural hydrocarbon gases, it constitutes up to 7 percent. These hydrocarbon gases are principally found in southern parts of the United States.

Helium is the second lightest element (hydrogen is the lightest) and being nonflammable is used in weather balloons and airships. Helium is also used as a pressurizing gas in liquid-fueled rockets and as an inert atmosphere in arc-welding operations. Divers sometimes use oxygen–helium breathing mixtures rather than the conventional oxygen–nitrogen mixtures, because helium is less soluble in blood than nitrogen and is therefore less likely to cause the bends. This condition arises when dissolved gas is released from the blood as the diver ascends. Helium forms no known stable chemical compounds.

One of the more unusual properties of helium is superfluidity. At 2.17 Kelvin (−455.76°F, −270.98°C), which is close to absolute zero 0 K (−459.67°F, −273°C), the isotope helium-4

▼ Argon gas from the cylinder on the left is used in arc welding to prevent atmospheric oxygen from oxidizing the hot metal.

becomes superfluid. Under these circumstances the viscosity of helium almost disappears, resulting in some unusual behavior. Not only does its conductivity of heat increase dramatically, but the helium fluid flows up the sides of its container and over the top as if unaffected by gravity.

Neon and argon

Both neon and argon (chemical symbols Ne and Ar, respectively) are present in Earth's atmosphere and are produced commercially by fractional distillation of liquid air.

Argon accounts for almost 1 percent of air and is the most abundant of the noble gases. Argon is used in inert-gas-shielded arc welding of aluminum. When in the molten state, the metal titanium is extremely reactive, and no refractory material can withstand it, so a specially designed furnace employing an arcing process in an argon atmosphere is used. Argon is also used to fill ordinary domestic light bulbs, in Geiger counters, and as an inert atmosphere for producing silicon to be used in the electronics industry.

Neon was discovered in 1898 by the British chemists Sir William Ramsay and Morris W. Travers. It constitutes about 0.0018 percent of Earth's atmosphere and is used in discharge tubes, wave-meter tubes, and gas lasers and also as a cryogenic refrigerant.

Like helium, argon and neon do not form any known stable chemical compounds. Clathrate compounds, however, are known. They are compounds in which the noble gas atom is trapped in a cagelike cavity formed of molecules of an organic compound such as hydroquinone.

Krypton and xenon

Both krypton (Kr) and xenon (Xe) were identified in 1898 by the British chemists Sir William Ramsay and Morris W. Travers. Xenon constitutes about 0.0000086 percent of dry air, while krypton constitutes about 1 part in 900,000 of Earth's atmosphere. These elements are extracted from air by liquefaction. Xenon is also produced in nuclear reactors as a product of the neutron fission of uranium. Xenon and krypton are used to fill high-intensity arc lamps and in discharge tubes capable of producing high-intensity flashes of very short duration. Such tubes are employed in electronic flash apparatus used in photography. Radioactive krypton-85 is also used to detect leaks in containers. Unlike helium, neon, and argon, krypton and xenon do form a few chemical compounds, for example, krypton difluoride (KrF_2), xenon tetrafluoride (XeF_4), xenon oxyfluoride ($XeOF_4$), and xenon oxide (XeO_3). Krypton is also found in certain clathrate compounds.

Radon

Radon (Rn), the heaviest of the noble gases, is a highly radioactive gas that is formed in the radioactive decay of radium. Its most stable isotope, radon-222, was discovered in 1900 by the German chemist Friedrick E. Dorn and has a half-life of only 3.8 days. Because of its short half-life, little is known of its chemical properties. Radon is considered to be a health hazard in many homes built on areas containing underground deposits of uranium minerals. Radon gas may leak from the deposits and accumulate in houses that lack adequate ventilation. Over many years, the occupants may develop lung cancer as a consequence to exposure of high levels of radon.

▲ The color provided by neon lights is used to advertise products of all sorts—from hot dogs to hotels and circus entertainment.

◄ The extremely low temperature of liquid helium causes water vapor in the air to freeze out onto the discharge pipe. Liquid helium is transported in large tanker trucks, and vacuum flasks are used for storing it. One of its most common applications is in arc-welding operations.

SEE ALSO: AIR • AIRSHIP • ATOMIC STRUCTURE • DISCHARGE TUBE • GAS LAWS • LIGHTBULB • PERIODIC TABLE • RADIOACTIVITY

Noise Measurement

◀ Chronic exposure to noise at work can cause irreversible hearing impairment. The use of noise-measuring devices helps identify the acoustic protection necessary to prevent such damage.

Acoustic noise is sound that is disharmonious, random, and frequently disagreeable to hearing people. In some cases, noise can be damaging to the ability to hear, particularly where there is chronic exposure to high volumes of noise.

The potential of acoustic noise to cause discomfort, distress, and damage to health has stimulated the development of equipment and systems of measurement that allow noise to be classified and quantified. The availability of such data underpins noise regulations and guidelines that help ensure healthy and comfortable conditions in leisure and working environments.

Signals and noise

A broader definition of noise is that of acoustic or any other form of energy flux that has no discernible information content. The opposite of noise in this context is a signal, which has a recognizable structure and information content.

When listening to music on a beach, for example, the sounds that correspond to musical notes and percussion form a signal, while the sound of crashing waves is noise. In the case of radio reception, the electromagnetic waves transmitted by a radio station form the signal, while atmospheric interference is a type of noise.

The ratio of signal and noise intensities in an electrical feed is of particular interest in the context of telecommunications and high-fidelity sound systems. The designers of such systems strive to maximize signal-to-noise ratios, whose measurement is an application of electrical metering and will not be described in this article.

Characterizing noise

Although acoustic noise has been defined as sound energy that has no information content, noise from a given source has a characteristic frequency distribution and intensity. Both of these values can be expressed as time averages, and intensity in particular is often expressed as its instantaneous peak value. (Sound intensity is defined as sound energy per unit area.)

Total sound intensity gives an overall figure of the strength of a noise and is important when considering, for example, its physical effects. Frequency analysis is important when comparing different types of sounds: a truck struggling uphill produces mainly low-frequency sounds, whereas the noise of a jet engine is characterized by a shrill high-frequency whine, for example.

The human ear is not equally sensitive to all sound frequencies, however, and low-frequency sounds tend to be less of a nuisance for this reason. To obtain a figure that represents the effect of a sound on an average person entails a process called weighting, whereby the magnitude of each frequency component of a noise is multiplied by a factor that corresponds to the sensitivity of the ear at that frequency. A figure of the receptiveness of the ear to the whole noise can be obtained by summation of all these weighted magnitudes.

Measurement of sound energy

Noise energy, E_N, is measured on a logarithmic scale relative to a reference sound energy, E_R. This reference energy is usually taken to be the quietest sound that can be heard by a person with average hearing. Noise, measured in decibels (dB), is taken from the following expression:

$$\text{noise (dB)} = 10 \times \log (E_N/E_R)$$

Since the effective area of the detector is the same for the noise and the reference sound, the ratio of energies in this expression is equal to the ratio of sound intensities (the detector areas that divide energy to give intensity values cancel out).

Sound energies are difficult to measure directly, however, whereas the pressure of a sound wave is easily determined using a pressure transducer. Since sound energy is related to the square of the amplitude of pressure variation in a sound wave, an alternative expression for the decibel rating of a noise is as follows:

$$\text{noise (dB)} = 10 \times \log (P_N^2/P_R^2)$$
$$= 20 \times \log (P_N/P_R)$$

In this expression, P_N and P_R are the pressure amplitude values for the noise and reference sounds, respectively. The quietest sound that can normally be heard—the reference pressure, P_R—corresponds to a pressure amplitude of 0.00002 N/m², which is 20 billionths of normal atmospheric pressure, or 100,000 N/m².

A sound wave with a pressure amplitude equal to P_R therefore rates as 0 dB, since the logarithm of 1 is 0. The maximum reading of many noise meters is 120 dB, which corresponds to a pressure amplitude of 20 N/m²—one million times the reference pressure, P_R. Nevertheless, the pressure variation at this maximum reading is only ⅕₀₀₀ of normal atmospheric pressure.

Conveniently, a difference of 1 dB is usually the minimum discernible difference in noise level for much of the audible range. Also, an apparent doubling of loudness corresponds to a change of 10 dB, which represents an increase in pressure amplitude by a factor of 3.2.

Weighting filters

The awareness of noises and reactions to them are highly subjective—they vary greatly between observers. Consequently, the total intensity of a particular noise may not relate directly to its physical or psychological effects. A number of frequency-weighting systems produce noise figures that correlate well with the impact that different noises have on people.

All noise-measuring systems take an electrical input from a microphone and produce noise-level readings, in decibels, on an analog or digital sound meter. The diaphragm of the microphone moves in response to pressure fluctuations in the air—sound waves—and the microphone converts those movements into an electric signal.

Weighting circuits are sets of electrical filters whose frequency responses are such that certain frequencies are emphasized relative to others. The four weighting circuits used for most noise measurements are labeled A, B, C, and D.

Weighting A is the most widely used, and sound levels measured in this way are referred to as decibels A, or dB-A. The advantage of the A weighting is that dB-A levels have been found to correspond fairly closely with subjective effects, since it places less emphasis on low-frequency sounds, to which the human ear is less sensitive. The B weighting is of little contemporary use, while the C weighting is used when wideband noise measurements are needed.

The D network was designed to monitor aircraft noise. It emphasizes frequencies around a few thousand kilohertz and has been found to match subjective assessments of such noise.

Data logging and dosimeters

Some noise-monitoring devices store a constant stream of noise readings that can then be analyzed for noise peaks and overall exposure. Such devices can be placed in remote stations from which their data are accessed by telephone lines, or they can be used as personal noise dosimeters.

TYPICAL NOISE LEVELS

The dB-A scale is convenient for comparing noises from different sources. The threshold of hearing is 0 dB on this scale, and the threshold above which continuous noise is painful is around 130 dB. An interval of 10 dB corresponds to a doubling in the perceived sound intensity, or volume of noise.

Background noise in a rural setting is around 20 dB, whereas normal conversation is around twice as loud—30 dB. A home entertainment system functions at around 40 dB, while the noise in a busy office setting can reach 60 dB. The average noise level in an urban street is around 80 to 85 dB, reaching as much as 100 dB when pneumatic jackhammers and car horns are taken into account. An aircraft at takeoff produces around 120 to 125 dB for nearby observers, which is a value similar to the noise level of a thunderclap.

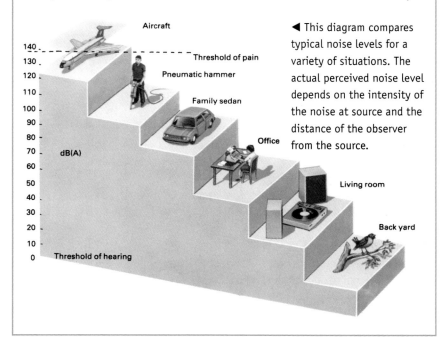

◄ This diagram compares typical noise levels for a variety of situations. The actual perceived noise level depends on the intensity of the noise at source and the distance of the observer from the source.

SEE ALSO: ACOUSTICS • MICROPHONE • SOUND • TRANSDUCER AND SENSOR

Nonlethal Weapon

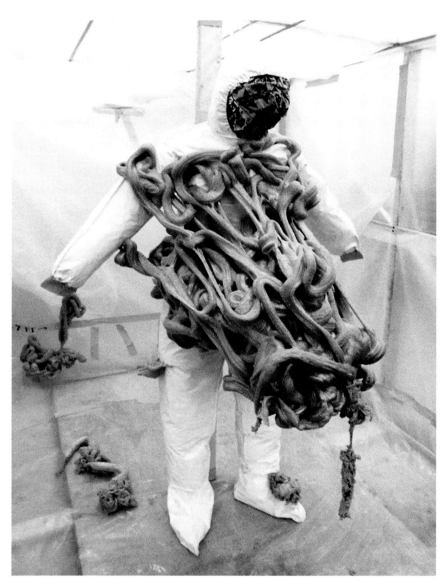

▲ A test dummy wearing protective clothing is covered with "sticky foam," an extremely tacky, tenacious material used to entangle and impair an individual. Sticky foam was created as a prototype less-than-lethal weapon by Sandia National Laboratories.

The intended effect of nonlethal weapons is to temporarily disorientate or incapacitate a human target without causing permanent injury. Security forces, such as the police, use nonlethal weapons to disperse illegal gatherings and riotous mobs, and individuals—civilian or otherwise—sometimes use nonlethal weapons to repel aggressors or to stun them for sufficient time for the user of the weapon to flee or to restrain the aggressor.

Tear gases

Tear gases are among the most widely used tools for riot suppression and crowd dispersal. They are called tear gases because they have a lachrymatory effect—they cause tear production by irritating the eyes. Additional effects include spasms of the eyelids and coughing and choking resulting from inflammation of the upper respiratory tract. The combination of these effects compels exposed individuals to flee from the source of irritation—hence the effectiveness of such substances in crowd dispersal. The effects of tear gases pass within a few minutes in fresh air.

The active components of tear gases are organic compounds that contain chlorine or bromine atoms. These atoms are bound in such a way that they form hydrochloric acid or hydrobromic acid—potent irritants—in contact with the water in the moist tissues of the eyes and respiratory tract. CN gas—the active component of mace sprays—is based on chloroacetophenone, which is a liquid at room temperature. CS gas is an off-white powder based on *ortho*-chlorobenzylidenemalononitrile; CS has a stronger immediate effect than CN, but its effects generally wear off more quickly if moderate concentrations are used (high concentrations can be fatal).

Despite their name, tear gases are actually aerosols or fogs of liquid or solid agents. CN, being liquid, is most conveniently used in sprays, while CS, a solid, is dispersed by a pyrotechnic charge in a grenade or canister. The gas cartridges can be fired from standard 1.5 in. (38 mm) pistols and antiriot guns with a range of 330 ft. (100 m). After a delay of about two seconds, the cartridge releases gas for 5 to 25 seconds.

Pepper sprays

Pepper sprays are based on capsaicin, a natural substance responsible for the heat of chili peppers and derived from such plants in the form of a substance called oleoresin capsicum, or OC. A typical spray contains 2 to 10 percent OC in a nonflammable dispersant liquid that can be sprayed from an aerosol can. When droplets of OC spray come into contact with the mucous membranes of the eyes, nose, throat, or lungs, a painful inflammation ensues almost immediately, and the target of the spray is blinded for up to 30 minutes, when the effects of the OC wear off.

Fog sprays are most effective for repelling groups, whereas thin-stream sprays are more suitable for motorists, for example, since they can be directed through a partly open window. Foams have the advantage that they stick where they are sprayed, thereby reducing the chance of the person using the spray being exposed. Some sprays contain substances that fluoresce when exposed to ultraviolet light, thereby helping identify an aggressor from "invisible" marks on clothing.

Pepper sprays are widely used for personal protection from human aggressors and wild animals, since they tend to be legal in countries and states that classify CN- and CS-containing products as offensive weapons. Some authorities impose a maximum allowed strength of 2 percent OC, but products that contain this concentration of OC are at least as effective as more concentrated products, which are more viscous and therefore less penetrating than the diluted spray.

Baton rounds

Baton rounds are low-velocity projectiles that can be fired into crowds by guns. Some are intended to cause a painful blow when they strike a person but without penetrating or causing wounds or lasting injuries; others deliver tear gas.

The first baton rounds were wooden cylinders, used on rioting crowds in Hong Kong in 1958. By 1970, the baton round had evolved into a bullet-shaped rubber projectile. Although rubber bullets proved to be effective in dispersing crowds, they were extremely inaccurate and caused casualties among innocent bystanders.

The rubber round was later replaced by a plastic round made of polyvinyl chloride (PVC). Unlike rubber bullets, the PVC baton was flat at both ends. Although more accurate than rubber bullets, PVC rounds still tended to tumble and strike sideways-on. PVC rounds were also susceptible to temperature changes, becoming soft in warm weather and extremely hard at low temperatures. Modern polyurethane rounds are more stable in flight—and therefore easier to aim—than rubber or PVC rounds. In the same manner

▶ An armored vehicle equipped with a water cannon that shoots a jet of water under high pressure.

as their predecessors, polyurethane rounds are capable of causing severe injuries at close range, and they should not be fired on targets at distances less than 75 ft. (23 m).

Arwen 37

The Arwen 37—*anti*riot *w*eapon *En*field rifle, 37 mm (1.5 in.) bore—was developed by the British Royal Small Arms Factory to replace the single-shot smoothbore L67A1 weapon that had previously been used for firing baton rounds. Whereas the L67A1 had a slow rate of fire, the Arwen 37 has five-shot revolving magazine; also, its rifled barrel improved accuracy of fire.

The five types of rounds developed for use with the Arwen 37 are designated AR1 through AR5. The AR1 is a polyurethane baton round that weighs 2.5 oz. (70 g) and delivers 200 joules of impact energy at 230 ft. (70 m). The AR2 contains four CS-filled canisters in a plastic sabot that bursts to scatter the canisters over a 16 ft. (5 m) radius; each canister emits CS for 12 seconds. The AR3 frangible-nosed baton round delivers 150 joules at 6 ft. (1.8 m) and has a CS powder holder; the powder disperses when the polystyrene nose of the baton round is crushed on impact. The AR4 smokescreening round has the same structure as the AR2, but its canisters contain a compound that generates a dense smoke on impact. The AR5 is a barrier-penetrating irritant round: it has a tough plastic outer sleeve that enables it to penetrate windshields at 100 ft. (30 m) and hollow-core interior doors at 200 ft. (60 m); it then spreads CS over 3,530 cu. ft. (100 m³).

The Herstal XM303 is a Belgian-developed weapons system that uses compressed air to propel 0.3 oz. (8 g) projectiles with an effective range of 330 ft. (100 m). In addition to simple impact baton rounds, the XM303 can fire a variety of cartridge rounds to deliver CS or pepper spray, mal-

◀ A hand grenade that uses blinding light and a loud noise to immobilize those at whom it is thrown.

odorant ("stink-bomb") chemicals, or marker compounds. The weapon can be shoulder fired, or it can be attached to a standard rifle.

Electric-shock devices

A number of devices use electricity to stun and incapacitate assailants by interfering with the electrical impulses that cause their muscles to contract. Handheld battery-powered "stun guns" and stun batons deliver a 100 to 500 kV shock between two electrodes at a rate of 10 to 20 W. The electrodes need not be in direct contact with the assailant's skin—the manufacturers of high-voltage models claim effectiveness through up to 2 in. (5 cm) of clothing. The shock causes muscles to contract violently, thereby draining blood sugar and producing lactic acid, which causes cramps. The shock leaves the assailant disorientated for up to 15 minutes but causes no permanent injury.

A related device, called a Taser, uses a discharge of 18 to 26 W to completely override the nervous control of the skeletal muscles. An initial discharge of up to 7 seconds' duration forces the assailant into the fetal position as the skeletal muscles contract; shorter subsequent bursts delay the recovery of nerve control. A variant of the taser has a projectile probe head that can travel up to 15 ft. (4.5 m) powered by an explosive release of compressed air or nitrogen from a replaceable cartridge. Two flexible leads provide an electrical connection between the handheld power unit and the electrodes in the probe head.

Other devices

The KA-1 Power Staf is a pneumatic piston impact weapon powered by compressed air. It can deliver single blows or semiautomatic repeated blows on a target 7 ft. (2 m) away. The blow is delivered by a retractable shaft with a collapsible tip. The impact head is a specially designed load-spreading tip that, at the moment of impact, reshapes itself into an X configuration that prevents it from piercing the body.

Some law enforcement authorities have adopted the firefighter's water cannon for riot-control purposes. Water cannon are usually fired down from atop pumping vehicles onto unruly crowds. Depending on the force of the jet, a water cannon can either knock people over or drench them. In many cases, water cannon are used in conjunction with CS gas cartridges.

Future developments

The future promises a wide variety of new non-lethal weapons for peacekeeping based on existing and new technology. Lasers capable of dazzling or temporarily blinding hostile personnel were used in Somalia in 1995, although their intensity was reduced so as to illuminate rather than dazzle.

Other frequencies of electromagnetic radiation could also find use in nonlethal weaponry. Beams of microwave radiation could heat humans in their path to the temperature of a delirium-inducing fever. Low-frequency electromagnetic waves have been shown to induce the brain cells of chicks to release vast quantities of sleep-inducing opioids, which could be used as the basis for the most peaceful weapon ever: a sleep gun.

Some experts believe that the first new wave of nonlethal weapons will use pressure waves and sound to debilitate. Single pulses of pressure could deliver strong blows to humans and snap inflexible structures, whereas a beam of intense sound waves could be used to cause organ pain and incontinence for those in its path.

 SEE ALSO: AMMUNITION • CHEMICAL AND BIOLOGICAL WARFARE • GAS AND DUST MASK • POISON • RIOT CONTROL

Nuclear Emergency

Nuclear reactor designers attempt to prevent releases of radioactive reactor contents by a threefold approach to safety. First, many reactor designs are such that abnormal occurrences—the loss of coolant, for example—tend to slow the fission chain reaction rather than accelerate it. Second, reactors have numerous automatic and manually operated safety systems, such as backup coolant pumps and emergency "scram" buttons that stop the reaction by plunging control rods into the core. These systems are associated with alarms and probes that monitor the reactor core and its ancillary systems. Third, the reactor and its pressure vessel are in most cases enclosed in a containment building, constructed from steel and concrete, that is intended to withstand a reactor explosion and contain materials from the reactor.

All reactor emergencies to date have been traced to inadequate reactor designs or safety systems or to deviations from safe operating procedures. The lessons learned from such occurrences have contributed to the safety of later designs.

Windscale (Sellafield)

The first major reactor incident occurred in 1957 in Pile 1 of a plutonium-producing plant at Windscale (now Sellafield) on the northwestern coast of England. The pile consisted of a honeycomb of horizontal shafts in a graphite moderator into which fuel rods slotted. Huge fans forced cooling air through the reactor, and the hot air that resulted left the plant through a chimney.

During the operation of a graphite-moderated reactor, the graphite lattice becomes distorted by neutron bombardment. This distortion is the source of Wigner energy, which must be dispersed from time to time by running the reactor hot so as to allow the graphite to return to its normal structure—a process called annealing.

On the morning of October 8, 1957, a technician was performing such an annealing operation. Misguided by inadequate temperature probes, the technician took measures to raise the temperature of the already overheated pile. The resulting release of Wigner energy fueled an uncontrolled temperature increase. After a while, the graphite moderator, a form of carbon, started to burn in the stream of cooling air.

Firefighters' attempts to extinguish the fire using carbon dioxide failed, and the pile reached around 2350°F (1300°C) before it was extinguished using water—a risky operation that could have caused a hydrogen explosion within the reactor. Filters in the pile's chimney failed to con-

◀ Plexiglas safety area at the entrance to reactor Unit 2 at Three Mile Island nuclear plant near Harrisburg, Pennsylvania. Here, a man wears a special radiation suit and mask to dress and monitor other personnel passing into and out of the contaminated reactor, which experienced a meltdown in 1979. It is expected to take until 2020 for workers to fully decontaminate the site.

tain the fumes from the fire, spewing more than 20,000 curies of radiation into the air as radioactive iodine, cesium, plutonium, and polonium.

Three Mile Island

In 1979, a chain of minor events led to a partial meltdown of the reactor core at Unit 2 of the Three Mile Island power plant near Harrisburg, Pennsylvania. The sequence started at 4 A.M. on March 28 with a failure in a nonnuclear part of the plant: the secondary cooling circuit.

Unit 2 was a pressurized-water reactor that used liquid water at more than 150 atmospheres to remove heat produced in the core. Water leaves such a reactor at around 630°F (330°C) and then passes heat to a secondary cooling circuit to produce steam for power generation. With the secondary circuit disabled, heat accumulated in Unit 2, and pressure and temperature in the reactor started to rise. Automatic systems shut down the reactor and opened a valve to relieve excessive pressure in the cooling system.

As the pressure dropped, technicians pressed a button to close the relief valve to prevent further loss of cooling water. The valve failed to close, however, and coolant continued to escape. Fearing that the pressure vessel would overpressurize with the relief valve closed, they shut off the coolant injection pumps that had been activated automatically. The remaining water in the reactor started to boil, and the core started to melt, leading to fears that it would melt its way through the bottom of the containment building—a scenario called the China Syndrome.

Eventually, the relief valve was closed and sufficient water introduced to reduce the reactor temperature, although not before the formation of a hydrogen bubble that could have destroyed the containment building had it exploded. The hydrogen bubble was finally removed on April 3. In the course of the incident, some 400,000 gallons (1,800,000 l) of radioactive water were released into the Susquehanna River, and radioactive gases leaked into the atmosphere.

Chernobyl

The worst reactor explosion to date occurred in the early hours of April 26, 1986, at Reactor 4 of the power plant at Chernobyl, Ukraine. It resulted from a combination of design faults, violated safety rules, and poor understanding of the Soviet-designed RBMK reactor.

RBMKs rely to some extent on the neutron-absorbing properties of liquid water to prevent the chain reaction from running out of control. At low power outputs, they are prone to sudden power surges as pockets of steam, called voids, form within the reactor.

Steam is a weaker neutron absorber than water, so the formation of such voids increases the neutron flux. In other reactor designs, water promotes the reaction by moderating the speeds of neutrons so that they are more effective in causing fission. Void formation therefore slows the reaction, as steam is a poor moderator. In contrast, the graphite in an RBMK continues to moderate neutrons during void formation, so the reaction accelerates. Such reactors are said to have positive void coefficients, and the effect made the Chernobyl reactor prone to sudden power surges at thermal power outputs less than 700 MW.

Ironically, the explosion occurred as a result of a safety test intended to show that the coasting turbine shaft could provide power for the coolant pumps if their power supply failed. Technicians first disconnected automatic safety systems to prevent them from interfering with the test. They then inserted control rods to gradually shut down the reactor. An unexpected drop to 50 MW thermal power output prompted the technicians to withdraw all but around 6 to 8 control rods to reestablish a safe output—safety rules required a minimum of 15 rods to be in place.

A technician then reduced the flow of cooling water to maintain the normal water level in the steam separator—the action that primed the reactor for void formation. When the steam output

valve was closed for the test, a routine withdrawal of the automatic control rods caused the reaction to accelerate. A technician pressed the "scram" button to plunge the graphite-tipped boron-carbide control rods into the core, but their moderating graphite tips—a design weakness—instead boosted the reaction at the base of the reactor.

The power surged to 100 times the normal output within seconds, and two explosions ensued. First, a steam explosion blew the cap off the reactor and ripped open the roof of the reactor building, exposing the red-hot graphite in the core to the atmosphere. The inrush of air then caused the graphite to ignite. More than 30 people died as a direct result of the blasts, and the open core burned at more than 2800°F (1500°C) for several days until it was extinguished by boron, lead, and clay dropped from helicopters. The explosions scattered some 9 tons (8 tonnes) of core material around the site, and the explosion and subsequent fire sent a plume of radioactive iodine and cesium over northern Europe and Scandinavia. An effective containment building would have reduced this leakage.

Tokaimura

On September 30, 1999, an incident occurred at the JCO fuel-production plant at Tokaimura, Japan. Three workers were dissolving enriched uranium oxide in buckets of concentrated nitric acid and then tipping the buckets' contents into a tank. The tank was not appropriate for the task, and a chain reaction started when the critical mass was exceeded. Two of the workers died shortly after owing to the effects of intense radiation.

▼ A nuclear fuel flask (the red cylinder) undergoes impact testing. Such tests are intended to show that the flasks would remain intact and prevent their contents from leaking in the event of a road accident during transport.

SEE ALSO: ATOMIC STRUCTURE • FISSION • NUCLEAR FUEL CYCLE • NUCLEAR REACTOR • NUCLEAR WASTE DISPOSAL • RADIOACTIVITY

Nuclear Fuel Cycle

Nuclear reactors exploit the fissile nature of the element uranium to produce power. Uranium occurs naturally in ore deposits all over the world, the main sources being North America, Russia, China, South Africa, Australia, and eastern Europe. The ore is found near the surface and in deep deposits, where it can be recovered by strip mining or traditional vertical-shaft mining techniques. Some mines have turned to in situ leaching methods, which dissolve the uranium from the ore underground and bring it to the surface as a solution.

Ore refining process

The ore is then taken to a mill for further processing. Concentrations of fissionable uranium (the isotope U-235) are typically 0.7 percent in natural ores, so the ore must undergo a series of concentration stages to reach the 3 to 5 percent level needed for most commercial reactors or the 20 percent and above required for naval propul-

▲ Pellets of uranium oxide being loaded into a fuel rod. The pellets are placed end-to-end into a thin trough and then slid into tubular cladding. The fuel rods are flushed with helium to expel air from between the pellets, and the tubes are welded shut.

sion reactors and nuclear weapons. Because the ores are not suitable for conventional metal-smelting methods, they are first roasted to remove the clay content and any carbonaceous material or reductants that would interfere in the next stage of processing. Acid or alkaline leaching follows, depending on the nature of the ore and whether or not the uranium is present in its more stable hexavalent state. Acid leaching usually employs sulfuric acid and manganese dioxide or a chlorate ion to oxidize the tetravalent uranium ion U^{4+} to the hexavalent uranyl ion UO_2^{2+}. The sulfuric acid reacts with the oxidized uranium to form a complex anion, uranyl sulfate $[UO_2(SO_4)_3]^{4-}$. Ores containing alkaline minerals, such as basalt and dolomite, undergo treatment with sodium carbonate solutions to form a readily soluble uranyl carbonate ion, $[UO_2(CO_3)_3]^{4-}$.

After leaching, the complex ions are removed from solution using ion-exchange resins and then eluted with sodium or ammonium chloride. Acidic leachates can also be treated by solvent extraction when the uranium concentration is greater than 1 g/l. Neutralizing solutions such as sodium hydroxide, aqueous ammonia, or magnesia are then added to precipitate out the uranium as ammonium diuranate $(NH_4)_2U_2O_7$ or sodium diuranate $Na_2U_2O_7$. The resulting precipitate, known as yellow cake, is dried and shipped for further purification.

Enrichment

Upgrading processes are used to convert the uranium in yellow cake to the metal or increase the U-235 isotope concentration. The cake is dissolved in nitric acid, and the uranium is selectively extracted from the solution using tributyl phosphate to give a highly purified uranyl nitrate, $UO_2(NO_3)_2$. Calcining the nitrate and then reducing it with hydrogen gives uranium dioxide (UO_2), which is then reacted with hydrogen fluoride to form uranium tetrafluoride (UF_4). From this point, the uranium tetrafluoride is either reduced with magnesium to produce uranium metal or further fluorinated with fluorine gas at 660°F (350°C) to give a volatile gas, uranium hexafluoride (UF_6).

A number of methods can be used to enrich the U-235 content for use in reactors. Gaseous diffusion is the most common process used in the United States; other countries prefer gas centrifugation. The end result is the same: the uranium hexafluoride is divided into two streams, one enriched in U-235, the other "depleted" contain-

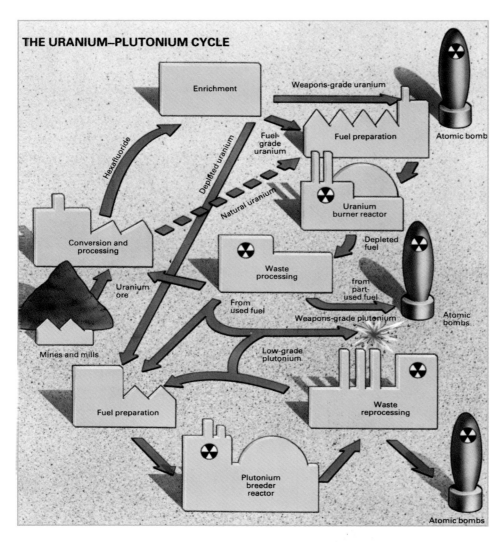

THE URANIUM–PLUTONIUM CYCLE

Enrichment

Weapons-grade uranium

Hexafluoride

Fuel-grade uranium

Depleted uranium

Natural uranium

Fuel preparation

Atomic bomb

Uranium burner reactor

Conversion and processing

Waste processing

Depleted fuel

Uranium ore

From used fuel

from part-used fuel

Weapons-grade plutonium

Atomic bombs

Mines and mills

Low-grade plutonium

Fuel preparation

Waste reprocessing

Plutonium breeder reactor

Atomic bombs

ing mostly U-238. Both streams are then reacted with water vapor to produce a hydrated uranyl fluoride and reduced with hydrogen to return it to powdered uranium dioxide, the enriched form being turned into ceramic fuel pellets. The depleted form can be converted back into uranium tetrafluoride and from there into uranium metal, or it can be bombarded with neutrons and gamma rays to convert the nonfissile U-238 into fissile plutonium-239.

Uranium fuels

Before the enriched uranium can be used for fission, it must be fabricated into a form suitable for use in a nuclear reactor. The powdered uranium dioxide is blended with natural or depleted uranium to provide the required percentage of U-235. It is then mixed with an organic binder and compressed into pellets. The pellets are then sintered at 2700 to 3250°F (1500–1800°C) to burn off the organic binder, leaving a dense ceramic pellet. Mixed uranium-plutonium dioxide (MOX) fuels suitable for use in fast breeder reactors are made in a similar way. Such fuel pellets contain 20 to 30 percent plutonium dioxide.

▲ This diagram shows the uranium-plutonium cycle from the early mining, conversion, processing, and enrichment stages to the production of fuel, nuclear waste, and atomic bombs. Strict safety precautions must be adhered to during this production cycle to prevent the leakage of radioactive materials.

Uranium oxide fuels are typically used in light water reactors but are less suitable for use in high-temperature reactors. Instead, other uranium and plutonium compounds are used. Carbides are highly refractory and are used in high-temperature gas-cooled reactors. The carbide is mixed with thorium, and the pellets are encased in a dense form of graphite. Uranium and plutonium nitrides can operate at temperatures greater than 3600°F (2000°C), making them potentially useful as high-performance reactor fuels.

After sintering, the pellets are loaded into tubes made from a zirconium alloy. The tubes are flooded with an inert gas and welded shut. These fuel rods, or pins, are assembled into hexagonal or square bundles by inserting them through grid plates at the top and bottom, thus ensuring that the rods are kept at an even distance apart. Bundles of rods are called a fuel assembly.

Metallic uranium can also be used as a nuclear fuel, though it is generally used to produce plutonium-239 in breeder reactors. Here, it is rolled into billets 20 in. (52 cm) long and 9 in. (23 cm) in diameter. For commercial reactors, the uranium metal is extruded into zirconium alloy tubes. Uranium can be mixed with other metals, such as aluminum and molybdenum, which give the metal greater strength and resistance to corrosion.

Fueling the reactor

Maintaining the power output of a nuclear reactor requires careful monitoring of the performance of the fuel rod assemblies. A typical reactor will contain several hundred fuel assemblies in its core. During the reaction, the uranium burns up and becomes degraded, so it contributes less energy to the process. To keep the reaction critical, the fuel needs to be replenished at regular intervals. Approximately one-third of the fuel rods are replaced every year, and each batch remains in the reactor for three or four cycles. When the oldest rods are removed, the remainder are shuffled around to keep the energy output evenly distributed in all parts of the reactor. The new fuel rods are then inserted into the reactor.

Reprocessing

Reprocessing of spent fuel is a controversial practice currently undertaken only in Britain and France. Spent fuel still contains about 96 percent of its original uranium, though its U-235 content is reduced to less than 1 percent. The remainder of the fuel rod comprises waste products and about 1 percent plutonium produced during the reaction but not fissioned.

Reprocessing separates the uranium and plutonium from the waste products so that they can be reused as fuel. Uranium is returned to the conversion plant, where it is converted back to uranium hexafluoride so that it can go through the enrichment process again. The recovered plutonium can be used as fuel for fast-breeder reactors or mixed with uranium for use in MOX reactors.

At the reprocessing plant, the fuel-rod cladding is removed by mechanical or chemical means. The fuel is then dissolved in nitric acid. The acid solution is then brought into contact with an oil in which tributyl phosphate (TBP) has been dissolved. TBP is a complexing agent for uranium and plutonium, forming compounds with them that remain in the oil. Waste fission products and nonradioactive components are left in the aqueous phase. The two liquids are then separated physically.

Plutonium and uranium are removed from the oil using an aqueous solution containing reductants that separate the two elements. Uranium is stripped from the TBP solution into a dilute nitric acid solution, where it forms uranium nitrate. A number of extraction-stripping cycles are performed to ensure purification of the products and to remove any trace contaminants.

When the uranium nitrate has reached the required degree of purification, it is calcined to an oxide (UO_2 or U_3O_8) and sent for enrichment. Plutonium nitrate is converted to plutonium dioxide and mixed with enriched uranium for reuse in a reactor or converted into weapons-grade plutonium metal. Metallic plutonium can be obtained in a similar way to uranium metal by heating plutonium fluoride at a high temperature with metallic calcium. A direct oxidation-reduction process is also used in which plutonium dioxide is reduced with metallic calcium.

The aqueous fission-product solution left after reprocessing is highly radioactive and must be converted into a more manageable form for storage. First, the solution is evaporated to a solid residue, which is then heated to convert the nitrate salts into oxides. The oxides are powdered and added to borosilicate glass, which immobilizes the radioactive waste. Molten glass is then poured into steel canisters and allowed to solidify. The canisters are packed into bentonite clay and sealed into drums for storage. Each canister can hold up to 0.45 tons (0.4 tonnes) of glass. There are currently five vitrification plants in operation.

Advanced fuels

Despite public concern over nuclear power, it remains a viable form of energy production, and it is likely that many reactors will have their licences to operate renewed when they expire in the early 21st century. Research is therefore continuing into more efficient reactor design and new fuel cycles that will produce less waste, enhance performance, and reduce the proliferation risks of plutonium buildup.

A novel fuel being tested is thorium, which has the advantage of being cheaper and more plentiful than uranium. However, natural thorium lacks any fissile content, so a neutron source is necessary to convert the thorium into the highly fissile U-233. A seed-blanket arrangement is being tested in which thorium dioxide fuel rods are surrounded by standard enriched uranium rods. The U-233 produced is burned in situ and denatured to U-238, preventing it from being used for nuclear weapons. The amount of plutonium produced is significantly reduced and comprises the isotopes Pu-238, Pu-240, and Pu-242, which are impractical for weapons use. Thorium has other economic advantages in that it can stand much-higher burn-up rates, the fuel can stay in the reactor for nine or ten years before it has to be replaced, existing light water reactors can be retrofitted to take the new fuel, and there is no need for reprocessing.

▲ After removal from the reactor, the fuel rods have to be dismantled using robot arms in sealed chambers because they are highly radioactive. The glass screens contain elements that block the leakage of radiation.

▼ A lump of uranium ore containing U-235 in low concentrations, radioactive owing to spontaneous fission.

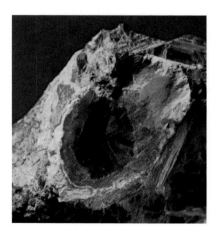

SEE ALSO: FISSION • NUCLEAR REACTOR • NUCLEAR WASTE DISPOSAL • NUCLEAR WEAPON • RADIOACTIVITY • URANIUM

Nuclear Magnetic Resonance

Nuclear magnetic resonance (NMR) is a technique for measuring the magnetic properties of individual atomic nuclei. Since its discovery in 1946, NMR has become widely used in chemical analysis to determine the detailed structures of solids and molecules in solution.

NMR is probably the most powerful single tool available to the chemist for determining the structure of a new compound and is used wherever new compounds are synthesized, especially in the pharmaceutical industry and in university research laboratories. NMR has provided a great deal of information about the structures of the synthetic polymers that are the basis of plastics. Another important application is in the analysis of natural products isolated from plants and animals. NMR is also used to investigate the metabolites or breakdown products of drugs in the body, although the small quantities in which they can be obtained present great difficulties. Increasingly, NMR is being applied to biological problems, for example, studying the structure of proteins and investigating the mode of action of enzymes. Another important application is in magnetic resonance imaging (MRI) body scanners, which make it possible to noninvasively image the soft tissues of the body.

The basis of NMR

The basis of the NMR method is the interaction between certain kinds of atomic nuclei and magnetic fields. Some nuclei behave as if they are spinning about an axis, and because they carry an electric charge, they have a magnetic moment. These nuclei align themselves with a magnetic field in a way that resembles the alignment of a compass needle in the Earth's magnetic field. In accordance with quantum theory, nuclei can take up only particular preferred orientations in a magnetic field. The most important cases are those nuclei that behave like magnetic dipoles and have just two orientations in a magnetic field. Among these nuclei are the common isotopes of hydrogen (H-1, where the nucleus is a single proton), fluorine (F-19), and phosphorus (P-31) and the rare isotope of carbon (C-13).

Each orientation of the nuclei corresponds to a different energy state, the energy difference between the states being proportional to the strength of the magnetic field. If the nuclei are subjected to electromagnetic radiation with a frequency exactly equivalent to the separation between the energy states, the nuclei will be induced to change from one state to the other. The overall effect is that energy is absorbed and released by the nuclei at a frequency called the resonance frequency. The magnetic field strengths usually employed are such that absorption occurs at radio frequencies.

Absorption frequencies

The importance of NMR in chemical analysis is that for any isotope there is a range of absorption (or resonance) frequencies, depending on the chemical environments of the nuclei. The nuclei experience a magnetic field that differs slightly

◀ An NMR spectrometer. The spectrum produced by a sample is ordinarily a straight line broken by peaks at the resonance frequencies.

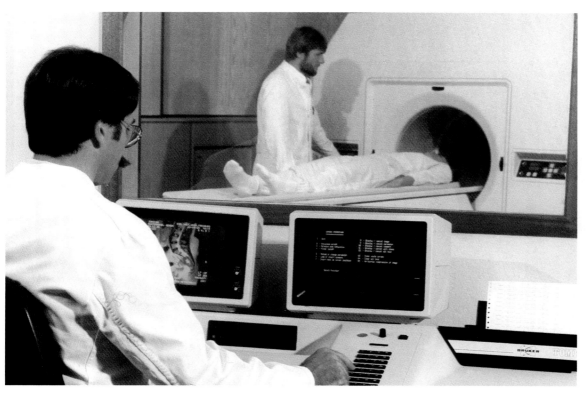

◄ A whole-body magnetic resonance imaging system. The MRI scanner is a noninvasive method that can show thin slices through body tissues by measuring the nuclear magnetic moments of hydrogen nuclei contained in water and fats in cells. The images MRI produces are so sensitive that doctors can differentiate between healthy and damaged tissues.

from the applied field because of shielding by the surrounding electrons. Different resonance frequencies are found for different compounds and also for nuclei in various locations within the same molecule. For example, the hydrogen resonance of ethyl alcohol (CH_3CH_2OH) shows three separate absorption frequencies, according to how the hydrogen atoms are coupled to the molecule by different types of bond. The separate absorptions have intensities proportional to the number of nuclei contributing.

NMR spectrometers

The instrument used for these measurements is an NMR spectrometer. It consists of a magnet, a radio frequency source, and a detector. The signals can be obtained by varying either the magnetic field strength or the frequency and thereby sweeping through the spectrum.

Alternatively, the signals can be stimulated at a fixed field strength by applying a short pulse of radio-frequency radiation, causing all the nuclei to resonate at the same time. The resulting mixture of frequencies is detected, stored in a computer, and unraveled by the process of Fourier transformation. The result is a spectrum similar to that obtained by sweeping the field or frequency. The advantage of the pulsed Fourier transform technique is that all the signals are detected simultaneously so that the procedure can be repeated rapidly and the individual spectra added in computer memory. The spurious noise peaks tend to cancel out over a number of scans.

For maximum separation between signals, a strong magnetic field is desirable. Permanent and electromagnets have been used, giving field strengths in the range 1.4 to 2.4 tesla (corresponding to hydrogen resonance frequencies between 60 and 100 MHz). Earth's magnetic field is only 5×10^{-5} tesla, substantially lower than fields used in NMR. Superconducting solenoids are used for higher field strengths up to 12 tesla (hydrogen resonance frequencies up to 500 MHz), giving better sensitivity and signal separation.

The magnetic field has to be extremely uniform, because variation leads to broadening of the signals. The sample is usually contained in a glass tube 0.2 to 0.6 in. (5–15 mm) in diameter, and the magnetic field must vary across it by less than one part in 1 billion. To achieve this accuracy, the magnet is fitted with a series of correcting coils that generate magnetic fields to cancel out non-homogeneity (unevenness) in the basic field produced by the magnet.

In addition, the field must be stable, particularly for signal averaging of larger numbers of scans, where precise alignment is important. For continuous control and correction of magnetic field, a reference NMR signal is used to detect attempted changes and to compensate for these via a feedback system known as an NMR field-frequency lock.

 SEE ALSO: ATOMIC STRUCTURE • BODY SCANNER • ELECTRONICS IN MEDICINE • MAGNETISM • QUANTUM THEORY • SPECTROSCOPY

Nuclear Reactor

The discovery of radioactivity in 1896 revealed that the elements thorium and uranium release energy spontaneously. The release accompanies a series of radioactive transformations in which atoms emit particles or rays and change their chemical identity. The rate of energy release is too slow to be of much practical use, and it seemed that nothing could be done to hasten it.

A breakthrough occurred in 1919, when the British physicist Ernest Rutherford discovered that alpha rays could shatter the atomic nucleus. Further research led to the discovery of the neutron in 1932 and of the fission of uranium in 1939. That year it became clear that a nuclear chain reaction could probably be set up, using uranium, and that this might be the means not only of releasing vast amounts of energy but also of producing a new element, plutonium. There was the possibility that an atomic bomb could be developed, and it led to the first artificial nuclear reactor at the University of Chicago in December 1942. The Hanford Works were then built beside the Columbia River, becoming the world's first industrial-scale nuclear reactor and starting operation in 1944 for the production of weapons-grade plutonium.

At Hanford, the heat of the nuclear reaction was carried away by river water. The next step was to develop reactors from which the heat could be converted into useful power, for which higher operating temperatures would be needed.

In the United States, the first objective was submarine propulsion, and the *Nautilus* commenced sea trials in 1955. In Britain, Calder Hall was being built for the dual purposes of plutonium production and electricity generation, and a program of nuclear power was put before Parliament. In the former Soviet Union, an atomic power plant had commenced operation at Obninsk in 1954. Twenty years later, nearly 250 seagoing nuclear propulsion plants and about 120 full-scale industrial nuclear power reactors were in operation by 16 nations, with subsequent development proceeding at a slower rate. However, reduced energy demand coupled with public concern about the safety of nuclear plants resulted in an effective halt in the expansion of nuclear power in the United States during the 1980s, although work had continued in other countries. By the end of the 20th century, the United States had 104 operating nuclear plants producing 20 percent of the country's energy requirement. Worldwide production of electricity from nuclear energy is expected to peak at 367,000 MW in 2010 but drop to 300,000 MW by 2020. Though most countries are reducing their nuclear programs, others such as India and China see it as a cheap means of providing their populations with energy.

Fission

The energy produced by a nuclear reactor is released by the fission of atomic nuclei in a controlled and self-sustaining manner and appears as heat, which is then converted to electricity using more or less conventional steam turbine generators. Nuclear fission occurs when the nucleus of an atom splits into two parts, and some nuclei can be made to split by bombarding them with neutrons. More neutrons are produced as a result of the splitting process and under the right conditions go on to split further nuclei, giving a continuous chain reaction. Generally speaking, the chances that a neutron will interact with a nucleus are much higher when the velocity of the neutron

is slow rather than when it is moving fast. For this reason, a moderator is used in the thermal reactor to slow down the neutrons emitted by the fuel to the velocities of thermal agitation. The slowing down occurs because the neutrons lose their energy of motion to the moderating nuclei, as they are scattered by them. The energy transfer is more effective the lighter these nuclei are. The most commonly used moderators are graphite, a form of carbon (nuclear mass approximately 12 times that of the neutron), and ordinary or light water, which contains hydrogen (mass approximately equal to that of the neutron).

The effect of neutron capture depends on the type of nucleus involved. The atomic nuclei of

▼ Diagrams of six different types of nuclear reactor. Pressurized-water reactors (PWRs) and boiling-water reactors (BWRs) are the most common type of reactor in use, and variations of this technology can be found in many countries around the world.

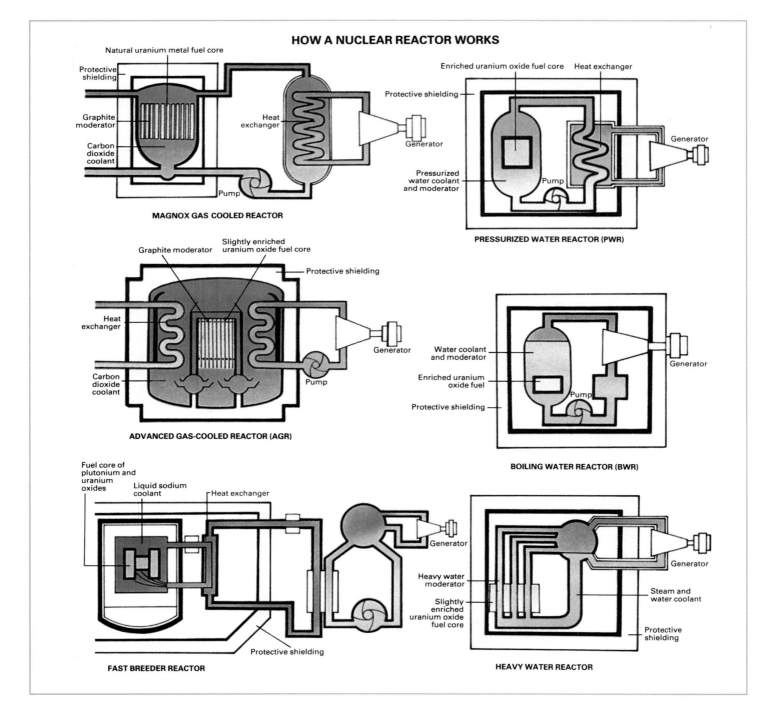

HOW A NUCLEAR REACTOR WORKS

MAGNOX GAS COOLED REACTOR

PRESSURIZED WATER REACTOR (PWR)

ADVANCED GAS-COOLED REACTOR (AGR)

BOILING WATER REACTOR (BWR)

FAST BREEDER REACTOR

HEAVY WATER REACTOR

◄ The temperature of the fuel elements inside a reactor core must be constantly monitored by thermocouples or banks of thermocouples (thermopiles) in the top of the reactor.

uranium, the most common reactor fuel, are of two types, or isotopes, containing different total numbers of nucleons (neutrons and protons). About 99.3 percent of the atoms have 238 nucleons, but 0.7 percent have 235, and it is the uranium-235 that is the active fuel in a nuclear reactor.

Some thermal reactors are fueled with uranium of natural isotopic composition, but for most, the uranium is first put through an isotope separation process to remove some of the uranium-238. The use of this enriched uranium, usually with between 2 and 4 percent uranium-235 content, gives greater freedom in the design of a reactor.

When a neutron hits the nucleus of a uranium-235 atom, a compound nucleus is formed. This nucleus (uranium-236) may remain intact but is more likely to undergo fission, splitting into two fission product nuclei of approximately equal mass and emitting fast-moving neutrons. Because it is so likely to undergo fission, uranium-235 is called a fissile material.

Capture of a neutron by uranium-238 yields, as compound nucleus, uranium-239. This does not split, but it undergoes spontaneous radioactive transformations, increasing the positive electric charge of its nucleus by emitting two beta rays and so becoming plutonium-239. This nucleus, an isotope of the second element beyond uranium in the periodic table, is fissile.

In practice, the ratio of the number of plutonium-239 nuclei produced to the number of uranium-235 nuclei consumed, in a thermal reactor, is less than one. If the plutonium is required for A-bomb manufacture, the fuel may be discharged at an early stage. Otherwise, it is left in the reactor for three to five years, during which some of the plutonium-239 is burned up by fission and some is converted to higher isotopes, plutonium-240, -241 and -242. Of these, only plutonium-241 is capable of fission.

Reactor design

In some reactors, the fuel is uranium metal, but uranium oxide and carbide stand up better to high temperatures and to the accumulation of fission products. Rods or pellets of fuel are sealed into thin-walled metal tubes that, in some designs, are grouped into clusters of 36 to form a fuel element. For the highest temperatures, graphite is used instead of metal for cladding the fuel. Because the fission products that build up in the cladding are good neutron absorbers, about one-third of the fuel rods have to be replaced every two to four years, otherwise the nuclear reaction would stop.

The fuel elements are assembled to form a core along with the moderator material and control rods. Heat produced by the nuclear reaction is removed by a coolant—either gas or liquid—that is circulated through the core and then through heat exchangers, where the heat is used to boil water into steam for driving electricity-generating plant. Normally, the coolant is circulated under high pressure, so the core is enclosed in a pressure vessel made from steel or prestressed concrete. Surrounding the core assembly is a safety vessel to contain the radioactivity of the working core. Some reactors, particularly research reactors, include a reflector, which is used to scatter stray neutrons from the core and reflect some of them back. In small reactors, the reflector surrounds the core, though it can be used inside the core to act as a island of high neutron intensity for experimental purposes. Larger power reactors do not need reflectors as they do not leak many neutrons, but they are used occasionally to keep the power density uniform.

Key to controlling the rate of the fission reaction are the control rods. These rods are made from a material that absorbs neutrons and can be moved in and out of the core to regulate the speed of the reaction. There are three types of control rods—safety rods used in start-up and shutdown of the reactor, regulator rods to adjust the rate of the nuclear reaction and the power produced, and shim rods, a coarse type of control used to compensate for radioactivity changes as fuel rods become used up.

Safety rods are vital in shutting down the reactor, whether in the case of an emergency or a scheduled shutdown for refuelling. The rods contain enough absorber to be able to stop the reaction completely no matter how critical the situation may be. Many have a fail-safe design that makes them fall into the reactor in the event of a mechanical or electrical failure.

While reactors are designed to operate safely without any release of radioactivity, contingency measures are necessary to contain radiation within any part of the reactor system should a leak occur. A series of barriers, starting with the cladding on fuel rods, a primary containment vessel, and thick shielding material are built up to confine the reactor's core. The reactor building acts as a last line of defense, and it is carefully constructed and tested to ensure there can be no more than a minor escape of radiation over a period of several days.

Types of reactors

Several types of reactors exist, but only two are used commercially: the thermal reactor and the fast breeder reactor. A number of different designs of thermal reactor are available, the main differences being in the cooling arrangements and the types of fuel elements. In the United States, most of the power-producing reactors are of the light-water type, originally developed for use in nuclear submarine power plants, with two main variations. The pressurized water reactor (PWR) uses the water as both a coolant and a moderator, and the working pressure is high enough to prevent the water from boiling at the core temperatures—for example, a core temperature of 570°F (300°C) needs a system pressure of more than 1,000 lbs. per sq. in. (68 atmospheres). The coolant water will absorb some of the neutrons, so the fuel has to be slightly enriched to contain about 4 percent uranium-235.

In the boiling water reactor (BWR), the water is allowed to boil in the reactor core to produce superheated steam, which is then fed directly to external steam turbines. Operating pressures are about half those of the PWR. The steam produced is radioactive, but the radioactive elements in the steam have a short half-life, so maintenance work can be carried out safely on the turbines once the steam supply has been cut off.

Heavy water (deuterium oxide) has the advantage that it is a poor absorber of neutrons and thus allows the heavy water reactor to use natural (nonenriched) uranium as a fuel. In the Canadian CANDU reactor, heavy water is used both as the moderator and the coolant, the coolant being contained in a separate high-pressure circuit to extract heat from the fuel. The CANDU reactor has the advantage that it can be refueled without shutting down the reactor. Another design uses normal, light water as the coolant and heavy water as the moderator.

◀ Nuclear fusion is the joining together of two nuclei of light atoms to form the nucleus of a heavier atom. Because of the different binding energies required to hold together the particles in the different nuclei, the process can release energy. Experiments in controlled nuclear fusion are continuing in several countries, and if they are successful, nuclear fusion reactors could one day provide an inexhaustible source of energy without any of the usual problems of nuclear fission.

Gases can also be used as the cooling medium, with designs such as the British magnox reactor using carbon dioxide under high pressure with a graphite moderator and natural uranium fuel. As with PWRs, the heat from the coolant is used to generate steam in a heat exchanger. More efficient steam generation can be achieved by the use of higher temperatures and this end is achieved in the advanced gas-cooled reactor, which uses uranium oxide fuel in stainless steel casings. The stainless steel cases act as neutron absorbers, so the fuel has to be slightly enriched.

Fast breeder reactors

An alternative design of reactor, the fast breeder reactor, uses the fast neutrons produced by fission without slowing them down as in the thermal reactor. The fuel used has a higher concentration (15 to 20 percent) of fissile material, usually plutonium-239 and uranium-235, with the high concentration resulting in a smaller core size. Coolants such as molten sodium or high-pressure helium, which offer good heat transfer efficiency and do not absorb or slow down the fast neutrons, are employed.

By surrounding the core of a fast reactor with fertile material, such as uranium-238, the excess fast neutrons from the core can be used to breed more fissile plutonium-239 so that the reactor makes more fuel than it burns. By reprocessing the fuel burned in this type of reactor, it becomes possible to use up to 60 percent of the energy in the uranium, as opposed to a few percent with thermal nuclear reactors.

Propulsion reactors

Nuclear reactors are still used to power naval vessels, particularly submarines. Unlike oil-based fuels, nuclear reactions do not need oxygen to produce power, so nuclear submarines can stay underwater almost indefinitely. Surface vessels too can spend long periods at sea without having to rely on tankers for refueling.

Little is known about the exact design of naval reactors for security reasons, but they are known to be moderated and cooled with light water and use highly enriched uranium as a fuel. Special design features include the ability to restart quickly after shutdown and to burn fuel for long periods without replacement.

Fuel cycles

The simplest fuel cycle used in nuclear reactors is the once-through cycle, in which the mined uranium ore is processed into pure uranium or uranium oxide, enriched if necessary and formed into fuel elements. These elements are then used to

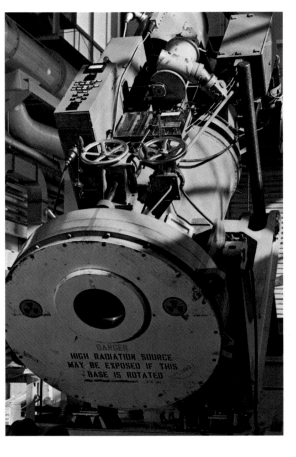

◄ A handling flask for irradiated fuel for the Dragon reactor at Winfrith, England. Dragon was an experimental high-temperature helium-cooled, graphite-moderated reactor that has now been decommissioned.

fuel a reactor and are removed when they are spent. The removed elements are radioactive and still producing a large amount of heat (because of the continued decay of fission products), so they are enclosed in lead-shielded flasks and immersed in storage ponds close to the reactor where the water provides cooling. Radioactivity and heat-production levels are considerably reduced after a few years, when the used elements may be left in storage ponds or disposed of in a permanent store of some kind. This once-through cycle is the one followed by the U.S. nuclear power industry following President Carter's moratorium on fuel reprocessing in 1977.

In the once-through cycle, only a small proportion of the fuel is actually burned up in the reactor, and much more efficient use can be made of the fuel by reprocessing the spent elements. In reprocessing, used elements are held in storage ponds until the level of radioactivity falls to a level at which the elements can be safely transported to the reprocessing plant. At the reprocessing plant, the fuel is removed from its casings and put through a sophisticated separation process to give uranium, plutonium, and various fission products that can then be reused.

SEE ALSO: FISSION • FUSION • NUCLEAR EMERGENCY • NUCLEAR FUEL CYCLE • NUCLEAR WASTE DISPOSAL • RADIOACTIVITY • URANIUM

Nuclear Waste Disposal

Nuclear reactors offer an efficient and safe means of electricity generation but have the peculiar disadvantage of producing waste products that are highly radioactive and difficult to dispose of safely. Radioactive waste products are also produced as a result of the use of radioactive materials in medicine and for industrial processes, and they also need safe disposal.

Radiation levels

In assessing risks due to the radioactivity of wastes, both the level of the radiation and the time it remains active have to be considered. The level of radioactivity is normally measured in curies or becquerels; one curie = 3.7 x 10^{10} Bq (where one becquerel is equivalent to one disintegration per second). Radioactive isotopes gradually decay as they emit radiation, the level of activity falling until the material becomes stable and nonradioactive. The time that it takes for the level of radioactivity of a substance to fall to half of its initial level is known as the half-life of the substance. The half-life may be many thousands of years. For example, plutonium-239 has a half life of 24,000 years. In general, ten half-lives of a highly radioactive element have to elapse—reducing the radioactivity to less than one-thousandth of the original level—before a material is no longer considered dangerous.

The rate at which radioactive particles are emitted varies considerably according to the element concerned; short-lived, highly active isotopes give out many particles over a short period. The same amount of a longer-lived isotope would emit fewer particles per second and so is less likely to cause damage. The cumulative effects over a long period, however, are likely, for example, to damage a living cell and perhaps cause cancer or mutation.

Nuclear waste is generally divided into three categories according to the amount and type of radioactivity present: low-level waste, intermediate-level waste, and high-level waste.

Low-level waste

By far the greatest volume of nuclear waste is low level and consists of material such as slightly contaminated protective clothing and equipment, for example, glassware, and pipework. Although most of this type of waste is produced by nuclear plants, much is also produced as a result of the use of radioactive substances for medical and industrial applications. This type of waste is disposed of by sealing it into steel drums and burying it in shallow trenches at special sites. Because of the rising costs of storing low-level wastes, more effort is being taken to separate contaminated wastes from uncontaminated waste and compacting the wastes into smaller volumes before disposal. However, compaction concentrates the radioactivity of the waste so that more stringent safeguards are necessary for landfilling. It has been estimated that in the United States nearly 280 million cu.ft. (8 million m³) of low-level waste will have been disposed of by 2020. Sea dumping has also been used for the disposal of low-level wastes, but it was discontinued in 1985 following concern about the environmental impact of this practice.

A related problem lies in the disposal of waste material, or tailings, produced during uranium mining. These tailings have a low level of radioactivity (less than most low-level waste), but the large volumes of the tailings heaps—one estimate puts the U.S. total at over 220 million tons (200 million tonnes)—makes the total radioactivity involved significant. The main danger from such tailings lies in the fact that some of the radioactive elements in the tailings have long half-lives—80,000 years in the case of thorium-230—thus causing particular problems. In addition, the decay products of the thorium are radium and radon gas, both of which are known to cause cancer. To minimize the risks, tailings piles are constructed with liners, to prevent radioactive elements from leaching into groundwater, and covered with earth and rock.

▼ Sites for storing nuclear wastes, such as that under investigation at Yucca Mountain in Nevada, must be geologically stable with little permeation from rain or groundwater that might corrode the waste drums. Underground galleries (1) would be excavated and diggings conveyed to surface dumps (2). Canisters of waste would travel from the receiving station (3) via an entry shaft (4) for deposit in newly cut galleries (5). Once filled, the gallery would be packed with diggings (6). To be safe, formations would have to maintain stability for at least 1,000 years while radioactive isotopes decay to less harmful products.

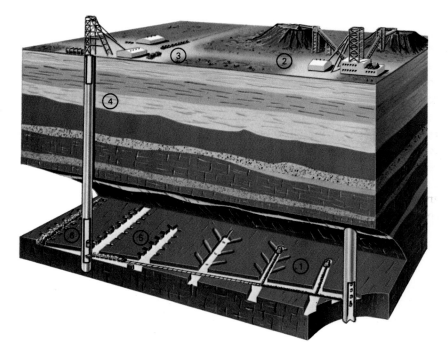

◀ Synroc (synthetic rock), developed in Australia for the safe disposal of nuclear waste is capable of being compressed to 98 percent of its theoretical density. In the process, liquid wastes are mixed with a mineral Synroc base, calcined, and packed into bellows-shaped stainless steel cans. The cans are sealed, preheated, and then compacted in a press that collapses the can bellows to give a pancake of Synroc. The material produced is a dense crystalline ceramic that is stable under the action of heat and radioactivity and has particular resistance to leaching of the radioactive elements. This canister has been cut away to show its inner layers of Synroc.

Intermediate-level wastes

Much of the intermediate-level waste is produced by the irradiation of reactor components and includes the remains of fuel element cladding materials, together with exchange resins used in fuel processing and contaminated equipment. A particular type of intermediate-level waste is the transuranic waste, which consists of elements heavier than uranium in the periodic table, in particular, plutonium. These transuranic wastes are generally poisonous and highly radioactive and are separated out during the reprocessing of spent fuel. The main danger from transuranic wastes is from ingestion or inhalation of radioactive particles, which can cause damage to internal organs. However, it can be stored safely as long as it is kept in secure containers.

The higher level of radioactivity from intermediate-level waste makes it necessary to shield it during handling (low-level waste does not require

such shielding). In some cases, the intermediate-level waste is disposed of by burial in concrete-lined repositories, and underground dumps in deep mines have also been used. One such dump is the Asse salt mine waste disposal facility in Germany. Here drums of low-level and intermediate-level waste are encased in concrete and buried in salt in the large underground caverns of the mine. Pending the development of suitable disposal sites, most intermediate waste is being held in store at fuel reprocessing plants and nuclear power stations.

In the United States, there are plans for the disposal of transuranic waste in salt beds in the Waste Isolation Pilot Project (WIPP) at Carlsbad, New Mexico. The projected capacity of this plant is about 6 million cu. ft. (175,500 m³). Regular shipments are expected to start in 2002 and will continue until 2035. The excess will continue to be held above ground until further safe disposal sites are developed.

During the early development of nuclear power and military nuclear establishments, intermediate waste was not treated as a separate category and was handled with the low-level wastes. This practice resulted in long-lived (transuranic) intermediate wastes being dumped in shallow surface trenches; thus, in the United States, there is an estimated 35 million cu. ft. (1 million m³) of such waste in unsuitable dumps. According to the U.S. authorities, much of this waste will have to be dug up and put into storage until safer burial grounds have been found.

High-level wastes

Most of the radioactivity in nuclear waste is in the high-level waste products, and it is the disposal of this type of waste that has aroused the greatest controversy. This waste is the result of reprocessing spent fuel from reactors and is highly radioactive. The decomposition of short-lived isotopes generates considerable heat, particularly during

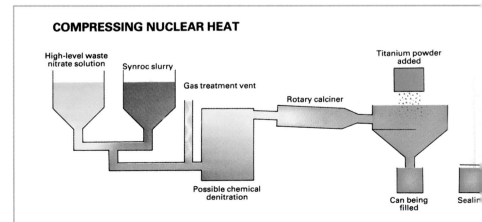

COMPRESSING NUCLEAR HEAT

High-level waste nitrate solution

Synroc slurry

Gas treatment vent

Rotary calciner

Titanium powder added

Possible chemical denitration

Can being filled

Sealin

the first few years after removal from the reactor. In the United States, the used fuel elements from reactors are not reprocessed but simply stored in water-filled holding pools on the reactor sites. This approach was adopted following President Carter's 1977 moratorium on fuel reprocessing (prompted by fears about the safety of the plutonium separated out during reprocessing), and by 1997, some 40,000 tons (36,500 tonnes) of spent elements were in storage, with this total expected to rise to 57,000 tons (52,000 tonnes) by 2005. At a number of power plants, the storage pools are reaching the limit of their capacity, so permanent means of disposal have to be found. Substantial amounts of high-level wastes are held at military reprocessing plants, though they are mainly in liquid or solid form. These wastes are now being stored in underground tanks and stainless steel silos while processes to solidify and stabilize them for storage in a national repository are developed.

Reprocessing of fuel from power reactors is being carried out in various countries, notably in Britain and France, which are developing techniques for high-level waste disposal commercially, and other countries, such as Sweden, Australia and Germany, are also developing techniques for disposing of their own accumulated wastes.

In reprocessing, the spent fuel elements are first split to separate the casings from the fuel itself, which is then submerged in concentrated nitric acid. The acid dissolves the uranium, plutonium, and fission products, leaving any solid wastes, and the resulting solution is put through a separation process. The unburned uranium and plutonium are recovered from the solution for reuse, and the highly radioactive fission products remain as a hot, acid liquid, which is concentrated by evaporation. This liquid is held in storage tanks for a period of several years to allow the initial high levels of heat (produced by the decay of short-lived isotopes) to fall and radioactivity to decay to more manageable levels.

In the long-term, two main approaches are proposed: to deposit the material in mined cavities or boreholes in stable geological structures below ground or to store the material above ground for tens of years while the long-term stability of burial sites is investigated and to allow further reductions in the rates of heat production and radioactivity. Above-ground storage has the advantage that the wastes are readily accessible if improved means of treatment are developed.

Storage

The prime requirement for underground storage is that the chosen site is geologically stable, because long storage times are needed for the waste to decay to safe radiation levels—comparable with the natural background radiation. In addition, the material of a suitable site should be resistant to the action of ground water and able to withstand the heating effects of the wastes. One proposed site is Yucca Mountain in Nevada, on which a decision is expected in 2001. The site has already been used for testing nuclear weapons and has a suitably dry climate and a very low water table that is geologically isolated from surrounding areas. Waste would be buried 1,000 ft. (300 m) below the surface after being packaged inside metal containers.

Much thought is being given to the structure and design of the storage casks to be used in the nuclear waste repository. The casks must be robust enough to survive being moved and accidentally dropped. They must also be leakproof and resistant to corrosion. An alloy of gadolinium and stainless steel is being tested for its mechanical and corrosion-resistance properties as a potential cask material. Gadolinium is a low-cost metal that has the advantage of absorbing more neutrons than boron. It is also resistant to corrosion, making it a good choice for nuclear packaging. Research is also underway on methods of reducing the amount of water in spent nuclear fuel using a very high vacuum at a low enough temperature that will not melt the fuel.

Solidification

Several processes have been developed to reduce the liquid wastes to a solid form for easier handling and reduced risk of leakage, with one of the favored techniques being vitrification, by which the wastes are incorporated into glass. In this process, the liquid waste is sprayed into a high-temperature furnace where it is dried and oxidized to give a calcine similar to fine sand. The calcine is then mixed with borosilicate glass-forming materials, or frit, melted, and cast to form borosilicate glass blocks.

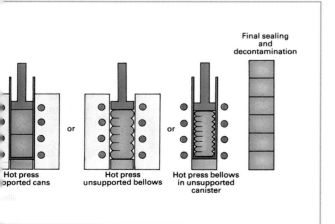

◄ Radioactive nitrate solution is mixed with Synroc oxide to form a slurry, which is then denitrated and injected into a furnace. After one hour of concentrated heat, titanium metal powder is added, and the mixture is loaded into metal cans, which are sealed and decontaminated, then disposed of permanently.

Final sealing and decontamination

Hot press supported cans

Hot press unsupported bellows

Hot press bellows in unsupported canister

◀ Nuclear waste is most dangerous in liquid form, because it can move through natural waterways into the food chain. At this French plant, liquid waste is reduced to a safer, solid form then incorporated into glass in a process called vitrification.

cladding. Some of the sodium has become incorporated into the fuel elements, making it difficult to remove by mechanical means. An electrometallurgical process being developed at Argonne National Laboratory may provide a solution by converting spent fuel into metallic and ceramic waste forms. Plutonium and other transuranides will be locked into the ceramic form while the sodium is converted into common salt. The rest of the coolant sodium from the reactor, which was only mildly radioactive, was exposed to moisture under controlled conditions to form sodium hydroxide and allowed to solidify before being shipped to a low-level radioactive waste dump.

Accelerator transmutation of waste is another technology being studied as a means of reducing plutonium, actinides, and fission products by changing their atomic structure. First, chemical separation techniques are used to separate long-lived isotopes and transuranics from the spent fuel. The process uses a linear accelerator to produce a powerful proton beam that is then converted by spallation reactions into an intense neutron flux. The neutrons react with the fission products and transmute them into stable nuclei or short-lived isotopes. These less radioactive isotopes can then be stored safely. A major benefit of the process is its ability to reduce the stockpile of plutonium that could be used for weapons.

The glass blocks retain their properties well at high temperatures, resist radiation damage, and are generally insoluble. Radioactive elements, however, can be leached out of the blocks by water, so the blocks are packed in corrosion-resistant canisters before being disposed of.

Further protection is given by surrounding the containers with overpacking material to prevent ground water from reaching the waste canisters in geologic depositories. The first commercial-scale vitrification plant, at Marcoule, France, started operation in 1979 with a capacity of up to 9.5 gallons (36 l) of liquid waste per hour, giving 44 lbs. (20 kg) of glass. The glass blocks produced are loaded into steel casks, and the lids are welded on, then the casks are stored in concrete vaults with forced cooling to keep their temperature down.

Advanced waste treatment

Some high-level wastes that can not be dried or vitrified or that contain transuranic elements require special processing techniques before they will be accepted into a geologic repository. Among these wastes are materials from an experimental fast breeder reactor where elemental sodium was used between the fuel pins and the

FACT FILE

- Between 1946 and 1970, the U.S. Atomic Energy Commission dumped tens of thousands of metal canisters containing low-level nuclear waste into the Atlantic and Pacific Oceans. Less than ten years after the last canister had been dumped, a piloted submersible discovered some canisters to be crushed and leaking.

- Nuclear waste exists in tailings, the heaps of pulverized ore from which uranium has been extracted. Once considered harmless, the tailings were used as foundation material for houses and other buildings in Colorado. In fact, the tailings emit radon gas, and dangerous alpha particles seep through building structures.

SEE ALSO: ATOMIC STRUCTURE • CERAMICS • FISSION • NUCLEAR FUEL CYCLE • NUCLEAR REACTOR • PARTICLE ACCELERATOR • RADIOACTIVITY • URANIUM

Nuclear Weapon

◀ Nuclear warheads being loaded into a missile. Many nuclear missiles contain several reentry vehicles, each with its own warhead.

Nuclear weapons are devices that use the energy contained within the nuclei of atoms to create massive explosions. This energy may be released by the fission, or splitting, of atoms or the fusion of atoms, in which small atoms are joined together to make larger ones. Both fission and fusion release huge amounts of energy and radioactivity. Broadly, there are three main types of nuclear weapons. They are the atomic bomb, or A-bomb, which uses nuclear fission, the hydrogen bomb, which uses nuclear fusion, and the neutron bomb, which also relies on fusion.

Nuclear weapons have been deployed only twice in war, at Hiroshima and Nagasaki in Japan. A single atomic bomb was released over each of these cities toward the end of World War II, causing their total destruction.

Nuclear fission

The huge power of an atomic bomb comes from the forces holding each individual atom of a substance together. These forces act over tiny distances deep within the atom itself. Every atom of every substance that exists is held together by them. The energy released by splitting one atom is tiny, but there are so many billion atoms in even the smallest piece of material that a great deal of power can be released from large quantities.

Most naturally occurring elements (pure substances) have very stable atoms that are impossible to split except by using such techniques as bombarding them in a particle accelerator. However, there is one natural element whose atoms can be split comparatively easily: this is the metal uranium. Its special property comes from the comparatively large size of its atoms; they are too big to hold together firmly.

There are two common naturally occurring isotopes of uranium: an isotope is a form of an element distinguished by the number of neutrons in its atom. Natural uranium consists mostly of the isotope U-238, but mixed in with this is about 0.7 percent of the other isotope, U-235. This isotope, unlike U-238, is fissionable (its atoms can be split), and so it is the one used for making bombs.

Both isotopes of uranium, and certain other heavy elements, are naturally radioactive, that is, their big, unstable atoms slowly disintegrate over the course of thousands of years. Atoms of U-235 can be made to break up much faster, however, in a chain reaction. Instead of disintegrating slowly by themselves, the atoms are forcibly split by neutrons forcing their way into the nucleus. When a U-235 atom splits, it gives off energy in the form of heat and gamma radiation, the most powerful form of radioactivity and the type that is most harmful to life. It also gives off two or three free neutrons. These may collide with other nuclei, causing them to fission.

In theory, it is necessary to split only one U-235 atom, for the neutrons from this will split other atoms, which in turn will split more, and so on. In practice, however, there has to be a certain weight of U-235 present before the chain reaction will sustain itself. If there is less than this amount, there will be too few atoms to ensure that neutrons from every atom that splits will hit other atoms. The minimum amount is known as the critical mass. The theoretical critical mass is about 2 lbs. (1 kg) of pure U-235. In practice, the degree of purity is so low that 110 lbs. (50 kg)—the effective critical mass—is required in order to sustain a chain reaction.

Uranium is not the only material used for making nuclear weapons. Another material is the element plutonium, as its isotope Pu-239. Plutonium is not found naturally (except in minute traces) and is always made from uranium.

▶ The initial explosion of an air-burst atomic bomb releases about 35 percent of its energy as intense heat followed by a supersonic shock wave. Around 50 percent of the bomb's output is felt as a highly destructive high-pressure air blast followed by a low-pressure wave of equal intensity.

U–235 BOMB LITTLE BOY

◀ A cutaway view of the U-235 Little Boy atomic bomb that was dropped on Hiroshima, Japan, in August 1945. This was a uranium gun-type bomb and killed over 80,000 people. The different parts of the bomb are illustrated as follows: (1) tail cone, (2) stabilizing tail fins, (3) airstream deflectors, (4) air inlet tube, (5) air pressure detonator, (6) pressure sensors, (7) detonating head, (8) packing, (9) conventional explosive charge, (10) electronic conduits and fusing circuits, (11) neutron reflector, (12) battery stores, (13) cast bomb casing, (14) telemetry monitoring probes, (15) lead shield container, (16) fuses.

Mechanism of the bomb

A bomb cannot be made simply by putting a piece of uranium larger than critical mass into a casing, because this would cause it to go off immediately. Instead, two or more pieces are inserted a safe distance apart and assembled, or shot together, to start a chain reaction.

The simplest possible atomic bomb is one of the type dropped on Hiroshima. It is known as a gun-type bomb, since it actually contains a type of gun. At one end of the barrel, there is a target, a piece of U-235 slightly smaller than critical mass and shaped like a sphere with a conical wedge removed from it to form a tapering gap.

At the other end of the barrel, there is another, smaller piece of U-235 in the shape of a cone with its apex pointing toward the gap in the target. It is the exact shape of the piece missing from the sphere. Together, the two pieces exceed the critical mass. The smaller piece is backed by a charge of ordinary high explosive. When it is set off, the cone is shot into the sphere, and the force of impact welds the two pieces together solidly. The explosion follows instantly.

Plutonium bombs are slightly more sophisticated. Plutonium is even more easily fissionable than U-235, and its critical mass is lower: 35.2 lbs. (16 kg) for pure Pu-239.

The mass can be reduced further, to 22 lbs. (10 kg), by making a sphere of this weight of plutonium and surrounding it with nonfissionable U-238, which reflects neutrons back into the center of the sphere and minimizes loss to the outside.

Plutonium cannot be exploded so easily by a gun-type device. It has to be assembled with much greater speed, or it will not explode properly. Plutonium is therefore assembled by a technique known as implosion. A number of wedge-shaped pieces of plutonium, which together will build up into a sphere, are arranged at equal intervals around a neutron source. Explosive charges of exactly equal weight are placed behind each wedge, and all are detonated together. The wedges shoot toward the center and touch each other at the same moment. This technique was used for the second American atomic bomb, which was dropped on the city of Nagasaki.

Hydrogen bomb

A hydrogen bomb is an explosive device in which energy from the nuclear fusion of hydrogen isotopes is released in an uncontrolled manner. Nuclear fusion is a process in which nuclei of small atoms combine to form the nucleus of a larger atom, and energy is released because the binding energy of the particles in the larger nucleus is greater than the sum of the binding energies holding together the small nuclei. The energy set free by the almost instantaneous fusion of many millions of nuclei results in an explosion of enormous power. Indeed, the hydrogen bomb is the most destructive device ever produced, many times more powerful than an atomic bomb.

Fusion

Nuclear fusion cannot occur spontaneously. Normally two nuclei repel each other because they both carry a positive electric charge, so if they are to fuse, they must be forced together. In order to force nuclei together, the nuclei must be as close together as possible to start with, and they must be moving toward each other at very high velocities. High velocities can be achieved by heating the components to temperatures of several hundred million degrees, and for this reason, the hydrogen bomb is often called a thermonuclear bomb. Once the critical temperature is achieved, fusion will begin, and the energy released will maintain the temperature and hence the reaction until either all the fusionable material has been used or the whole reaction mixture has expanded to such an extent that the temperature has fallen below the critical level.

Two isotopes of hydrogen—deuterium and tritium—are used in hydrogen bombs, rather than ordinary hydrogen. Deuterium occurs in nature, for example, as deuterium oxide (D_2O, or heavy water) to the extent of about one part in 5,000 of ordinary water, from which it can be extracted and purified. Tritium, a radioactive isotope, does not occur naturally and must be produced artificially: it is made by bombarding lithium-6 (an isotope of the alkali metal lithium with atomic weight 6) with neutrons, causing it to split into helium and tritium.

Development of hydrogen bombs

Primitive hydrogen bombs consisted of an atomic bomb and a supply of hydrogen isotopes in liquid form. The atomic bomb acted as a trigger by sup-

▼ Diagram showing the stages in the development of a mushroom cloud caused by an air-burst nuclear explosion. Detonating the bomb above the ground results in the maximum amount of damage.

DEVELOPMENT OF AN AIR-BURST ATOMIC EXPLOSION

5% initial radiation

10% residual radiation

ENERGY RELEASED

35% heat

50% blast

Fission products injected into atmosphere

Mushroom cloud

Blast wave

Detonation

Fireball develops

Fireball

Reflected shock front

Mach wave

Formation of mushroom cloud

Winds

Mushroom stem

plying the heat necessary to initiate the fusion reaction. (This method is still the only practical means of supplying the enormous heat required, although the possibilities of using lasers as triggers are being explored.) Liquid isotopes were used because atoms in a liquid are closer together than atoms in a gas, but this approach was abandoned because liquid hydrogen is highly volatile and, therefore, is very hazardous to store.

Modern hydrogen bombs consist basically of an atomic trigger surrounded by a lining of lithium deuteride, a compound of deuterium and lithium (lithium-6). Lithium deuteride has two main functions. First, it serves to hold deuterium nuclei very close together (atoms are even more closely packed in a solid than in a liquid) so that they undergo fusion readily when heat is supplied. Second, the lithium-6 will produce tritium when bombarded with neutrons, and the tritium can then fuse with the deuterium. Neutrons for this process are supplied by the atomic bomb so that the trigger has more than one function. In addition to the main reactions—deuterium with deuterium and deuterium with tritium—other fusion reactions may contribute to the explosion. For example, a lithium nucleus can fuse with a deuterium nucleus to release energy.

This type of hydrogen bomb is said to be relatively clean, meaning that it produces only small quantities of radioactive debris, or fallout. The fallout, which can remain radioactive for months or years, is composed chiefly of radioactive fission products from the trigger—but only in limited amounts, as only a small atomic bomb is used—together with unburned tritium. Often, however, a hydrogen bomb is surrounded by a layer of uranium (uranium-238). As well as acting as a container to keep the bomb together and the fusion reaction going a little longer, this uranium, when bombarded by fast neutrons generated by the fusion reaction, is a further source of fission energy. This type of bomb—called a fission-fusion-fission, or Triple-F, bomb—produces considerable amounts of radioactive fallout and is therefore described as a "dirty" bomb.

The explosive power of a hydrogen bomb is much greater than that of an atomic bomb, for two main reasons. First, because hydrogen is the lightest of all elements, a given mass of deuterium or tritium contains many more atoms than the same mass of uranium or plutonium, and thus, weight for weight, there are more deuterium or tritium nuclei available for fusion than there are uranium or plutonium nuclei able to undergo fission. In fact, the complete fusion of a given mass of deuterium would theoretically yield almost three times as much energy as the complete fission of the same mass of uranium-235. Second, the size of a hydrogen bomb, unlike that of an atomic bomb, is theoretically almost unlimited.

Neutron bomb

Neutron bombs, also called enhanced radiation fusion bombs, are a type of hydrogen bomb that produce a smaller explosion than other nuclear weapons. This explosion effects an area of only a few hundred yards radius but releases very large amounts of gamma and neutron radiation to a wider area. It does not, however, produce the radioactive fallout that results from fission explosions and which affects much larger areas. The gamma and neutron radiation produced by neutron bombs is relatively short lived but very destructive to life and is able to penetrate armored vehicles as well as making earth and water radioactive. For this reason, neutron bombs are intended as tactical weapons for use on battlefields rather than as strategic weapons for destroying large urban areas.

SEE ALSO: ATOMIC STRUCTURE • BOMB • ELECTROMAGNETIC RADIATION • FISSION • FUSION • NUCLEAR REACTOR • RADIOACTIVITY • SPACE WEAPON • URANIUM

Number Theory

Number theory is the study of the properties and interrelationships of numbers and, in particular, integers. The integers are a class of numbers formed by the natural numbers—positive whole numbers such as 1, 2, 3, and so on—the negatives of those numbers, and zero (0).

Number theory is characterized by equations and statements that are observed to hold true for any chosen combination of numbers and, on that basis, are proposed to hold true for any set of numbers. The creation of concrete mathematical proofs for such propositions is a great intellectual challenge, but much of the appeal of number theory lies in the appreciation of the curious relationships that exist between numbers.

Composite and prime numbers

Most integers can be expressed as multiplication products of other integers, so 20 is the product of 4 and 5, or 2 and 10, for example. Conversely, such integers can be divided by the appropriate integers—their divisors—to give whole-number results, as is the case when 20 is divided by 1, 2, 4, 5, 10, or 20. Such numbers are called composites.

Prime numbers differ from composites in that their divisions give only a whole-number result if the divisor is 1, the prime number itself, or the negative of either of those values. Numbers 3, 5, and 7 are examples of primes. The irreducibility of prime numbers makes them particularly interesting for number theorists.

The distribution of prime numbers among the integers is highly irregular, although there tend to be fewer primes to composites as the size of integers increases. There is a difference of 2 between some pairs of adjacent prime numbers—59 and 61, for example; such pairs are called twin primes.

For clarity in analysis, composites can be expressed as products of their prime factors raised to the appropriate powers, so $4,200 = 2^3 \times 3^1 \times 5^2 \times 7^1$, for example. One application of such analyses is in identifying coprimes, which are composite numbers that share no divisors besides 1—14 (divisors 1, 2, 7) and 15 (1, 3, 5), for example.

Testing primality

An integer can be proven to be a prime by checking that its division by any of the possible primes results in a nonzero remainder. This is a laborious task, but one that is well suited to execution by computers. The test ceases at prime number p, where $(p + 1)^2$ is greater than the number under test because a greater divisor would require a smaller prime to be cofactor of the test number

for that test number to be composite and all smaller primes have already been ruled out in earlier divisibility checks.

Euclid's proof of infinite primes

Around 300 B.C.E., the Greek geometer Euclid set forth in his book *Elements* a simple and elegant proof that there is an infinite number of primes. For any group of primes, represented by p_1, p_2, p_3,...p_n, a new prime number is given by adding 1 to the product of all the primes in the first group, so $p_{(n+1)} = p_1 \times p_2 \times p_3...\times p_n + 1$. Dividing $p_{(n+1)}$ by any of the original primes, represented by p_m, gives a remainder $1/p_m$. Hence, $p_{(n+1)}$ has no divisors among the original group of primes and is therefore a prime number in its own right.

Perfect numbers

Perfect numbers are integers that are the sums of all their divisors with the exception of the number itself. An example is 6, whose divisors are 1, 2, 3, and 6; the perfect-number property is revealed in the sum $1 + 2 + 3 = 6$. The divisors need not be primes, as is exemplified by 28: in the sum $28 = 1 + 2 + 4 + 7 + 14$, only 2 and 7 are primes.

▲ The seed head of this sunflower bears testament to the relevance of number theory to nature. The Fibonacci series starts 1, 1, 2, 3, 5, 8..., and each of its members is the sum of the two numbers that precede it. The seeds of this flower form 34 clockwise and 55 counterclockwise spirals; larger flowers have 89 clockwise and 144 counterclockwise spirals—34, 55, 89, and 144 are Fibonacci numbers. Other examples of Fibonacci numbers in nature include the arrangement of petals in daisies and that of the scales of pineapples.

Curiously, only even perfect numbers are known to date, although some number theorists believe high-valued odd perfects could exist.

Euclid produced a formula for generating even perfect numbers: $n = 2^{(p-1)} \times (2^p - 1)$, where n is the perfect number and p is a prime number such that $(2^p - 1)$ is also a prime. This condition excludes $p = 11$, since $2^{11} - 1 = 2{,}047$—the multiplication product of 23 and 89 and hence a composite. The lowest primes that can be used in this formula are therefore 2, 3, 5, 7, and 13.

When $p = 2$, Euclid's formula gives $2^{(2-1)} \times (2^2 - 1) = 2 \times 3 = 6$ (perfect); when $p = 3$, the formula gives $2^{(3-1)} \times (2^3 - 1) = 4 \times 7 = 28$ (perfect). The solutions to this equation increase almost exponentially with increasing p: $p = 5$ gives $n = 496$ ($= 2^4 \times 31^1 = 1 + 2 + 4 + 8 + 16 + 31 + 62 + 124 + 248$) and $p = 7$ gives $p = 8{,}128$ ($= 2^6 \times 127^1 = 1 + 2 + 4 + 8 + 16 + 32 + 64 + 127 + 254 + 508 + 1{,}016 + 2{,}032 + 4{,}064$). The "solution" for $p = 11$ would be $n = 2{,}096{,}128$, which is not a perfect number.

Mersenne numbers

At first, some theorists believed that a new prime number, p_2, could be generated from a known prime, p_1, by the formula $p_2 = 2^{p_1} - 1$. This formula works for the lower primes—$2^2 - 1 = 3$, $2^3 - 1 = 7$, $2^5 - 1 = 31$, and $2^7 - 1 = 127$—but has problems with $p_1 = 11$, which gives a composite.

In the early 17th century, the French monk Marin Mersenne published a list of prime numbers, p, for which $2^p - 1$ is also prime and can therefore be used in Euclid's perfect-number formula. Although his list was incomplete, solutions of $2^p - 1$ are called Mersenne numbers; those solutions that are also prime numbers are called Mersenne primes.

In the 1870s, the French mathematician Edouard Lucas devised a procedure for testing Mersenne numbers for primality. This test, refined in the 1930s by the U.S. mathematician Derrick Lehmer, has since become the basis for computer-executed primality tests. The largest number so far confirmed prime by the Lucas-Lehmer test is $2^{6,972,593} - 1$, verified in 1999, which has 2,098,960 digits.

Pythagorean triplets

In the 6th century B.C.E., the Greek philosopher Pythagoras developed the equation $x^2 + y^2 = z^2$ to relate the lengths x and y of the shorter sides of a right-angled triangle to the length z, its longer side, or hypotenuse. There is a set of three formulas for generating integral values of x, y, and z that fit this equation: $x = p^2 - q^2$, $y = 2pq$, and $z = p^2 + q^2$, where p and q are integers.

Fermat's last theorem

Fermat's last theorem is concerned with equations similar to those that generate Pythagorean triplets. Around 1630, the French mathematician Pierre de Fermat jotted a comment in a textbook to the effect that equations of the form $x^n + y^n = z^n$ have no whole-number solutions for values of n greater than 2, but that there was insufficient space for the proof in the margin of that page.

Fermat indeed proved his theorem for $n = 4$, and that proof can be extended to all even values of n. In 1770, the Swiss mathematician Leonhard Euler published a "proof" for $n = 3$, although that proof was later shown to be flawed. Other mathematicians produced proofs for special cases of the theorem, and calculations using computers demonstrated the validity of Fermat's theorem for values of n up to 4,000,000 by 1993. Nevertheless, a general proof remained elusive for many years.

A breakthrough in the quest for a general proof of Fermat's last theorem came from an unexpected area. In the 1980s, the German mathematician Gerhard Frey perceived that Fermat's last theorem could be proven if proof could be established for theorems of elliptic curves proposed by the Japanese mathematicians Yutaka Taniyama and Goro Shimura. The theorems were based on work started by Taniyama in 1955 and refined by French mathematician André Weil.

In 1993, the British mathematician Andrew Wiles put forward a supposed proof for the Shimura-Taniyama-Weil conjecture but soon withdrew his proposal, having become aware of a flaw. Undaunted, Wiles revised his proof and announced the result in 1994. The Wiles proof has since become widely accepted by mathematicians as proof for Fermat's last theorem and so has concluded almost 370 years of research.

 SEE ALSO: COMPUTER • MATHEMATICS • STATISTICS

Nutrition and Food Science

Nutrition is concerned with the way an organism takes in food and turns it into substances that can be used by the body. These substances, called nutrients, are essential for building and repairing body tissues and regulating body processes and act as fuel to provide the body with energy.

Thousands of chemicals are found in the foods commonly eaten by humans, but comparatively few are essential to health. Nutritionists classify these nutrients into six groups: water, fats, carbohydrates, proteins, vitamins, and minerals. Of these, the first four are termed *macronutrients*, because they are needed in large quantities by the body. Vitamins and minerals, though required in much smaller quantities, are just as important to growth and regulation of body functions and are termed *micronutrients*.

Water is of vital importance, because it acts as a solvent for transporting other nutrients around the body and carries waste materials away from cells. Humans can go for several weeks without taking in any of the other nutrient groups but can survive only one week without water. Adults should consume at least 4 pints (2.4 l) of water a day to maintain fluid balance and replace losses from excretion.

Types of nutrients

Nutrients used by the body fall into two categories; essential and nonessential. Essential nutrients cannot be synthesized by cells and so must be supplied to the body through food. These substances include inorganic compounds and a limited number of organic compounds. Nonessential

▲ Fresh fruit and vegetables are increasingly recognized as a vital part of a healthy diet, helping to combat a variety of medical disorders.

nutrients can be made from other substances in the body, though organisms will tend to use these nutrients directly if present in food rather than expend energy synthesizing them.

The main source of energy comes from carbohydrates. Carbohydrates include sugars and starches and are found in a wide range of foods, including bread, cereals, pasta, potatoes, and rice. Fats are a more concentrated source of energy but require more effort by the body to convert them into useful smaller molecules. Fats are made up of an alcohol (glycerol) and a fatty acid; the type of fatty acid determines whether the fat is classed as saturated, monounsaturated, or poly-unsaturated. Some polyunsaturated fatty acids cannot be manufactured by the body and must be included in the diet for the building of cell membranes. Typical sources include plant seed oils and oily fish, such as mackerel. Meat and dairy produce are the main sources of saturated fats. Monounsaturates are found in olives and various species of nut.

Proteins are of vital importance in a healthy diet because they supply the body with substances called amino acids. There are 20 amino acids, 11 of which can be manufactured by the body for creating hormones, enzymes, muscle, and antibodies. The remaining nine amino acids, called the essential amino acids, either can not be manufactured by the body or are manufactured in insufficient quantities. A number of foods, such as eggs, milk, lean meat, and cheese, can provide all the amino acids and are termed complete proteins. Vegetables, nuts, legumes, and cereals lack one or more amino acids and are described as incomplete proteins. However, eating two or more incomplete proteins together can usually provide the complete range of amino acids.

Micronutrients

Minerals are inorganic compounds needed in small amounts for the metabolism of the other nutrients. Most animals obtain minerals by eating plants, which absorb them from the ground, or by eating herbivorous animals. The major minerals needed by humans are calcium, magnesium, and phosphorus, which are essential for building the skeleton and teeth; iron and copper for regulation of the blood; and manganese and zinc for the action of key enzymes. Other minerals include sodium, sulfur, chromium, iodine, selenium, fluorine, and molybdenum.

Vitamins are also essential in small amounts for regulation of the chemical reactions in which food is turned into energy for use by the body. Vitamins are organic compounds and are denoted by a letter. Some are fat soluble (vitamins A, D, E, and K), and the others dissolve in water (vitamin C and the B group of eight vitamins). No food-stuff contains the entire range of vitamins, though some foods may contain several—green leafy vegetables, for example, are good sources of vitamins A, B_2, B_{12}, and K.

Balanced diets

To stay healthy, nutritionists and dieticians advise that humans eat a range of foods that can provide the body with all the chemical compounds it needs to function efficiently. They advocate that a certain number of portions of fruit and vegetables, dairy products, meat, fish and pulses, and bread and cereals be eaten per day to provide the recommended dietary allowances (RDA) of key nutrients. RDAs vary from country to country and are determined by age, sex, and occupation. Men working in very physical jobs, for example, have a greater need for energy-providing fats and carbohydrates than those in sedentary occupations. Children also need more calories than might be expected from their height and weight because they are growing. Similarly, pregnant women increase their intake of food temporarily because of the demands of the growing fetus.

Diets that consistently lack a key nutrient or group of foods can lead to a number of deficiency diseases. Such diseases predominate in developing countries, where food supplies may be irregular or inadequate. A major problem is protein-calorie malnutrition, which affects young children and is aggravated by common infections such as diarrhea. Lack of protein leads to a slow rate of growth, susceptibility to infections, and even death. A common mineral deficiency found in both developed and developing countries is a lack

▶ Mealtime aboard the space shuttle. Much research remains to be done on methods of providing a sustainable food supply on long-duration missions, such as those to Mars. Astronauts lose weight, muscle protein, and bone calcium while in space despite a seemingly adequate diet. Research into their nutritional needs to overcome these problems could have applications in degenerative diseases on Earth, such as osteoporosis and aging.

▼ Worries over the link between cholesterol and heart disease have led to the development of low-fat dairy products and fat substitutes in an effort to reduce the amount of saturated fats in Western diets. Some synthetic fats have been developed that cannot be broken down by digestive enzymes and are therefore not metabolized by the body.

of iron, leading to anemia, which causes tiredness, headaches, and dizziness through a lack of hemoglobin in the blood. A shortage of certain vitamins can lead to complaints like scurvy (lack of vitamin C), rickets (vitamin D), pellagra (a combination of the B vitamin niacin and the amino acid tryptophan), and xerophthalmia (vitamin A).

The concerns of the nutritionist and the food scientist are wide ranging. In the developing countries, they are concerned with developing strategies to solve the seemingly ever present food shortages and nutritionally related diseases (such as malnutrition, blindness, anemia, and goiter) that cause endless suffering. In Western countries, on the other hand, they are researching the effects of a very different kind of diet on what are commonly called the diseases of affluence: obesity, heart disease, cancer, and even dental caries.

Antioxidant vitamins

Since the 1990s, people in Western countries have been urged by nutritionists to eat more fruits and vegetables. The National Academy of Sciences in their 1989 report *Diet and Health* recommended that the U.S. population should eat five or more servings per day, especially yellow and green vegetables and citrus fruit. This is not simply a call to add some color to the country's dinner table but has much more serious implications for the health of the nation. One vital reason is that fruit and vegetables are major sources of important antioxidant nutrients—vitamin C, beta carotene (a precursor of vitamin A), and vitamin E. There is clear scientific evidence also that these nutrients can protect the body from a wide range of degenerative diseases, such as cancer, atherosclerosis, coronary heart diseases, and

rheumatoid arthritis, that are thought to involve agents known as free radicals. Free radicals are produced in the body as part of normal metabolism and are generally dealt with by the body's own array of defense mechanisms. They include the antioxidant vitamins, which are thought to prevent oxidation damage inside the body by stabilizing some of these free radicals and quenching the effect of others.

The greatest risk of disease seems to arise when production of these free radicals is increased by external factors such as air pollution, radiation, and cigarette smoke, and in such circumstances, the need for antioxidant nutrients becomes even more imperative. Smokers, in particular, are more likely to be deficient in vitamin C.

Research into these complex and wide ranging areas is still in its infancy, and much work needs to be done. Experts cannot agree, for example, whether supplements of antioxidant vitamins are as effective as increasing the intake of foods containing those vitamins (there may be other substances in the plant foods themselves that are also protective, such as glucosynilates found in green vegetables). The exact mechanisms relating to specific disease processes are not fully understood.

Beyond cholesterol

Antioxidant vitamins are also linked with another important area in nutrition research—the role of cholesterol in atherosclerosis and coronary heart disease. High levels of vitamin E may play an important role in preventing free radical damage

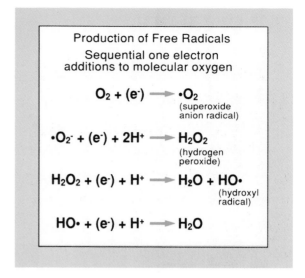

How free radicals—shown by the dot—are produced from molecular oxygen. Their unpaired electrons make them highly reactive.

Production of Free Radicals
Sequential one electron additions to molecular oxygen

$$O_2 + (e^-) \longrightarrow \cdot O_2$$
(superoxide anion radical)

$$\cdot O_2^- + (e^-) + 2H^+ \longrightarrow H_2O_2$$
(hydrogen peroxide)

$$H_2O_2 + (e^-) + H^+ \longrightarrow H_2O + HO\cdot$$
(hydroxyl radical)

$$HO\cdot + (e^-) + H^+ \longrightarrow H_2O$$

of cholesterol and the subsequent production of oxidation products that are more damaging to arteries than cholesterol itself. It has even been suggested that it may be low levels of antioxidant vitamins rather than high levels of cholesterol that are of greater importance in the development of heart disease.

The 1990s have certainly seen a move away from the view that dietary cholesterol is the "bad guy" in the heart disease story. While high levels of cholesterol in the blood are predictive of heart disease, this condition is not a result of eating foods high in cholesterol. Most cholesterol is in fact made within the body itself. The most important dietary influences on heart disease are surplus weight and eating a diet high in fat, particularly saturated fats: meat and dairy fats. The introduction in the 1960s of unsaturated soft vegetable margarines and the increasing use of (again, unsaturated) liquid vegetable oils for cooking certainly heralded the start of a decline in rates of heart disease in the United States. However, American diets are still seen as being too high in fat—a factor that increases the tendency of blood to clot and hence the risk of heart attack.

Some of the most recent research in this field has shown that fish oils can protect against heart disease by mechanisms that do not involve lowering blood cholesterol. The specific protective agents are two unsaturated fatty acids called eicosapentanoic acid (EPA) and docosahexaenoic acid (DHA). Long-term studies in several countries including the United States have shown that eating fish (especially oily varieties) just two or three times a week reduces rates of heart disease compared with eating none at all.

FACT FILE

- *Astronauts tend to eat more carbohydrate and less fat when in space. Favorite foods are peanut butter, flour tortillas, and fresh fruit. Most space foods are preserved by canning, freeze drying, or thermovacuum packing. The only foods not allowed are alcohol, carbonated drinks, foods that produce excessive crumbs, and those that do not store well at room temperature.*

- *NASA encourages the use of food as the primary source of nutrients whenever possible, rather than using vitamin and mineral supplements, because natural foods contain essential non-nutritive substances such as fiber and carotenoids. Natural food also provides an important sense of psychological well being.*

SEE ALSO: AMINO ACID • CARBOHYDRATE • FAT • METABOLISM • PROTEIN • VITAMIN

Observatory

The word *observatory* is commonly applied to a building in which astronomical observations are made, but it is also used for places where other physical phenomena are observed. There are, for example, meteorological, geomagnetic, volcano, and tidal observatories. The location and design of an observatory are decided in relation to the type of observation that is to be made.

History

Astronomical observatories have existed for thousands of years. One of the earliest and best known of these is Stonehenge in England. This ancient stone circle was built and added to over a period ranging from 3100 to 1100 B.C.E. Although its exact function is unknown, archeologists have shown that the northeast axis of Stonehenge is in line with the sunrise on the summer solstice, indicating a sophisticated awareness of the movement of the Sun. Similarly, it is known that 5,000 years ago the Babylonians observed the movement of the stars from the top of towers called ziggurats. In South America, the Maya built pyramids dating back as far as 500 B.C.E. that many archeologists believe had a function related to astronomical observations. All of these observatories, however,

▲ The Hubble Space Telescope is a cooperative project between the European Space Agency and NASA. Operational since the 1990s, this remarkable observatory has the advantage of being able to view images of celestial bodies with greater clarity and brightness than telescopes on Earth, because the Hubble telescope is not affected by the obscuring effect of the atmosphere.

permitted viewing celestial bodies only with the naked eye. It was not until the construction in 1608, by the Dutch spectacle maker Hans Lipperhey, of the first telescope that astronomers had the opportunity to observe the night sky in greater detail. Over the following centuries, many observatories using telescopes were constructed throughout the world, including those in Paris, Greenwich, England, and Washington, D.C.

Gradual improvements in technology have led to much larger telescopes, and the introduction of radio telescopes and space telescopes has expanded the range of activities possible in an astronomical observatory.

Choosing the site

When planning an astronomical observatory, it is necessary to find a site that provides frequent clear skies far away from the adverse effects of light pollution. In the past, astronomical observations were not affected by artificial lighting. William Herschel, for example, discovered the planet Uranus using a telescope set up in his backyard. Many amateur astronomers still observe the night sky in this way, though with increasing difficulty unless they live away from street lights. Clouds and atmospheric dust also interfere with optical astronomical observation, and there are advantages in observing from high altitudes, although many mountains attract clouds and high winds.

A study of meteorological conditions worldwide has shown that there are areas near the western coasts of the continents where clouds tend to remain at comparatively low levels in the atmosphere, and there are mountains which project above the clouds into air that is clear and dry and largely free from turbulence for many nights in the year. Most of the world's largest optical telescopes are located in these areas: in California and Mexico on the western coast of North America; in the Andes Mountains of South America; on the western side of South Africa; and in the Canary Islands, off the western coast of North Africa. The observatories in these places are mostly at heights of 1 to 2 miles (1.6–3.2 km) above sea level. One of the world's largest observatories is at a height of more than 2.5 miles (4 km) on the extinct volcano of Mauna Kea on the island of Hawaii in the Pacific Ocean.

Designing the building

Large optical telescopes are put out of adjustment by quite small temperature changes, so the observatory buildings are designed so that the telescopes are kept at the temperature of the air through which they will be observing. Vibrations must also be avoided, so the building is constructed in such a way that the effects of movements of people and machinery (such as elevators) are not transmitted to the piers on which the telescopes are mounted.

Observatories in space

By using rockets, astronomical instruments can be placed in orbit around Earth above the atmosphere. Several remote-controlled telescopes of specialized types have been functioning in that way for some years, including the Hubble Space Telescope. This space observatory has the advantage over earthbound observatories of a clear view without the distorting and obscuring effect of Earth's atmosphere. In addition, many parts of the electromagnetic spectrum cannot penetrate Earth's atmosphere, and some objects can therefore be observed only from space.

Optical telescope

The optical telescope is rightly regarded as the basic instrument of modern astronomy. Soon after its invention in the early 1600s, it was used by Galileo Galilei to make a number of significant observations. Through the years, the telescope has been improved and developed. With the invention first of photography and then of electronic detectors, the optical telescope has continued to lead to new discoveries, and it is as important to astronomy in the Space Age as it was in the Renaissance.

Telescopes can make distant objects appear nearer, and so larger, and can reveal details that are too small to be resolved by the unaided eye. But for astronomy, the facility of the telescope that is most significant is its ability to gather light so that objects can be detected and studied that are otherwise too faint to be visible.

Refractor telescopes

The first telescopes used a lens as the objective to collect the light from the distant object and bring it to a focus. Another lens was then used as the eyepiece to magnify and display the image formed by the objective. Such a telescope is called a refractor. Because a simple lens brings light of different wavelengths to different focal positions, the image has colored fringes, an effect called chromatic aberration. Thin lenses with long focal length produce less chromatic aberration than thick, short-focus lenses. For this reason, astronomical telescopes were usually made very long, the objective being suspended high above the eyepiece by an arrangement of poles and pulleys.

▼ An aerial view of Mauna Kea, Hawaii, showing (from left to right) the 1.9 ft. (0.6 m) University of Hawaii telescope, the 9.8 ft. (3 m) NASA infrared telescope (standing alone on the upper left of the picture), the 12.4 ft. (3.8 m) British infrared telescope (in the building with the dome shutter open), the 7.2 ft. (2.2 m) University of Hawaii telescope, and on the far right, the 11.8 ft. (3.6 m) telescope jointly funded by Canada, France, and Hawaii. The summit of this extinct volcano (seen to the extreme right of the picture) is 14,000 ft. (4,300 m) above sea level—well above the clouds, which lie at about 10,000 ft. (3,000 m).

Modern lenses are achromatic, producing an image that is virtually free of chromatic aberration. They are composed of two or more lenses made of different types of glass chosen so that the aberration of one component cancels out that of the other. It was a refractor with an achromatic lens that was used to discover the tiny, faint, white dwarf star that accompanies the brightest star in the night sky, Sirius.

The largest refractor ever built has an aperture of 40 in. (1.01 m) and is at Yerkes Observatory. It is unlikely that larger refractors will ever be used for astronomical work.

Reflector telescopes

A lens is not the only optical device that can be used to collect and focus light; a concave mirror will do the same, reflecting the incoming light to the focal position. Reflector telescopes do not have chromatic aberration, and they can be made with larger apertures than refractors. The focus to which incoming light is brought by a concave mirror is not conveniently placed for observation, and two, three, or more other mirrors may be used to bring the light to a convenient focal point. Although the mirror of a reflector is usually

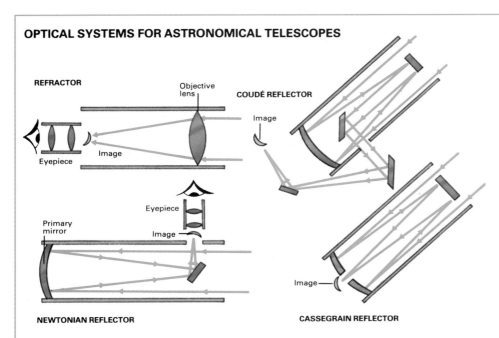

OPTICAL SYSTEMS FOR ASTRONOMICAL TELESCOPES

REFRACTOR

Objective lens

COUDÉ REFLECTOR

Image

Eyepiece

Image

Eyepiece

Image

Primary mirror

Image

NEWTONIAN REFLECTOR

Image

CASSEGRAIN REFLECTOR

◄ The principles of the optical system of four types of astronomical telescopes: the refracting, Newtonian, Coudé, and Cassegrain. Newton's telescope represented a breakthrough in that it used a mirror rather than a lens to form the image. Mirrors do not require the same degree of high optical standards that lenses need and, in addition, do not cause chromatic aberration (the colored fringes in an image caused by the splitting of light into its spectrum by a lens). The Cassegrain mirror was proposed by the French scientist N. Cassegrain in 1672, and a century later, it was found that this design reduces the spherical aberration that produces blurring. This type of design has also been used in radio transmitters and receivers.

made of glass, the reflecting surface is actually a thin layer of metal (usually aluminum) deposited on shaped glass.

The mirrors and the camera (or other type of detector used) have to be held rigidly in relation to one another within the telescope, and the whole instrument has to be able to swing around so as to point to any part of the sky. It must also be able to drive steadily in a direction opposite to the rotation of Earth, so long-exposure photographs can be taken. Large modern telescopes are driven by electric motors controlled by microcomputers, and many of the observations are made with electronic detectors.

Wide-field telescopes

A reflector or refractor telescope generally gives high-quality images only close to the central axis, and so the field of view is small. In 1930, Bernhard Voldemar Schmidt, an Estonian lens and mirror maker, designed a telescope that combined special lenses and a main mirror so as to give a wide-angle view with high-quality images over the whole field. Schmidt telescopes have been used to produce photographic atlases of the sky. A typical photograph taken with a large Schmidt telescope in an hour-long exposure covers an area of sky of perhaps 6 degrees by 6 degrees and contains approximately a million images of stars and galaxies. To study and measure such a photograph by eye would take an extremely long time. Automatic scanning machines have been developed to extract the information recorded in these photographs in a form suitable for computer processing. Hubble uses a wide-field camera to photograph the planets.

Radio telescopes

The radio telescope was invented in 1931 by a U.S. radio engineer, Karl Jansky. Because radio telescopes are not dependent on the night sky for their observations, they can be used during the day as well as the night. They must, however, be located on sites that are not affected by local artificial sources of radio waves.

▶ The 4 ft. (1.2 m) U.K. Schmidt telescope is, effectively, a large camera that provides a wide-angle view of galaxies. Faint objects in distant clouds have to be probed with giant remote reflectors.

SEE ALSO: ASTRONOMY • LENS • LIGHT AND OPTICS • MIRROR • RADIO ASTRONOMY • TELESCOPE, OPTICAL • TELESCOPE, SPACE

Obstetrics and Gynecology

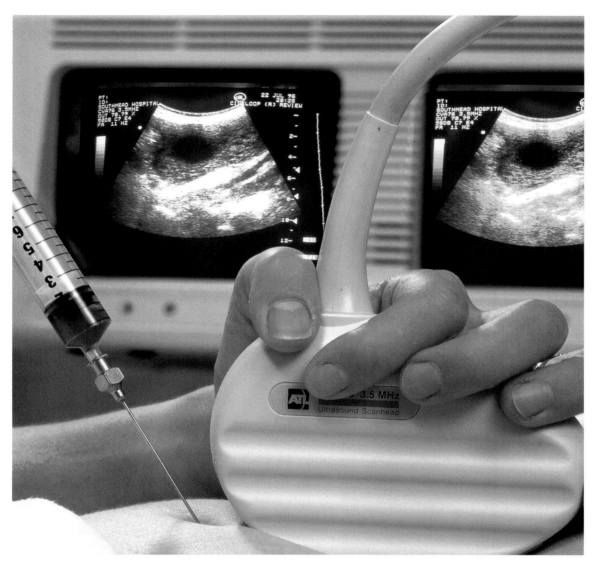

◄ Chorionic villus sampling is usually conducted between 9 and 12 weeks into a pregnancy to evaluate the possibility of any abnormality in the fetus. The doctor holds an ultrasound emitter on the woman's abdomen while drawing a sample into a syringe. The ultrasound scanners in the background enable the doctor to see the position of the fetus and guide the needle to the chorionic villi tissue located in the placenta.

Obstetrics and gynecology are two closely related medical specialties concerned exclusively with women. Obstetrics is concerned with all aspects of pregnancy and childbirth, gynecology with disorders that affect the reproductive system in women, whether or not they are pregnant.

Obstetricians are involved with pregnancies from the earliest stages to give maximum safety to mother and child. As soon as a woman becomes pregnant, the obstetrician wants to know as much as possible about her physical and psychological state and about the genetic health of the embryo.

Later, as the embryo develops into a fetus, it is vital to check that everything is proceeding normally. One of the most valuable ways of monitoring fetal development is by ultrasound screening. Modern, high-resolution ultrasound scanners can safely monitor fetal vitality and rate of growth, diagnose twin pregnancies, check the position of the fetal feeding organ (the placenta), detect vari-

ous abnormalities, and toward the end of pregnancy, check whether the fetus is lying in a suitable position for safe delivery.

It is not only when a woman is pregnant that checkups are needed. Gynecologists are often concerned with problems associated with menstruation. They also investigate and, if possible, treat many cases of infertility. They deal with many cases of pelvic pain and backache and of infection and tumors of the pelvic organs. Since the female reproductive system is so much under the control of hormones, the gynecologist must also be an expert on endocrinology and will often prescribe hormone therapy.

Laser treatment

Women who suffer from menstrual problems may benefit from removal of the endometrium—the lining of the uterus, which normally comes away at each menstrual period. The original procedure involved dilation of the cervix so that the obstetrician could scrape away the endometrium using a sharp-edged wooden spoon. The technique that replaced this method, laser ablation of the endometrium, became widely used in the 1990s. It involves inserting a fine catheter, which can be undertaken with much less dilation and risk of pain, and the use of a laser to destroy the lining.

In vitro fertilization

One way in which many infertile couples can have children is by the technique of in vitro fertilization—popularly called the "test tube" baby method. In this situation, both partners are fertile but the process of conception is prevented because, for some reason, the sperm cannot reach the egg. To overcome this, the woman's eggs are taken from her and placed in fluid in a warm sterile dish (in vitro means "in glass"). Her partner's sperm are then added, and fertilization occurs in the dish. In a development announced in 1993, some clinics are offering a choice of the child's sex. Though there are slight differences in behavior of the XX chromosomes in female-producing sperm and the XY chromosomes in male-producing sperm, distinction has not yet proved to be reliable enough to confidently predict sex.

Obstetricians can watch the early development of the fertilized egg under a microscope. If all goes well, they place the fertilized ovum in the uterus to develop normally.

Chorionic villus sampling

Recent developments have included screening fetuses for inherited diseases and for tissue or blood type. Very early in pregnancy, the fertilized egg divides into a part that will form the fetus and a part that will form the structure that nourishes the fetus throughout the pregnancy (the placenta). The latter starts off in the form of small fingerlike structures that grow out from the embryo into the wall of the uterus. These structures are called chorionic villi. Because both the villi and the fetus come from the same fertilized cell, they have exactly the same chromosomes. Therefore, a microscopic sample of chorionic villi provides detailed knowledge of the genetic constitution of the future baby.

Chorionic villi can be obtained from about the eighth week of the pregnancy onwards, either by passing a fine tube through the neck of the uterus (the cervix) or by passing a needle into the uterus through the abdominal wall. The obstetrician can then study the future baby's chromosomes. Conditions such as Down's syndrome, in which there are visible chromosome abnormalities, can immediately be detected.

Other conditions that can be diagnosed by villus sampling at an early stage of pregnancy include sickle cell disease, cystic fibrosis, Duchenne muscular dystrophy, hemophilia, phenylketonuria, retinitis pigmentosa, and retinoblastoma. All these conditions are serious, and some may prove fatal. Chorionic villus sampling provides parents with the possible option of agreeing to early termination of the pregnancy, a moral consideration that concerns obstetricians and parents alike. Additional moral considerations arise in cases where parents have selected an embryo whose tissue or blood type is similar to an older sibling's with a view to providing tissue or blood cells to cure a disease.

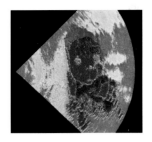

▲ This false-color ultrasound scan shows a frontal view of a human fetus in the uterus at approximately six months.

Amniocentesis

Pregnant women over the age of 35 are now commonly advised to undergo an amniocentesis. The fluid that surrounds the growing fetus is called amniotic fluid. The fetus swallows some of this fluid. It also urinates and casts off skin cells into it. A sample of the amniotic fluid can thus provide material for testing for various abnormalities.

To obtain the sample the obstetrician passes a long needle attached to a syringe through the wall of the abdomen (which is under local anesthesia) and into the fluid in the uterus. A sample is then sucked out. The whole process can be viewed in real time on an ultrasonic scanner, which shows the uterus, the amniotic sac, and the needle.

An important finding may be the presence of raised levels of a substance produced by the fetus called alpha-fetoprotein. Abnormal levels alert doctors to the possibility of such conditions as Down's syndrome or spina bifida.

Ultrasound is also used to give the obstetrician a clear picture of the fetus. Although minor defects cannot be spotted, it is routinely used because it is nonintrusive and cannot harm the fetus.

◄ Routine ultrasound imaging of the fetus is used to monitor growth and detect problems.

SEE ALSO:	Blood • Hormone • Pediatrics • Population • Reproduction • Ultrasonics

Oceanography

◀ Relief map of the seafloor obtained using satellite altimetry. The deepest areas are shown in purple. The Mid-Atlantic Ridge, an area of seafloor spreading can clearly be seen as a pale green line between the continents of America and Africa. The deeper regions just off the continental shelves are a source of nutrients, which are brought nearer the coastline by upwelling, making the coastal waters the most productive areas of the sea.

Oceanography is the study of all aspects of the sea. It includes the physical and chemical properties of water itself, the plants and animals that live in it, and the geology of the seabed. The oceans of the world remain the least explored regions of the planet. It is only in the last 50 years that mountains and canyons higher and deeper than any on the surface have been discovered beneath the waves. Ecosystems that exist in these regions are largely unexplored and populated with unknown species that could provide clues as to how organisms survive in hostile environments in other parts of the Solar System. However, discovering the secrets of the deep poses a greater technological challenge than getting a man into space.

Types of oceanography

Oceanography is a wide-ranging subject divided into smaller disciplines. Physical oceanography is concerned with the physical nature of the water itself—including salinity, temperature, density, pressure, electric conductivity, and transmission of light, radio, and sound waves.

Dynamic oceanography looks at the motion of seawater—waves, tides, and deep-sea currents. More especially, it studies the energy that is carried by this motion. Already, waves and tides have been used as renewable sources of energy.

Chemical oceanography emphasizes the chemistry of seawater, especially the trace elements dissolved in it. Several chemical and biological cycles take place in the ocean, and the study of these cycles gives clues to the origin and development of the oceans.

Biological oceanography focuses on the diverse forms of life that exist in and on the sea. It looks at their life cycles, their interrelations, and their relationships with their environment. The overall ecology of the sea and the survival of endangered species is its particular concern.

Finally, geological oceanography is concerned with the geology of the seabed and the rocks and the marine sediments that make it up. It looks especially at ocean ridges and troughs, the magnetism of the rocks, heat flow from the ocean floor, and underwater volcanoes.

More than 70 percent of Earth's surface is covered by water, and oceanography has contributed much to the total scientific understanding of Earth. However, it was not until the 1960s that much effort was made to study and explore the ocean depths, and it was then that the concept of seafloor spreading was first postulated. The concept was developed into the theory of plate tectonics, which maintains that the continents move around the globe on huge crustal plates. Between these plates, magma from Earth's core spews up, forcing the plates apart. Where the plates collide—for example, where the African plate forces Italy into Europe—mountains are formed.

This revolutionary theory led teams of scientists from all disciplines to turn their attention to the sea and coastal environments. As a result, the 1970s were designated the International Decade of Ocean Exploration (IDOE).

The oceans and seas contain about 35 million cubic miles (1.5 billion km³) of water, and its average depth is about 2.5 miles (4 km). The greatest depth does not occur in the middle of the oceans but in trenches at the continental margins. The deepest is the Marianas Trench in the Pacific Ocean, which drops to more than 6.9 miles (11 km) below sea level. The continental shelves are about 656 ft. (200 m) below sea level.

The sea level itself has varied considerably since the oceans were first formed, mainly because of the spreading of glaciers from the polar ice cap and their subsequent melting. The current level of the sea stabilized about 5,000 years ago. Since then, it has risen by only about 15 ft. (5 m). At present, the overall level is rising by around 0.04 in. (1 mm) per year. The effect on the coastline appears more dramatic though, because of erosion and the tilting of the tectonic plates, which is especially prevalent along the Pacific coast. Around New England, the records since 1940 show the coastline submerging at about 0.12 in. (3 mm) annually, and the submergence rate along the Gulf coast is about 0.6 in. (15 mm) a year.

Temperature

The mean temperature of the oceans is about 39°F (4°C). Between the tropics, the temperature of the surface water is between 75 and 80°F (24–27°C). However, the temperature drops markedly toward the polar regions, where it reaches 28°F (−2°C), except where it is warmed by strong currents from the equator.

▲ A sediment trap being deployed at a mooring on the Ross Ice Shelf in the Antarctic. The Antarctic is one of the most productive regions of the ocean, but comparatively little is known about life in its inhospitable waters.

▼ This Pisces class submersible is capable of diving to depths of 6,000 ft. (2,000 m).

It was once thought that, apart from the influence of such currents, the temperature of the sea was uniform. The IDOE program discovered enormous pools of water that are between 34 and 35°F (18–19°C) warmer or cooler than their surroundings. These pools are up to 984 ft. (300 m) in depth and 932 miles (1500 km) in diameter.

Density and salinity

The density of seawater is determined by its temperature and salinity—that is, how much salt is dissolved in it. Seawater—like pure water—has its maximum density at around 39°F (4°C). As it cools, it becomes denser and sinks, displacing warmer water to the surface. Once it becomes colder than 39°F, it becomes less dense again and rises. This explains why water does not freeze at the bottom.

The salinity of the sea varies too. It is affected by the dissolved minerals brought into the sea by rivers. The mean salt content of seawater is about 3.5 percent by weight. About 78 percent of the dissolved salt is sodium chloride, but magnesium chloride, magnesium sulfate, calcium sulfate, potassium sulfate, magnesium bromide, and calcium carbonate are also present in seawater. It is this dissolved salt that is the most undesirable characteristic of seawater, making it useless for drinking and irrigation and highly corrosive.

Salt also makes seawater a good conductor of electricity, which makes it practically impenetrable to radio waves. Submarines can communicate with the surface only by using low-frequency radio waves, which carry information very slowly. Sound waves, however, travel well through seawater. An explosion that can be heard half a mile away on land can be heard for thousands of miles underwater. This characteristic is exploited by sonar and animals such as dolphins and whales.

A SUNLESS OASIS ON THE SEABED

What is the difference between a hot desert and the deep-sea floor? One is hot and dry, and the other cold and wet. It may seem remarkable, but apart from these basic differences, the two environments are very similar. Both are exposed to extremes of temperature; both include huge tracts of completely barren land where there is almost no food. So when a group of scientists descended 1.5 miles (2.5 km) down to one part of the Pacific Ocean floor, they were astonished to find the area teeming with life.

Surrounding small circular vents in Earth's crust was a strange community of creatures: huge worms with scarlet crowns protruding out of white tubes attached to rock, clams and amber-colored mussels, an extraordinary red fish that hovered with its head inside the vent, and a host of other bizarre creatures.

The reason for the scientists' astonishment is easy to understand. The basis for the production of food and the sustaining of life is photosynthesis. In the sea, the Sun's rays grow progressively weaker the farther they penetrate. At a depth of 325 ft. (100 m), they are so diminished that photosynthesis can no longer take place. So what could such a dense concentration of life possibly live on, when the source of food had dried up 1.5 miles above?

Part of the answer to this puzzling enigma came from a side effect of the formation of new crust—the temperature of the water. The temperature of ocean water at this depth should be around freezing point, but the geophysicists found it to be a surprisingly warm 68°F (20°C). The closer they got to the vent, the warmer the water became, and when they measured it directly over one particular vent, they found it was as high as 662°F (350°C). The enormous pressures at these depths prevent the water from boiling.

One theory to explain this phenomenon is that the cold water seeps through porous rock in the crust, meets the molten rock underneath, becomes superheated, and shoots out through the vents at high speed, warming the whole area.

Laboratory analysis of the water showed that it contained up to three or four times more bacteria than typical surface water—as much food as any surface fish would need, and certainly enough for the vent colony.

The bacteria grow in clumps on the walls and sides of the vents where the temperature is at its highest. When a clump is large enough, it breaks free and is carried upward by the hot water rushing out of the vents. Some clumps of bacteria are large enough to be eaten by filter feeders.

The filter feeders of the vents are called vestimentifera and include huge worms—some more than 10 ft. (3 m) long—anemones, and mussels. Some of the worms cling to the sides of the vent chimneys in temperatures of about 68°F (20°C), and others, called Pompeii worms, live in really hot water near the vent openings. Higher in the food chain are crabs and fish,

▲ Giant tube worms near an undersea vent. They live by filter feeding but ultimately, as all vent creatures, depend on the presence of sulfur bacteria for nourishment.

which scavenge on the sea floor or in the mouths of the vents for large clumps of bacteria or other animals.

The discovery of this extraordinary environment at the bottom of the sea, however, was to prove only the first surprise for the explorers. Study of the creatures themselves was to yield even more baffling questions. As soon as the biologists got one of the worms to the surface, they started laboratory work on it and found that it had no mouth, no gut, and no anus. How did it feed, digest, and excrete?

When they cut the worm open, they found a large organ called the trophosome. The trophosome is also found in the class Hydrozoa, which includes various jellyfish, and plays a role in providing nutrition.

In it they found enzymes that are active in the production of food by chemoautotrophy. They were even more surprised when they found another set of enzymes, because they turned out to be photosynthetic.

It is difficult to reach hard and fast conclusions about exactly what goes on in such complex food chains, but scientists believe that some of the bacteria are free floating, and others live inside the bodies of the giant tube worms. The worms are able to transport the sulfides from the water via their blood to the bacteria, which, in turn, supply their hosts with food. Both the vestimentifera and the bacteria need each other to survive. If this is so, the vestimentifera will be the first animals found to depend on the heat inside Earth rather than that directly from the Sun. Further research showed that other vent animals, including clams, also obtain food in this way.

◄ The submersible *Alvin* is capable of withstanding pressure at extreme depths of the ocean. The *Alvin* is the deepest-diving submersible currently in use by the U.S. Navy.

The immense hydrostatic pressures at great depths can crush all but the strongest vessels. At the mean sea depth of 13,124 ft. (4,000 m), the pressure is equivalent to 388 atmospheres; at the bottom of the Marianas Trench, it reaches more than 1070 atmospheres. The pressure increases at a rate of around one atmosphere for each 33.9 ft. (10.3 m).

Oceanic studies

The systematic exploration of the ocean depths started with the Deep Sea Drilling Project, when the specially built craft *Glomar Challenger* began drilling and recovering ocean-floor samples from nearly 500 deep-sea sites. Thirty years on, the Ocean Drilling Program, as it has now become, using its research ship, the *JOIDES Resolution*, has drilled over 2,000 holes into Earth's crust and has made several significant discoveries. It has proved that plate tectonics is responsible for continents moving and the creation of ocean basins through seafloor spreading. Drilled cores have shown that Earth's climate has alternated between a freezer and a greenhouse repeatedly in cycles lasting from hundreds to thousands of years. The program has also found evidence that a giant meteorite hit Earth 65 million years ago, leading to the extinction of most life forms on the planet, including the dinosaurs. In 1998, millions of bacteria were found in sediments half a mile down on the seafloor off New Guinea. Experts predict that life will soon be found at even deeper levels.

▶ The Gulf Stream is a western boundary current that originates along the east coast of the United States. Boundary currents result from the interaction of the ocean basin topography, the direction of prevailing winds, and the motion induced by Earth's rotation. The estuaries of Chesapeake and Delaware Bays and the Grand Banks region off Nova Scotia show areas of high productivity (red), resulting from nutrient runoff from land sources. The blue eddies are warm core rings that form when a meander separates from the main current.

New research is focusing on ways to safely exploit vast reserves of gas hydrates lying under the seabed, which have the potential to be a major energy resource in the 21st century. Studies will also be carried out in the Arctic Ocean to investigate its role in ocean heat circulation and its implications for climate change.

The part played by the oceans in climate change has been the subject of a major research program since the 1990s. The World Ocean Circulation Experiment is a cooperative study by 30 nations to determine the global movement of water bodies and their thermodynamics. The density of the oceans is determined by their temperature and salinity. As ocean water evaporates, it makes the water more dense, thus lowering the temperature and making the water more saline. Generally, the upper layer of the ocean is less dense than the lower level because it is warmed by the Sun. The effect of Earth's rotation induces currents in the oceans that force these two layers to mix and carry warm surface waters from the equator toward the poles.

From their observations, scientists have been able to draw up a circulation map of a "global conveyor belt" for heat. Cold water travels down the east coast of the Americas to the Antarctic, becoming colder and saltier before it begins to move northward along the east coast of Australia. As the current passes the equator, it begins to warm. This warm current loops back as it reaches the coast of Japan, passing through the islands of Indonesia into the Indian Ocean. From there, it travels down and around the tip of South Africa

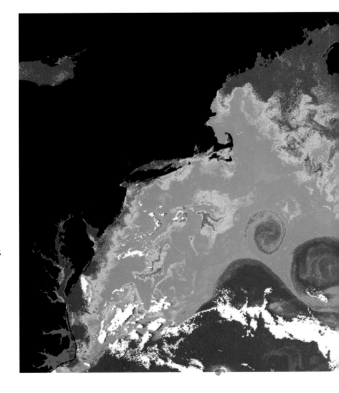

before rising northward again along the west African coast to the Arctic, where the warm current gives up its heat to the atmosphere and the cycle begins once more. This global circuit can take up to 1,000 years to complete.

Satellite observations

Oceanographic satellites are used to study the sea. The first, Seasat, was launched in 1978. It circled Earth 14 times a day and observed 95 percent of the ocean every 36 hours. It used radar altimeters, visible, infrared, and microwave radiometers to study sea-surface winds, sea-surface temperatures, wave heights, ice, and the varying height of the sea.

It was followed by the SeaStar satellite, which carried an instrument called SeaWiFS (Sea-viewing Wide Field-of-view Sensor) to record the "color" of the oceans. The sensor, being more sensitive than the human eye, can pick up the distribution of phytoplankton, sediments, and dissolved organic chemicals, which show up as different colors against the blue of the oceans. Phytoplankton are an important indicator of the health and productivity of the sea, because they are the beginning of the food chain for other marine animals. They are also critical to the balance of carbon dioxide in the atmosphere, absorbing it for photosynthesis and releasing oxygen as a by-product. Furthermore, phytoplankton act as a carbon "sink," locking it into sediments when they die and descend to the seafloor, thus preventing it from accumulating in the atmosphere as carbon dioxide.

The TOPEX/Poseidon satellite has been measuring changes in sea level since it was launched in 1992. Data obtained so far have indicated that contrary to the view that most ocean warming occurs in surface waters, midwater layers are heating fastest. If this finding proves to be the case, it could have a significant impact by altering ocean current patterns that mix nutrient-rich bottom waters with surface layers. In turn, any change in the direction of heat circulation could affect the climate as well as the biology and chemistry of the oceans.

Underwater exploration

There are about 70 submersibles in the world capable of descending to depths greater than 686 ft. (200 m), and only four are capable of descending to half the ocean's depth. Most of them are used in the oil and gas fields off the United States and in the North Sea. In most of them, the crew of two or three researchers, a pilot, and instruments are housed in a metallic sphere about 7 ft. (2.14 m) in diameter. Normal atmospheric pres-

▲ Biologists regularly trawl the seabed to ascertain the distribution of species that can tell them about environmental conditions in an area of the ocean. The main catch here is sea cucumbers and small crustaceans.

sure is maintained inside so no special suits are required. The U.S. Navy's *Trieste* dived to a depth of 6.2 miles (10 km) as early as 1962, but the deepest-diving submersible currently in use, the *Alvin*, can reach only 63 percent of the ocean floor. For coastal zone exploration, the DeepWorker, a one-person submersible, has been developed for depths up to 2,000 ft. (650 m), which is well beyond the depth that SCUBA can be used. Remote-operated vehicles are also used in conjunction with camera systems, shipboard tracking systems, and up-to-date navigation tools.

Resources

Oceanography has also been concerned with ocean resources, and one of the most economically important resources the oceans have to offer is its fisheries. Animal life of one kind or other exists at all depths of the oceans in great abundance. Nearly half of all classes of animals are marine and about 25 million tons of fish are harvested from the sea each year.

The oceans are also a rich source of minerals. Solar sea salt is produced in about 60 countries. Just over 38 percent of the world's salt consumption comes from evaporated seawater. Its estimated value is over $400 million a year.

Over 13 percent of bromine comes from seawater, as does 70 percent of the magnesium metal and 33 percent of the magnesium compounds used by industry. Sulfur is produced from two salt domes just off the coast of Louisiana. The sea is also a source of potassium and iodine.

SEE ALSO: AQUACULTURE • CLIMATOLOGY • DESALINATION • DIVING SUIT • FISHING INDUSTRY • GEOPHYSICS • HALOGEN • MARINE BIOLOGY • PLATE TECTONICS • SALT PRODUCTION • SATELLITE, ARTIFICIAL • SONAR • SUBMERSIBLE • TIDE • UNDERSEA HABITAT

Oil Exploration and Production

Oil exploration is the search for large natural reservoirs of crude oil by first locating the types of rock structures associated with oil deposits. Where suitable geological structures are found, the drilling of test wells is the only way to determine whether those structures hold oil and, if they do, whether that oil can be extracted in a commercially viable process. Test drilling is the greatest contributor to the development cost of a potential oil field—a cost that may be billions of dollars in the case of a large offshore oil field.

Oil production is the exploitation of an oil deposit through shafts drilled through its cap rock. In some cases, the pressure of the oil is sufficient to drive it to the surface; in others, pumping and a variety of other techniques are employed. Oil extracted by these techniques can be led from the wellhead to refineries by pipelines, or it can be loaded into ships that ferry it between offshore production platforms and oil-handling quays.

Initial exploration

Exploration starts with assessment of existing geological data of a region of interest, supplemented by studies of outcrops, which are the parts of inclined rock strata that break the surface. Fossils and associated material help to date and identify rocks, and accurate measurements of age can be obtained by analysis of the isotopic compositions of rocks. These techniques help identify rock strata that are of an age and type of material consistent with petroleum formation.

Observations of surface contours can give some idea of how these rock strata continue underground, and more precise details of the depths of rock strata near the surface are obtained by the analysis of carefully logged soil and rock cores taken from test bores. Geophysical exploration methods—principally, magnetic and gravimetric surveys and, above all, seismometric exploration—provide information about rock structures deep underground.

Seismometric surveying

The speed at which shock waves travel through different types of rocks varies according to the properties of each type of rock. Because of this variation, boundaries between rocks of different types cause shock waves to be reflected, just as light waves are reflected at boundaries between

▲ A line of drilling rigs being used to conduct seismic surveys on the Norwegian island of Spitsbergen. The specially designed rigs are mounted on sledge runners for maneuverability. Holes 60 ft. (20 m) deep are drilled at 150 ft. (50 m) intervals across the glacier surface. Charges detonated in the holes emit shock waves, which are reflected back from the rock strata below to provide a seismic profile of the area. The results can then be analyzed for signs of oil-bearing rock.

different transparent media, such as glass and air. Seismometric surveyors measure reflected shock waves and analyze them to determine the depths of boundaries between strata of different rocks. In particular, the time taken for an echo of a shock wave to arrive at Earth's surface helps determine the depth of the boundary between rock strata from which it was reflected.

The instruments that detect shock waves are called geophones; they are extremely sensitive accelerometers. Seismometers use signals from geophones to measure the time that shock waves, often produced by the detonation of solid explosives or combustible gas-and-air mixtures, take to reflect or refract from rock boundaries and reach the geophones. A good impression of the underground rock structure can be built up by combining a large number of seismometric tests.

Apart from controlled explosions, means for producing shock waves for seismometry include the use of falling heavy weights. Some surveys use "vibroseis" trucks that thump the ground beneath them at specific frequencies.

Magnetometric surveying

Earth's magnetic field varies with position and with time and also as a consequence of magnetic storms. Igneous and metamorphic rocks are slightly magnetic, and the orientations of their magnetic fields correspond to the orientation of Earth's magnetic field at the time of their formation. In contrast, sedimentary rocks are essentially nonmagnetic. Sedimentary rocks are the only type capable of holding petroleum deposits, so the presence of large "basins" of sedimentary rocks are of particular interest to oil explorers.

The "frozen-in" magnetism of igneous and metamorphic rocks modifies the local magnetic field. The size of the distortion at Earth's surface helps determine the depth of magnetic rock strata below nonmagnetic sedimentary rocks, thereby indicating the thickness of the sedimentary layer.

The results of magnetometric surveys are not easy to interpret, but such surveys have the advantage that they can be done rapidly and economically from an aircraft flying over land or sea. The survey aircraft carries the magnetometer in its tail or, more usually, trails it on a lead. The instrument measures minute variations in magnetic field as the aircraft flies at constant altitude along a set pattern of flight lines. Meanwhile, the magnetic readings are recorded continuously.

Gravimetric surveying

Gravitation is an attraction between masses; the greater the concentration of mass in an object, the stronger its gravitational field. Accordingly, Earth's gravitational field varies from place to place according to the densities of the rocks near the surface. Dense base rocks make a greater contribution to the gravitational field than do less dense sedimentary rocks. Consequently, a localized dip in the gravitational field indicates the likely location of a sedimentary basin, and the size of the dip gives an indication of the likely thickness of the sedimentary layer.

Instruments that measure gravitational fields are called gravimeters. They may be used on land or mounted on gyroscopically stabilized platforms for use on board ships or even planes.

Satellite surveying

Images from satellites are useful in identifying regions where oil deposits might be found. Visible-radiation images show the relief of the land, which can hint at underground structures, as well as indicate types of surface vegetation, giving a clue to the type of rock or soil at the surface. Radar images also provide information about the surface topography, and they have the advantage of being able to penetrate cloud cover, which can obscure visible images. The images from satellites are particularly useful when correlated with the results of geophysical surveys.

Test wells

The combinations of results from geophysical and satellite surveys guide oil explorers in their choices of locations for drilling one or more test wells, which are the only way of determining with certainty whether a rock structure contains oil.

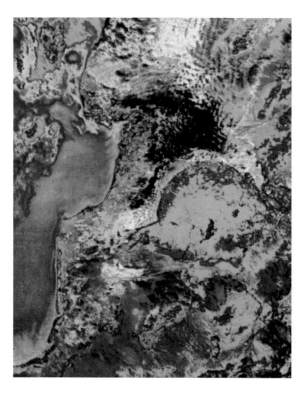

◄ Aerial surveys can be used to identify potential sites of mineral and oil deposits for further investigation using seismic surveys.

FORMATION OF OIL RESERVOIRS

The process that formed current reserves of petroleum—crude oil, natural gas, and bitumen—started many millions of years ago with the formation of silty sediments on the ocean floors. Bacteria converted the organic content of these silt beds—the remains of free-floating marine organisms called plankton—into an insoluble bituminous substance called kerogen.

As further silt deposited on these beds, the pressure and temperature in them increased to such an extent that the kerogen started to break down to form liquid and gaseous hydrocarbons—the components of crude oil and natural gas. The inorganic content of the silt and dead organisms formed a porous matrix through which these products could move.

The exact composition of the hydrocarbon mixture produced in this process depends on the temperature and pressure within the rocks. At greater depths and higher temperatures—depths approaching 16,000 ft. (4,900 m) and temperatures close to 300°F (150°C)—greater proportions of natural gas and low-molecular-weight (lighter) hydrocarbons form; at depths closer to 2,500 ft. (750 m), less gas is produced, and the mean molecular weight of the hydrocarbons is greater.

At one extreme of conditions, younger petroleum formed at lesser depths and lower temperatures tends to be darker and more viscous and has a greater proportion of aromatic hydrocarbons. Older oil from greater depths and higher temperatures tends to be lighter in color, have lower viscosity, and be more aliphatic.

Once oil has formed, it tends to migrate upward, since its density is less than that of the water and rocks around it. The oil moves as an extremely dilute solution or as an emulsion in water. The upward migration proceeds as long as the oil (and natural gas) encounter porous rocks. In fact, the vast majority of oil that forms escapes to the topsoil or seabed in this way and evaporates or is gradually digested by microorganisms. In some cases, however, rising oil encounters a capping layer of impermeable rock that prevents its escape from the porous rock and instead causes it to accumulate. Such rock structures are called geologic traps, and they are the targets of oil explorers.

▼ In an oil reservoir, a liquid mixture of crude oil and dissolved gas occupies the spaces between solid particles in a porous rock, such as sandstone. Water, which has a greater affinity for the minerals in rock than does oil, accumulates in layers around the rock particles (top left). Geologic traps where oil reserves gather include fault traps, where layers of porous and impermeable rocks have undergone a relative shift such that a cone of porous rock is capped by impermeable rock (top right); anticlines, where buckled rock strata form a trap of porous rock (bottom left); and salt domes, where a rising plug of salt has caused overlying rock strata to buckle (bottom right).

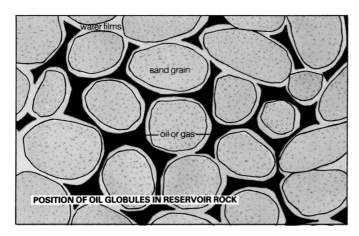

POSITION OF OIL GLOBULES IN RESERVOIR ROCK

water films · sand grain · oil or gas

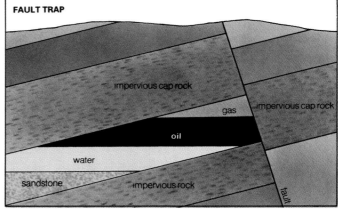

FAULT TRAP

impervious cap rock · gas · impervious cap rock · oil · water · sandstone · impervious rock · fault

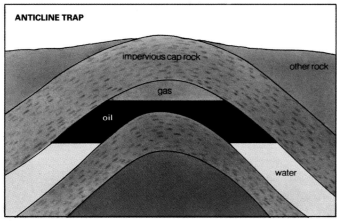

ANTICLINE TRAP

impervious cap rock · other rock · gas · oil · water

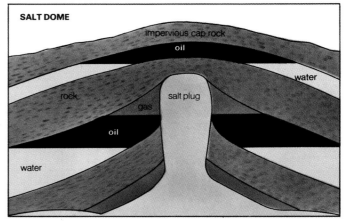

SALT DOME

impervious cap rock · oil · water · rock · salt plug · gas · oil · water

Where possible, wells are drilled vertically; if necessary, they can be drilled at an angle—to test for offshore deposits from an onshore drilling station, for example, or to investigate a geological structure that lies under a town.

Drilling starts with a single tube that has a drill bit at its lower end and that is gripped in a turning device at its top end. A popular type of drill bit consists of three conical cutting wheels. A lubricating mud is pumped down the drill tube to cool the cutting head and to carry the cuttings back up to the surface. Further tubes are attached as drilling progresses, and the assembly of tubes and the drill bit is called the drill string.

At the surface, the mud is filtered to remove cuttings before being pumped back down the drill string. Visual and chemical analyses of the cuttings provide information on the geological structure being penetrated; this information can be supplemented by the extraction and examination of rock cores. The condition of the mud is measured by a series of instruments to provide further information, all of which is monitored by the mud logger (normally a geologist) as drilling proceeds. Instrumentation probes can be fed down the well to take readings of parameters such as rock porosity, local temperatures, and rock density and to take samples.

Monitoring of the mud parameters is also important in the prevention of blowouts caused by the drill unexpectedly striking oil or gas under pressure. Adjusting the composition and density of the mud helps ensure that the weight of the mud balances the geologic pressures. Nevertheless, sudden changes in pressure can start to force mud out of the well; such changes trigger automatic blowout-prevention valves that temporarily seal the well while denser mud is prepared or other remedial action is taken.

When oil is found in a test field—the success rate is around one field in eight—the next stage is to determine the extent of the field and the measures necessary to extract the oil. These two factors determine the commercial viability of a field. Oil may be present in a number of rock strata within a field, and exploratory drilling has to be continued to find the vertical extent of the field. Additional wells may be drilled to determine the field area, and flow tests are also carried out.

Oil recovery

Oil may be recovered from a well in a number of ways, depending on the field characteristics. In general, several production wells are drilled into a single field to obtain a satisfactory yield rate. The simplest extraction technique relies on natural flow, whereby the pressure that acts on the oil is

◀ To meet the ever increasing demand for gas and oil, explorers are having to probe some of the most inhospitable regions of the world, such as the Antarctic.

◀ Natural gas, which is principally methane (CH_4), occurs in association with oil. If its quantity is insufficient for commercial exploitation, natural gas is often burned in a flare to minimize the risk of gas explosions or uncontrolled fires at the wellhead.

sufficient to force it to the surface. Much of this pressure stems from the greater densities of rock and water compared with oil, which therefore tends to rise when an escape route is available.

Part of the pressure in the underground oil results from dissolved natural gas. The drop in pressure caused by oil escaping through wells results in gas being released from the oil. A layer of gas forms above the oil reserve, and provided the well taps the reservoir below the boundary between gas and oil, the expansion of this gas helps drive oil through the reservoir to the well.

At the start of natural flow production, pressures at the wellhead can be extremely high. A system of valves, called a Christmas tree, has to be fitted to reduce pressure and control flow. Daily production for natural flow can exceed 10,000 barrels (a barrel is 42 gallons, or 192 liters).

Pumping

As the exploitation of an oil field proceeds, the natural pressure can subside to such an extent that it is no longer sufficient to force oil to the wellhead. Under such circumstances, the productive life of a well can be extended by pumps that apply suction and then pressurize the oil underground so as to enable the oil to reach the surface.

A common type of pumping system is the sucker-rod pump. In such a system, a plunger assembly installed near the bottom of the well is driven by a string of rods that pass up through the well tubing to a capping device where the top rod passes through a seal and the oil is collected. A "nodding donkey"—a walking-beam arrangement driven by a crank system—drives the sucker

rods with a stroke of up to 16 ft. (5 m) and a rate of 10 to 20 strokes per minutes. A nodding-donkey pump can extract several thousand barrels per day. Hydraulically driven sucker pumps with strokes of up to 30 ft. (9 m) are also used. Hydraulic and electrical centrifugal pumps are also used to drive oil to the wellhead.

Enhanced recovery

At the end of its primary production phase, an oil field may have yielded as much as 25 percent of its oil content, but the yield is often much less. A number of techniques exist for increasing the overall yield of an oil reservoir to as much as 33 percent. Each of these techniques increases the production cost of the oil, so the extent to which they are economically viable depends on the selling price of crude oil at any given time.

Some enhanced-recovery techniques concentrate on increasing flow rate to maximize oil production. Sometimes, increased flow is achieved by pumping acid down the well to dissolve the rock and enlarge existing flow channels; otherwise, explosive charges can be detonated in the oil-bearing strata to crack them and provide new paths for oil to flow to the bottom of the well.

Some techniques increase the amount of oil retrieved by taking some wells out of oil production and using them instead to inject water to increase the pressure in the reserve. For a while, natural gas separated from oil at the wellhead was used for a similar purpose; natural gas is now being used more as a fuel in its own right, however, and this practice is falling out of favor.

Tar sands and shale oil

Large quantities of heavy oil are locked up in tar sands; this oil cannot be extracted through conventional drilling and pumping techniques, because it is too thick to flow freely. Other available techniques include the injection of high-pressure steam, sometimes mixed with hot water, into a well over a period that can last for some weeks. The heat and pressure supplied by the steam reduce the viscosity of the oil and help force it out of a conventional well.

Oil shale can be mined and heat treated to liberate its oil. The cost of the process is greater than that of normal oil extraction; the process also produces large amounts of oil-contaminated waste shale that must be disposed of. Nevertheless, with a backdrop of high oil prices, the extraction of oil from shale becomes a more attractive proposition.

▲ Mobil's Beryl A oil production platform being towed to its site in the North Sea. Once secured to the seabed, the concrete platform can withstand waves up to 30 ft. (10 m) high and winds up to 115 knots. Offshore platforms have helped in the exploitation of large oil reserves, many of which lie deep beneath the ocean.

SEE ALSO: DRILLING RIG, OIL • GEOLOGY • OIL REFINING

Oil Refining

Oil refining is the processing of crude petroleum to produce useful materials such as fuels, lubricants, and raw materials for the manufacture of products as diverse as dyes, explosives, fertilizers, pharmaceuticals, and plastics. Refining adds value to petroleum by making petroleum derivatives that are well suited to their end uses; practically no oil is used in its crude state, an exception being the small amount of crude oil that is used to fuel remote pumping stations on oil pipelines.

Early developments

The first refinery started operations in 1861 to process crude oil from wells near Titusville, Pennsylvania. At that time, the goal of refining was to produce kerosene for use as a low-odor, smokeless replacement for the smelly and smoky animal fats and oils that were used as lamp oils. Refining consisted of batch distillation in simple pot stills at atmospheric pressure. As the temperature of the still increased, naphtha boiled off first, followed by kerosene; tar remained in the pot.

The production of kerosene generated large quantities of naphtha and tar, and refiners sought ways of commercializing these by-products to improve their profits. Naphtha found use as a solvent, notably, for rubber in the waterproofing process developed by the British chemist Charles Macintosh. Refiners soon found that vacuum distillation of the tar from primary distillation gave high-quality lubricants and fuel oils and left a black, sticky residue called bitumen, which found use as a sealant for wooden boats. The invention of the internal combustion engine toward the end of the 19th century created a further use for naphtha, but the demand for gasoline and diesel was at first small compared with the quantities of naphtha produced in kerosene manufacture.

The increase in car ownership in the early years of the 20th century caused a radical change in the priorities of oil refiners, as the demand for motor fuel from naphtha outstripped the amount available from kerosene production. Once again, the mixture of products from primary distillation—the "straight-run" products—was out of step with the requirements of the market.

The shortfall of gasoline eased to some extent with the introduction of thermal cracking in 1913. (Coincidentally, 1913 was the launch year of Henry Ford's mass-produced Model T automobile, which would add impetus to the growth in demand for gasoline.) Cracking improves the yield of gasoline by subjecting high-molecular-weight hydrocarbons to heat and pressure so that

▼ An oil refinery, such as this one near New Orleans, Louisiana, works without interruption for months at a time, only shutting down for maintenance breaks. Most of the round-topped towers in this picture are fractionation columns; in some cases, the pipes that lead gases from the tops of the columns are visible. The frame structures that protrude from the sides of these columns are ladders and walkways that provide access for inspection and maintenance workers.

they split into smaller molecules similar to those found in straight-run naphtha. The heavier fuel oil that results as a by-product of simple thermal cracking is useful as marine fuel, or "bunker."

The late 1930s and early 1940s saw the introduction of a number of processing techniques that improved the yield and quality of gasoline from crude oil. These techniques—catalytic cracking, alkylation, and isomerization—are still extremely important refinery processes. The fuels produced by these processes have higher octane numbers than straight-run gasoline, indicating their superior ignition characteristics in gasoline engines.

Catalytic reforming (platforming) and alkylation processes, introduced in the 1950s, provide a means for improving the octane numbers of low-grade naphthas. Hydrocracking, introduced in the 1960s, makes it possible to produce gasoline from fractions that are too heavy for conventional catalytic cracking, thereby improving the gasoline yield yet further. By the mid-1970s, even heavy distillation residues were being hydrocracked.

Modern refineries

A modern refinery combines several separation and conversion techniques to produce hydrocarbon mixtures for sale as such or for blending to produce mixtures tailored for specific uses. Some refineries convert as much as two-thirds of their intake into gasoline; others concentrate on the production of raw materials for other chemical processes. The choice of crude oil type and the

---

FRACTIONAL DISTILLATION

Fractional distillation—also known as fractionation—is the principal physical separation technique used in oil refining. After water-based impurities have been removed from crude oil, fractionation at atmospheric pressure is the first stage of the refining process. Fractionation also separates the products of catalytic and chemical modification reactors later on in the oil-refining process.

The liquid mixture for fractionation passes through a furnace and enters the column near its base in a continuous stream. On entering the column, most of that liquid vaporizes and rises through the column; the rest remains liquid and falls to the bottom of the column.

As the vapors rise through the column, they encounter a succession of bubble plates whose function is to collect liquids that condense from the vapors. Vertical pipes in the bubble plates allow vapors to pass to the space above while some of the liquid above the bubble plate overflows into the space below. Bubble caps at the tops of these pipes force the rising vapors to bubble through the liquid.

The mingling of liquid and vapor at the bubble caps encourages high-boiling components of the vapors to condense. As they do, they give up their latent heat of vaporization to lower-boiling liquid components, which can then evaporate and rise through the column. The bubble plates and caps therefore contribute to an efficient separation by boiling point.

Each bubble plate collects a different fraction, or liquid mixture of compounds that boil over a specific temperature range. The mean boiling temperatures of the fractions decrease up the column, and the lowest-boiling fraction leaves the top of the column as a mixture of gases. Some of the liquid that collects in a bubble tray is tapped off for subsequent processing or for use unmodified, the rest spills through the bubble caps into the space below. The efficiency of separation depends on the reflux ratio—the rate at which liquid falls back down the column relative to the rate at which it is tapped off. Higher reflux ratios lead to better separations.

High-boiling liquid mixtures are separated using vacuum distillation. The lower pressure reduces the boiling points of all the components of the mixture.

▼ The primary separation in an oil refinery occurs in a fractionation column that runs at atmospheric pressure. The residuum that collects in the bottom of this column is then separated in a smaller vacuum column.

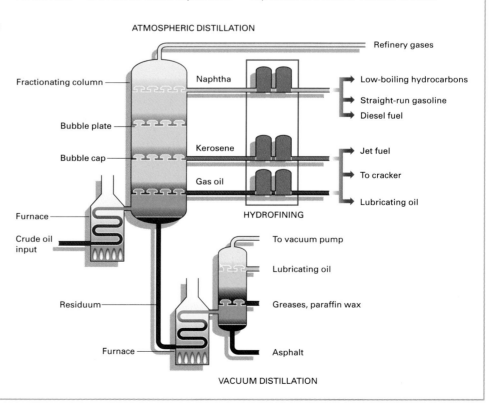

ATMOSPHERIC DISTILLATION

Refinery gases

Fractionating column

Naphtha

Low-boiling hydrocarbons

Straight-run gasoline

Diesel fuel

Bubble plate

Kerosene

Jet fuel

Bubble cap

To cracker

Gas oil

Lubricating oil

HYDROFINING

Furnace

Crude oil input

To vacuum pump

Lubricating oil

Residuum

Greases, paraffin wax

Furnace

Asphalt

VACUUM DISTILLATION

intended product range determine the exact nature of processes used in a given refinery. Moreover, these processes may change in response to variations in the availability and cost of different types of crude oil and the demand and achievable selling price for products.

In any case, the refining process starts with a water wash. Crude oil that arrives at a refinery contains salts, such as sodium, magnesium, and calcium chlorides, and sometimes clay or other inorganic materials. When water is agitated with crude, these materials form a water-based sludge that is immiscible with the hydrocarbon content of the crude oil. The sludge settles out and the washed crude is skimmed off for distillation.

The first distillation occurs at atmospheric pressure using crude oil heated to around 750°F (400°C) in a pipe furnace. Hydrocarbons that boil above this temperature fall to the bottom of the column. This mixture, called the residuum, is reheated in a second furnace before passing to a column that operates under a partial vacuum. The low pressure causes some of the heavier components to boil below 750°F (400°C), so they can be separated without heating the residuum to temperatures that could cause it to start cracking and forming coke in the pipe furnace.

Refinery gases

The lowest-boiling components of crude oil are propane (C_3H_8) and butane (C_4H_{10}). Although these hydrocarbons are gases at room temperature, they remain dissolved in crude oil until released from solution by boiling. The gases are tapped from the top of the column and subsequently compressed until they liquefy.

Propane, butane, and their mixtures are sold in pressurized containers as liquefied petroleum gas, or LPG. Some propane and butane from this stage is used for the alkylation process that forms branched hydrocarbons; some is used for heating purposes within the refinery.

Naphtha

The term *naphtha* describes hydrocarbons that boil in the range from around 90 to 315°F (30–155°C), although each refiner has its own definition of precise temperature ranges for this and other fractions. This fraction contains relatively light alkane, cycloalkane, and aromatic hydrocarbons in proportions that depend on the type of crude that has been distilled, since distillation causes no significant chemical change.

Naphthas from crudes that are particularly rich in aromatic compounds have high octane numbers and can be used directly in gasoline blends; this type is called straight-run gasoline.

CRUDE OIL COMPOSITIONS

A typical crude oil contains around 84 percent carbon by weight and 14 percent hydrogen—figures that correspond to an average formula of CH_2. The exact composition varies between oil fields, however: hydrogen-rich oils have higher paraffin (alkane) contents, while carbon-rich oils contain more aromatics. Naphthenes (cycloalkanes) have a C:H ratio of 1:2 exactly. Individual molecules in crude oil can contain as many as 60 carbon atoms.

Other elements present in crude oil include sulfur (1 to 3 percent) and nitrogen, oxygen, and metals (less than 1 percent each). Of these elements, sulfur is the most troublesome for refiners. Compounds of sulfur would poison some of the catalysts used in refining and produce sulfur dioxide (SO_2), a corrosive pollutant, if they were left in fuels and burned. These compounds must therefore be removed early in the refining process.

The compositions of some crude oils are tabulated below. Oils that contain large proportions of alkanes, such as Saudi light, yield more light petroleum products on primary fractionation than do low-paraffin oils. Aromatic crudes contain more benzene-related compounds.

Origin and type	Paraffinic (% volume*)	Aromatic (% volume*)	Naphthenic (% volume*)	Sulfur (% weight)
Nigerian light	37	9	54	0.2
North Sea (Brent)	50	16	34	0.4
Saudi light	63	19	18	2.0
Saudi heavy	60	15	25	2.1
Venezuelan light	52	14	34	1.5
Venezuelan heavy	35	12	53	2.3
West Texan sour	46	22	32	1.9

* percentage of the total volume of hydrocarbons

▼ Oil refineries are frequently located close to deep-water ports, where supertankers deliver crude oil for refining and smaller vessels accept refined products for shipment to customers and distributors. The plentiful water is also useful for cooling purposes.

CRACKING HYDROCARBONS

As a general rule, the proportion of high-molecular-weight hydrocarbons in crude oil is greater than required by the market for petroleum products. Various cracking processes are the means by which the excess of low-value, heavy hydrocarbons can be converted into high-value fuels and raw materials for the production of specialty chemicals and polymers.

The most basic crackers use heat alone to split straight-chain hydrocarbon molecules into fragments. Temperatures as high as 1500°F (around 800°C) cause the molecules to vibrate so violently that some carbon–carbon bonds rupture. Such bond ruptures, combined with hydrogen transfers, create double bonds as follows:

$$RCH_2-CH_2-CH_2R' \rightarrow RCH{=}CH_2 + H_3CR'$$

where R and R' are alkyl groups of the general formula C_nH_{n+1}. Examples of this type of reaction include the conversion of decane ($C_{10}H_{22}$) into octane (C_8H_{18}) and ethene ($C_2=H_4$) or into heptane (C_7H_{16}) and propene ($CH_3CH=CH_2$), among numerous other combinations of compounds.

Unsaturated cracking products—those that have double bonds—are useful raw materials, because they are capable of addition and polymerization reactions at their double bonds. The same property enables it to form high-molecular-weight tars and coke (impure carbon) within the cracker as a consequence of polymerization and loss of hydrogen to the lighter hydrocarbons that form there.

Operating conditions have a strong influence on the mixture of products that emerges from a cracker; the other main

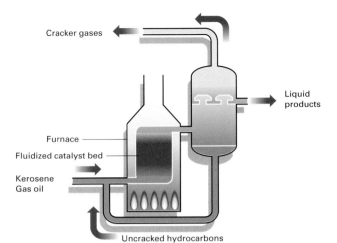

Cracker gases

Liquid products

Furnace

Fluidized catalyst bed

Kerosene
Gas oil

Uncracked hydrocarbons

◄ The simplified layout of a fluidized-bed catalytic cracker, or FCC. Medium- and high-boiling fractions boil as they enter the chamber that holds the catalyst. The upward flow of hydrocarbon vapors lifts the catalyst granules and agitates the bed like a boiling liquid. This motion ensures good contact between the reacting gases and the catalyst.

factor is the nature of the feedstock. One class of thermal crackers—called visbreakers, for *viscosity breakers*—heat the highest-boiling primary-distillation fractions to 900°F (around 500°C). Rapid cooling quenches the cracking reactions, giving lighter oils and heavy tars that are separated in a fractionation column.

Coking is a more extensive version of visbreaking. The cracking mixture remains at a high temperature (900°F, 500°C) in a coking drum until it forms coke and larger quantities of lighter oils than form in the visbreaking process. The coke is shattered and packaged for sale as solid fuel.

Some thermal crackers use lighter feedstocks and operate at higher temperatures—up to 1500°F (around 800°C)—sometimes with steam at high pressure. The product mixtures of such crackers contain large amounts of benzene, ethene, propene, and other hydrocarbons that are valuable raw materials for the production of polymers and other chemicals.

Catalytic crackers use fluidized beds of granular alumina (Al_2O_3) or zeolite catalysts that convert gas oil and kerosene into high-octane hydrocarbons for use in gasoline blends. Temperatures around 1000°F (550°C) convert a small proportion of the feedstock on each pass through the bed; the uncracked part separates out in a fractionating column to return to the cracker. Ethene and propene leave the same column as gases. The catalyst is continuously removed and steam cleaned to remove hydrocarbons. Roasting the catalyst in air burns coke deposits and reactivates it for return to the cracker.

In hydrocracking—a type of catalytic cracking in which hydrogen gas is included with the hydrocarbon feed—high-boiling fractions and distillation residues are converted into kerosene and lighter fractions. The addition of hydrogen to the cracking mixture promotes the formation of low-molecular-weight compounds and inhibits the formation of coke.

◄ Octane numbers for gasoline range from 87 (regular) to 93 (premium). The equivalent rating for diesel fuel is its cetane number. Unleaded gasoline contains oxygenated compounds that improve its ignition properties for use in automobile engines.

Naphthas from crudes that are more naphthenic or paraffinic can be upgraded for use in gasoline by catalytic reforming, which converts alkanes (paraffins) and cycloalkanes (naphthenes) into high-octane aromatics. Alternatively, straight-chain alkanes can be converted into branched alkanes by isomerization. The isomerization of straight-chain *n*-hexane (C_6H_{14}) to 2-methylpentane ($CH_3CH(CH_3)C_3H_7$) causes a change in octane number from 25 to 73, for example.

Naphtha is also a source of many important chemicals. Aromatics such as benzene (C_6H_6), toluene (methylbenzene, C_7H_8), and xylene (dimethylbenzene, C_8H_{10}) are present, as are cycloalkanes, such as cyclohexane. These chemicals are vastly important as solvents and as raw materials for many branches of the chemical industry. Hexane and other alkanes also have some use as solvents for chemical and industrial processes and as raw materials.

Kerosene

Kerosene is taken from the atmospheric fractionating column just below naphtha. It has a typical boiling point range of 315 to 550°F (155–290°C) and is classified as a middle-distillate product. Kerosene from the column is further fractionated and then blended according to specifications, such as flash point and wax-formation temperature.

Kerosene fuel for commercial jet aircraft boils between 375 and 525°F (around 190–275°C), while fuel for military jets includes some naphtha and boils over the range from 130 to 550°F (around 55–290°C). Other parts of the kerosene fraction are sold as fuel for oil-burning heaters, lamps, and stoves. The remainder is blended into diesel fuel or added to the feedstock for cracking.

Gas oil

The term *gas oil* broadly describes the heaviest of the hydrocarbons that boil in the atmospheric fractionating column. A typical boiling range is from 400 to 750°F (around 200–400°C). The fraction is sometimes subdivided into light and heavy gas oils according to boiling point.

CONVERSION PROCESSES

The yield and quality of gasoline from an oil refinery can be improved by the use of conversion reactions—reforming, isomerization, and alkylation. These processes transform low-octane hydrocarbons, such as unbranched alkanes, cycloalkanes, and low-molecular-weight cracking products, into high-octane hydrocarbons, such as branched-chain alkanes and aromatic compounds. The same mechanisms can be used to produce such compounds for sale as raw materials. The reactants are heated in the presence of a catalyst and then fractionated to separate conversion products from unchanged feedstock.

◄ At Britain's Stanlow refinery Platformer II, low-octane feedstock is converted to a high-octane output, then blended into gasoline to replace lead.

Heating fuel is a blend of gas oil with some kerosene; diesel fuel is a similar blend that is formulated to give a good cetane number (the equivalent for diesel of a gasoline octane number) and to resist the formation of engine-clogging wax at low ambient temperatures. The heavier parts of the fraction are used as light lubricating oils. What remains is cracked to form naphtha.

Residuum

The residuum from atmospheric fractionation contains the heaviest, highest molecular weight components of crude oil. Its lowest-boiling components are heavy fuel and lubricating oils. Aromatic compounds must be removed from lubricating oils to improve their resistance to thinning at high temperatures; the process involves solvent extraction with phenol and furfural.

A mixture of greases and waxes distil at higher temperatures than the heavy oils. Wax is stripped from this mixture and from oils by thinning with benzene and chilling to –4°F (–20°C). Adding butanone ($CH_3COC_2H_5$) then causes the formation of wax crystals that are removed by filtration.

The residue from vacuum distillation can be sold as bitumen for road surfacing or as a sealant for roofing felt. Oxidation lightens the color of bitumen, making it suitable as a binder for heavy-duty industrial coatings and tank linings.

Product mixes

The predominant product of oil refining is gasoline, which accounts for 46 percent of the refinery output volume of the United States. Diesel and home-heating fuel take second place with 22 percent, followed by aviation kerosene at 10 percent. Refinery gas is 9 percent, half of which is used for refinery heating, the rest is sold as LPG.

Heavy fuel oil for marine engines and power plants accounts for 5.5 percent, coke just over 4 percent, and bitumen just over 3 percent. Just under 3 percent of output goes to chemical manufacturing, and another 3 percent is taken up by lubricants, stove kerosene, and other products.

Hydrofining

The sulfur content of crude oil presents a number of problems for oil refiners. Some sulfur compounds have obnoxious odors, and all produce corrosive sulfur dioxide if burned. Furthermore, the presence of sulfur compounds in hydrocarbon streams can "poison" the catalysts used for processes such as reforming and isomerization, reducing their activity and useful life.

Malodorous sulfur compounds can be made inoffensive by treating the sulfur-containing hydrocarbon stream with air in the presence of a copper chloride catalyst. The offending compounds, called thiols, have –SH groups that become oxidized and couple together in odorless disulfides, which contain the –SS– linkage. This process is called sweetening (high-sulfur crudes are called sour in reference to their odors). Sweetening does not remove the problems of sulfur dioxide production and catalyst poisoning, however, since the sulfur content remains.

A more satisfactory solution is hydrofining, whereby sulfur-containing fractions are vaporized and passed over a metal catalyst with a stream of hydrogen gas. The hydrogen converts the sulfur content of the stream into hydrogen sulfide, which is then trapped by a solution of diethanolamine in water. Hydrogen sulfide can be converted into elemental sulfur—a useful and harmless by-product—by partial oxidation.

Hydrofining has long been used to treat distillation fractions before they pass to catalytic conversion reactors. The same process is now being used to produce ultra-low-sulfur fuels to conform to environmental regulations.

Planning and control

Although refineries can be huge manufacturing complexes, they are operated by few people. A refinery that processes 100,000 barrels per day may be staffed by a crew of only 25 engineers at any time, for example. Furthermore, the majority

◄ The catalytic reformer at Shell's Wood River refinery in the United States is used for making platformate.

of those engineers is likely to be performing routine maintenance rather than controlling the details of the refining process.

Low staffing levels are possible because of the high degree of automation of refineries. Sensors measure temperatures and pressures at critical parts of the refinery. Computers use these data to formulate commands for components such as heating and cooling circuits, compressors, and valves. Normal production is confirmed by automatic testing of feedstock and product compositions, and small deviations can be corrected without human intervention.

Abnormal conditions trigger alarms to attract the controller's attention and can initiate automatic safety measures. In the case of an emergency, a whole section of plant can be shut down and purged with inert nitrogen gas to render it safe. If this happens, flammable contents of reactors and pipework burn off at a flare stack.

Human intervention is necessary for planning production targets. Decisions on the balance of products from a range of crude oils are made in response to predicted changes in crude oil supply and demand for products. Some demand changes are short term and are dictated by existing orders from customers. Computers help with these orders by calculating gasoline blends on the basis of the stock inventory.

Other demand changes are seasonal—the increase in demand for heating oil in winter, for example. Such production bulges can be prepared for by building up stocks in advance. Long-term changes, such as the reformulation of gasoline blends to comply with environmental regulations, require more detailed planning and might even necessitate modifications of the plant.

SEE ALSO: CATALYST • CHEMISTRY, ORGANIC • DISTILLATION AND SUBLIMATION • GASOLINE, SYNTHETIC • HYDROCARBON • OIL EXPLORATION AND PRODUCTION • ZEOLITE

Operating Room

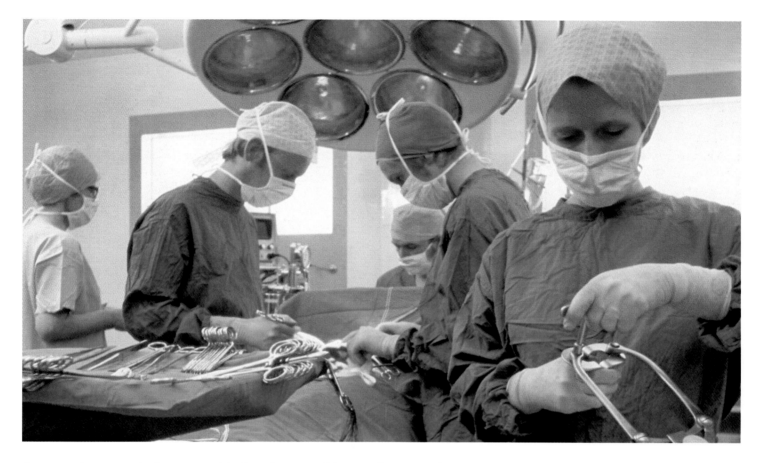

An operating room is the most critical environment most people ever experience. It must be designed to allow the surgical team to work with maximum efficiency, exposing the patient to minimum risk—especially from infection to the surgical wound. Design of an operating room starts with the design of the hospital itself, and its location within it is discussed by architects, hospital authorities, and the surgeons and nurses who will be using it.

An operating room must provide a completely aseptic (germ-free) area—near the surgical wards but isolated enough to be undisturbed by the day-to-day work of the hospital. Between the wards and the operating zone, there must be a transfer area, enabling movement of patients from the unsterilized general areas of the hospital to the operating department with no risk of spreading infection. After an operation the patient will go first to the recovery room, then back via the transfer area to the ward. Meanwhile, all unclean material must be hygienically removed from the operating area.

The details of how hospitals achieve these basic aims vary. The British system is based on three main zones: a transfer area, an anesthetic room, and the operating rooms themselves. In addition, there are changing areas and storage areas and the clean rooms related to the operating room itself: the scrub-up and preparation rooms. In the United States, surgical departments are planned in a similar way except that the anesthetic is given in the operating room itself.

Equipment carts for different kinds of surgery are kept in the preparation room, where they can be loaded with sterile instruments and supplies. These supplies are prepared in either the department or a dedicated sterilizing unit in the hospital. Samples taken for analysis from the patient during surgery are transferred to a utility room, which also serves as a depository for soiled linen and other waste material. Care must be taken when disposing of surgical waste, and strict safety procedures are enforced to prevent infection or contamination of those handling it.

Preparing for surgery

The surgeons, nursing staff, and patients approach the operating rooms via the main corridor from the wards. The surgical and nursing staff enter suites of anterooms with lockers, toilets, and rest facilities. There they change from day clothes into operating clothing, caps, masks, and boots or overshoes. They do not shower because shower-

▲ A nurse prepares sterile equipment for the surgical team. Complexities of modern medicine demand a high level of cooperation and communication between members of the team.

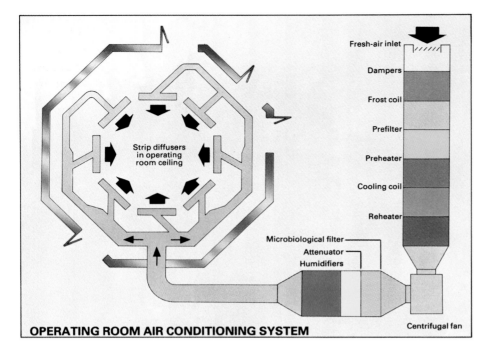

OPERATING ROOM AIR CONDITIONING SYSTEM

ing causes the body to increase the rate at which it sheds contaminated bacteria-bearing skin particles. From the changing area, the surgical teams go first to the scrub room and wash their hands and forearms. After hands are dried on a sterile towel, a sterile gown and gloves are put on, and the staff proceeds to the operating room.

Transfer zone

The patient, meanwhile, has entered the operating zone through a transfer zone. This critical area must be designed so that disease-causing germs are not carried into the clean zone from the rest of the hospital on the gurney wheels, on orderlies' shoes, or on the patient. The transfer area therefore has a demarcation line where the unclean and clean areas meet—this line can be a simple line on the floor. The patient can be transferred from the bed or gurney by the operating room staff on the unclean side of the line by whatever system is used in the hospital. Some gurneys are taken straight into the transfer area or anesthetic room. Some patients transfer to an operating room gurney, and some to an operating table top.

In the British system, the patient is anesthetized in the anesthetic room and then transferred to the operating room. The advantage of this system lies in fast turnover; one patient can be undergoing anesthesia while another is on the operating table. There is also a psychological advantage: some surgeons believe that it would disturb the patient to enter the operating room before being anesthetized.

In the U.S. system, which has no separate anesthesia preparation room, the patient is

▲ A clean-air system surrounds the surgical team in a column of filtered, sterile air that sweeps down continuously from overhead fans and filters. Contaminated air circulates upward and back to the ceiling.

▶ A hydraulically controlled operating table makes positioning of the patient quick and safe. A push-button panel controls the movements.

brought directly to the operating room and is surrounded by gowned and masked surgeons and nurses—plus lights, ancilliary equipment and instrument table—before being anesthetized.

Clean-room technology

All surgical procedures need to be carried out in a clean atmosphere to prevent bacteria from infecting the wound. We are covered in bacteria, which are seldom dangerous unless we are sick or undergoing surgery. Surfaces inside the operating room are therefore made of a washable plastic. Joins between the walls, floor, and ceiling are designed to be easy to clean, and floors are made of an anti-static material to prevent sparks from igniting the anesthetic gases.

Infection can be minimized by controlling the atmosphere, especially by use of an air conditioning system. Air that has passed through high-efficiency particle-arrest filters is pumped into the operating room and kept at a positive pressure. The air is also humidified and the temperature controlled. The air is changed a minimum of 20 times per hour to create a clean, comfortable, and safe environment for the patient and the staff. Some operations need to be carried out in an ultraclean area because of the difficulty in curing an infection in bones and joints, especially if an implant has been introduced.

One system developed in the 1960s envelops the patient and surgical team in a column of clean filtered air that sweeps downward from a canopy above the operating table, covering over an area of about 30 sq. ft. (2.8 m²). Contaminated air circulates upward away from the operating table back to the filtration plant in the ceiling.

Surgeons and other operating room personnel are also a source of potential infection. The human body, especially in the heat and stress of an

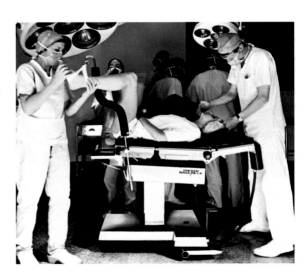

operating room, loses about 1,000 scales of skin per minute—all carrying organisms that could circulate on the convection currents of the operating room. A total body exhaust system can eliminate this source of potential infection. The surgeons and nurses do not wear the familiar cap and breathing mask. Instead, they wear an all-enveloping, one-piece hooded gown with a light-weight visor. The gown is made of closely woven material to prevent the passage of particles as small as 0.0002 in. (4 μm). Cloth in conventional gowns can keep out particles only ten times this size. The particles are drawn off through a flexible tube under the visor, putting a negative pressure under the surgical gown, so a continuous upward flow of purified air bathes the surgical teams' bodies, keeping them fresh and alert.

The operating table

The surgeon needs efficient equipment. The operating table is a main priority. At its most basic, it could be a simple, cleanable table. It should also be adjustable, so the surgeon can bring the patient's body to the exact position necessary for unimpeded access to the operating site. All tables have a facility for raising the patient's head or feet. Many include other devices to support the patient in the precise position required: leg and body supports and arm tables can all be attached to the sides of the main table if needed.

Many operating tables now have translucent tops so that the surgeon can have up-to-date X-ray information during the course of the operation. The table can also be covered with a water-filled mattress to keep the patient warm.

Some tables hinge at four points to divide into five supporting panels. Electrically controlled hydraulics adjust the table at points corresponding with the four main articulation points of the human body: neck, lumbar arch, hip, and knee. The surgeon can adjust the table to position the patient exactly. Controls include a lateral tilt to each side and a facility to raise and lower the entire table. A sophisticated operating table has a detachable top, which fits over a fixed, centrally supporting pillar. Oxygen, compressed air, and medical vacuum can be provided through this central column. A diathermy unit for cauterizing small blood vessels is also situated close by.

Surgical lamps

The operating room must be well lit. The main surgical light is directed onto the patient from several sources so that plenty of strong light passes around the surgeon's head and shoulders. In this way, the surgeon avoids throwing a shadow on the surgical wound when bending over the patient.

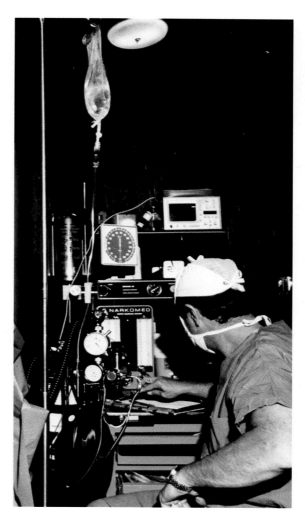

◀ During an operation in which the patient must be unconscious, the anesthetist monitors the condition of the patient constantly.

Surgical lamps are arranged to produce the right pattern of light, concentrating on an area about 10 in. (25 cm) in diameter, with reasonable brightness over a range of between 30 in. (75 cm) and 60 in. (150 cm) from the lamps. At one time, it was necessary to use a transformer to achieve the intensity of light needed for surgery. Now, quartz halogen lights allow the surgeon the right degree of intensity—ten times that of a domestic incandescent bulb—from the normal voltage supply. Modern lighting also employs solid-state intensity control so that the surgeon can adjust the light intensity.

The intensity of light is not the surgeon's only consideration. Surgeons can suffer serious eye fatigue in the course of a long operation, especially if their eyes are forced to move between highly contrasting areas—from shiny steel instruments and white swabs to the darker tones of the surgical cavity. Dark surgical drapes and surgical instruments with a satin finish help reduce their light-reflecting properties.

Accurate color rendering is also crucial: the lighting should produce results as near to daylight as possible. Ordinary lightbulbs give a yellowish light, lowering the eye's ability to distinguish sub-

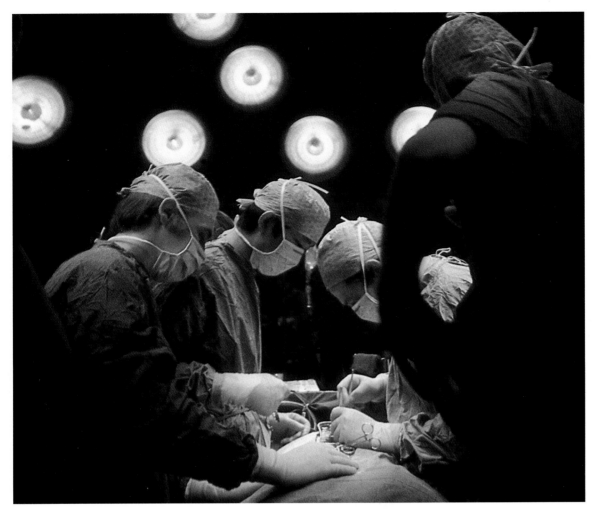

◀ The modern operating room is well equipped and sterile. Lighting is precisely positioned so the assistants have a clear, well-defined field of vision in which to operate.

tle color differences in the blue range. Modern surgical lights have a color rendering about as close to daylight as artificial light can get. For some time, operating rooms were built without windows, but the trend today is to allow in some daylight if building arrangements permit. Surgical teams tire less quickly and suffer less eyestrain under natural light, and of course, it helps color rendering. The design of the lamp also ensures that heat is deflected from the patient and the surgical team.

Operating procedures

Each member of the surgical team has precise duties to ensure the operation proceeds safely. To maintain sterile conditions, the surgeon and the scrub nurse are not allowed to leave the room. A scout nurse, who does not touch the patient, is used to take supplies and samples to and from the operating area. Anesthetists keep the patient unconscious throughout the operation and monitor vital signs with the help of sophisticated equipment. Items used during surgery, such as swabs, scalpels, sutures, and sponges are counted before and after surgery to ensure that none are accidentally left inside the patient.

Recovery room

After surgery, the patient will spend some time in a post-anesthetic recovery area, which is an integral part of the surgical department. This area is where the patient will recover consciousness from the anesthetic before returning to the ward. The recovery area is highly serviced and equipped with oxygen, suction, and monitoring equipment and has a high ratio of nurses to patients. With modern anesthesia, the time spent in the recovery area can be very short.

Some patients may be so critically ill that they go directly to the intensive care unit. It is helpful if the intensive care unit is close to the operating department to reduce travel time for the patient, but it also makes access easier for anesthetic and surgical staff who are working in the operating department and for resuscitation teams.

Within an accurately controlled and planned environment, safe conditions are available for patients during a critical period of their stay in the hospital.

SEE ALSO: ANESTHETIC • HEART SURGERY • MICROSURGERY • PLASTIC SURGERY • SURGERY • TRANSPLANT

Index

Page numbers in **bold** refer to main articles; those in *italics* refer to picture captions.